Praise for Julia Hob

"A must-read for anybody concerned about the f
Dieter Schwarz Associate Professor of AI & Work,

"Julia Hobsbawm offers characteristic wisdom and insight on one ~
questions of our time, how the workplace is being changed by technology a..
changing generational attitudes. This is a compelling guide to the future of work."
– John Gapper, Business columnist, *Financial Times*

"The book with its finger on the pulse of the world of work. Things are shifting fast – read *Working Assumptions* if you want to know what's happening and what matters right now." – Herminia Ibarra, Charles Handy Professor of Organisational Behaviour, London Business School

"Julia always seems to be three steps ahead on her thinking. This is THE user guide to the future of the future of work. A review of what everyone will be talking about in five years." – Nicholas Bloom, William D. Eberle Professor of Economics, Stanford University

"Julia Hobsbawm has done it again! In her new book *Working Assumptions*, our foremost futurist of the workplace crafts a savvy and succinct, lively, and deeply informed chronicle of where work is now. Not to be missed by anyone – other than people permanently at leisure." – Barbara Kellerman, Fellow, Center for Public Leadership, Harvard Kennedy School, Harvard University

"*Working Assumptions* is a masterclass for navigating and adapting to the challenging new era of work – in this essential guide Julia Hobsbawm does a magnificent job in translating the increasingly disruptive, complex and ever-changing Future of Work landscape." – Peter Miscovich, Global Future of Work Leader, Jones Lang Lasalle

"One of the many reasons why Julia Hobsbawm is the nonpareil guru of modern work is that she grasps the profound cultural significance of her subject, and is as likely to cite Murakami, Magritte or *Succession* as an economic or social theorist. This book is essential reading for anyone who wants to understand our rollercoaster of a century." – Matthew d'Ancona, Editor at large, *The New European*

"As one of the most respected voices on the future of work, Julia Hobsbawm has yet again taken a lead in explaining where we are and where we're heading. *Working Assumptions* provides an insightful, forthright perspective on this fast-moving topic. Anyone wanting to take stock of where we are should start here." – Bruce Daisley, bestselling author and speaker on work, including the podcast 'Eat Sleep Work Repeat'

"Julia Hobsbawm is my go-to thought leader when it comes to intelligent writing and speaking about how we work now." – Rachel Johnson, LBC broadcaster and writer

"*Working Assumptions* is a fascinating read from start to finish. Julia Hobsbawm eloquently explores the current debates, challenges, nuances and trends of the now and the future of work, challenging what we think we know along the way. This thought-provoking and absorbing book is an absolute must-read for anyone who is interested in the world of work – today and tomorrow." – **Gemma Dale, Senior Lecturer, Liverpool John Moores University**

"The definitive book on the state of work in 2024. At a time when work is changing more rapidly and significantly than at any time since the advent of personal computing, Julia Hobsbawm has managed to distill that complexity into a clear synopsis of where we are and where we're going." – **Rob Sadow, CEO & Co-Founder @ Scoop, Creator of Flex Index**

"A great book and a comprehensive exploration of the dramatic transformations reshaping our professional landscapes – what Julia Hobsbawm rightly calls 'The Amazing Age'. This book stands as a pivotal guide for professionals seeking to understand the nuances of the current work environment and seize the opportunities arising from these significant changes. It is an essential read for anyone looking to adapt and thrive in the evolving post-Covid, AI-driven work paradigm." – **Dr Gleb Tsipursky, author of the bestselling *Returning to the Office and Leading Hybrid and Remote Teams***

"Exploring the complex issues facing us about how we work and live, Julia Hobsbawm has written the book for tomorrow that we need today. Always ahead of the curve, *Working Assumptions* integrates multiple threads and the past, present and possible future, using data, stories and interviews as well as culture, politics, literature and music. The result is a highly engaging book that will help us keep our moral compass, clear sight, thinking and optimism, as we reach towards the potential of this time." – **Gabriella Braun, author of *All That We Are* and Director of Working Well**

"Written with deep insights and a sharp wit, Julia Hobsbawm's *Working Assumptions* is an indispensable guide to the future of work, in no small part because it roots every new trend in somewhere that we've been before. *Working Assumptions* is required reading for anyone who's leading the way forward in the world of work – or worried about where they're being led." – **Brian Elliott, co-founder of Future Forum, bestselling author of *How the Future Works***

"Whether it's the impact of AI, or bringing your 'authentic' self to the office, there is no better guide to the complexities of modern working life than Julia Hobsbawm." –**Alice Sherwood, author of *Authenticity: Reclaiming Reality in a Counterfeit Culture***

"Super timely and full of thought-provoking ideas from politics to popular culture and business – which is Julia Hobsbawm's trademark when it comes to looking at how we live and how we work." – **Giles Gibbons, Founder & CEO of Good Business**

WORKING ASSUMPTIONS

What We Thought We Knew About
Work Before Covid and Generative AI
and What We Know Now

JULIA HOBSBAWM

Other books by Julia Hobsbawm

The Nowhere Office
The Simplicity Principle
Fully Connected
The See-Saw
Where The Truth Lies

www.juliahobsbawm.com

*"The blue-collar blues is no more
bitterly sung than the white-collar moan"*

Studs Terkel, *Working* (1974)

First published in Great Britain and the United States in 2024
by Whitefox Publishing in association with Fully Connected Services Ltd.

© Julia Hobsbawm. A selection of essays as indicated first appeared on Bloomberg Work Shift in 2022 and 2023. Some of these essays have been edited for this edition. The originals are all on Bloomberg Work Shift Bloomberg.com/work-shift

Preface © Lynda Gratton 2024

Where Do We Park Our Spaceships? © Mr Gee 2024

A History of the Typewriter and A History of the Desk Diary
© Andrew St George

Selected Interviews reproduced from *The Nowhere Office* podcast
© Fully Connected Services Ltd and available on Apple Podcasts,
Spotify and podcast platforms.

Cover artwork: Hayden Brown at The Brown Studio

Inside line drawings: DALL-E-3 courtesy of OpenAI/ChatGPT-3
powered by Microsoft Bing

Inside graphics © Nicola Streeten see @nicolast.reeten on Instagram

Trade paperback
ISBN 978-1-916797-27-7
Also available as an eBook
ISBN 978-1-916797-28-4

A CIP catalogue record for this book is available from the British Library.

Julia Hobsbawm asserts the moral right to be identified as the author of this work.

All rights reserved. No part of this publication may be reproduced,
stored in a retrieval system or transmitted in any form or by any means,
electronic, mechanical, photocopying, recording or otherwise,
without prior written permission of the author.

While every effort has been made to trace the owners of copyright material reproduced herein, the author would like to apologize for any omissions and will be pleased to incorporate missing acknowledgements in any future editions.

Dedication

To the memory of three wise and infinitely kind souls whose work will live on after they have left us: Alessandra Cavalli, Derek Draper and Giulia Quintarelli, who all died between 2020 and 2024.

CONTENTS

Preface by Professor Lynda Gratton xi
About this book xv

Introduction 1

1. THE NEW JOB COLLAR 13

2. TASK FORCES 65

3. COMMUTER TRIANGLE 105

4. CULTURE CLUBS AND CLASHES 151

5. HEALTH AND SAFETY NETS 193

6. THE AMAZING AGE 223

Further Reading 275
Acknowledgments 281
Index 285

PREFACE

We are all fascinated by the future of work – or rather, *our* future of work. What sort of jobs should I prepare for? What skills will be most valuable, and what will be defunct and valueless? As more of us live urban lives, what will our cities look and feel like? How will our cultural norms and assumptions change, and how best can I prepare for this? How will I focus on my wellbeing and what can I expect my company to do to support me? And, given that so many people will live longer lives, how do I make the most of the generational benefits that could accrue while steering clear of generational stereotypes?

These are all questions that are being discussed when friends meet, when project teams work together, and when executives decide on their business strategy. They are crucial because they are indeed about *our* future of work, but also about our *everyday* experiences.

With this in mind, I am delighted to write this preface. For who better than Julia Hobsbawm to guide us, show us the potential contradictions, and draw our attention to the conversations we should be having? In her must-read Bloomberg column "Working Assumptions" she has brought to our attention the paradoxes around questions of jobs, skills, cities, culture, wellbeing and generations. As a consummate networker and expert interviewer,

Julia has reached far and wide on our behalf to find experts and executives with whom to converse. And more, she has traveled to many places to observe first-hand what is working – and what is not working.

Through her observations, asides, stories and narratives, Julia draws our attention to the turbulence we are all experiencing. Her descriptions, which go from granular detail to grandiose big picture, are never dull and often amusing. You can imagine Julia would be the perfect dinner party guest with whom to converse on questions of work, because she has many snippers and facts that would illuminate the dreariest of conversations.

Here you will find ideas to help you think through these questions, frameworks to guide your thinking, and examples of what others are doing. Taken together they give courage to imagine both what could be, and perhaps more importantly, what *should* be.

The underlying essence of this collection is *optimism*. Julia is positive about work, and the beneficial impact *good work* can have on wellbeing, connectivity and feelings of self-worth.

Yet she is clear-sighted that work only plays this positive role when it is good. As she describes, when work is *bad* – when tasks are precarious, schedules ever changing, bosses aggressive, colleagues uncaring – then the outcomes are deteriorating mental health and a fast denuded skill set.

So, this is an agenda, a point of view. It takes the momentum created after the pandemic to explore what a post-pandemic world can look like, and how some of the experiments of that period can be baked into how we work both now and in the future. And it considers how the technologies we are mesmerized by, like

ChatGPT, can play a positive role to support human work and creativity. It is a description of an inflexion point. As Julia asks: "Do we want to jump into new territory or retreat to the old?"

I, for one, want to jump into new territory, and I am delighted that in exploring the unknown, I have Julia as a guide.

Lynda Gratton

Professor of Management Practice at London Business School
and founder of HSM Advisory

> *The working assumption across all the chapters here is that we are at an inflexion point in two ways. Firstly, around how to identify and handle the undeniable changes already wrought. But secondly, around whether we want to be optimists or pessimists, and whether we want to jump into new territory or retreat to the old.*

ABOUT THIS BOOK

> "I give consent for my perceptual chronologies to be surgically split, separating my memories between my work life and my personal life."
>
> *Severance*, Episode 1, Apple TV, Dan Erickson 2022

Throughout the teeth of the Covid pandemic my living room became my place of work. Zoom and Teams became my constant companions. When I wasn't working, I was watching television, which seemed curiously obsessed with work: *The Office*, the multi-season global comedy hit, became the most streamed show in America during the pandemic, with 57 billion minutes watched.*

Every kind of screen offered us a connection to work. To our old lives. It made us miss it. We assumed that those who were not working on the frontline would rush "back" to the office. But I could not quite shake the feeling that work was a snowglobe being shaken up, and that it would settle back in a different place from before. Decades of observing corporate culture gave me a hunch and I set about reading what I could to verify it from the endless stretch of my sofa.

---

* *The Office* was the most-streamed TV in the US in 2020. Source: Nielsen SVOD Content Ratings (Netflix, Amazon Prime, Disney Plus and Hulu), Nielsen National TV Panel, US.

WORKING ASSUMPTIONS

The Nowhere Office: Reinventing Work and the Workplace of Tomorrow came out in 2022 and was something of a gamble as its central argument was that people would not go back to the office as they had before – an unpopular argument in some quarters, then and now. I argued that there were too many latent trends in the way people live, work and, crucially, *feel* about the way they live and work which were bubbling up between the end of the Second World War in 1945 and the arrival of Covid at the end of 2019. These included the way women work and the impossibility of having structured schedules around childcare and other care duties. *The Nowhere Office* also included a call I repeat in this book, namely to address how toxic the workplace is or feels for many people, as this is a factor in the rise of a desire for freedom from it.

Popular culture, meanwhile, had continued to brood on our relationship with work. By 2022 a far darker and more dystopian TV show on work was airing – *Severance*, on Apple TV, which played directly to our anxieties about two things: the point of corporate work and the ability to separate work and personal life.

Something was both on air and in the air.

The Working Assumption

The working assumption throughout the pandemic was that everyone would snap back into a pre-Covid way of working and living once it was all over. This would include resuming the commute and working five days a week. In *The Nowhere Office*, I argued that this liminal phase of time would not end up "back" anywhere, but in a new place, a new phase in the story of work. Clearly this has happened. Covid isn't over fully, and neither are its effects. This was before the new kid on the block – ChatGPT – had even arrived.

Some of my ideas caught on. In the summer of 2022 Bloomberg invited me to write a column for their new section examining the new world of work, aptly called Work Shift, which they launched in the autumn. They were generous in their brief: to write what interested me. When asked what I wanted to call my column I had no hesitation: "Working Assumptions".

What exactly is a working assumption? Well, it's like a work in progress combined with a rear-view mirror. It's a snapshot of views we make about the future, based on what is happening now and what has happened before. Society makes working assumptions all the time. The world was flat once, remember? And industry was small and made from a cottage. Women had to work in the home, not from home. A daily commute wearing a bowler hat was just "done". And no, the robots were not coming.

When history and experience change the facts, our working assumptions shift from something which has the ring of prediction to the clarity of hindsight.

WORKING ASSUMPTIONS

This book tries to do both. To future cast into the direction work is heading while being anchored in what has happened to date. To notice where the trends are moving. This book includes a combination of columns as they first appeared behind a paywall on Bloomberg (and are therefore available here more widely) plus new material, new ideas in this ever-evolving story. In addition, the book contains quotes from some of the scores of executives, academics and thinkers interviewed over five series of my podcast *The Nowhere Office*, with which I and my co-host Stefan Stern aim to shed light, as I say in the introduction to each episode, "on the world of work as it is, as it could be, should be, might be". In other words, working assumptions.

> *I think we have moved beyond the phase described in* The Nowhere Office, *with its uncertainty and liminal feel, into a new phase in which the evolution of work will be mediated by wonder and extraordinary opportunity.*

ABOUT THIS BOOK

The American Way Of Work

I hear America singing, the varied carols I hear,

Those of mechanics, each one singing his as it should be blithe and strong,

The carpenter singing his as he measures his plank or beam,

The mason singing his as he makes ready for work, or leaves off work,

The boatman singing what belongs to him in his boat, the deckhand singing on the steamboat deck,

The shoemaker singing as he sits on his bench, the hatter singing as he stands,

The wood-cutter's song, the ploughboy's on his way in the morning, or at noon intermission or at sundown,

The delicious singing of the mother, or of the young wife at work, or of the girl sewing or washing,

Each singing what belongs to him or her and to none else,

The day what belongs to the day—at night the party of young fellows, robust, friendly,

Singing with open mouths their strong melodious songs.

"I Hear America Singing", Walt Whitman,
1867 edition, *Leaves of Grass*

The locus of this book is mainly Anglosphere, and in particular the UK and the US. I live in London but travel so frequently to the United States that I have become the kind of nerd who not only has the perfect packing technique but knows which aircraft type is best. Virgin Atlantic has been my transatlantic buddy all my working life. I have had some of the most interesting chats on board mid-air, not just with fellow passengers but with the stewards. These snapshot chats up in the air always shed light on what's happening in the vast expanse below.

I first started to write seriously about how we live and work in 2017. Between 2019 and the end of 2023 I made more than ten visits to the US, including to the East Coast, the Midwest and the West Coast. In Utah, Miami, Baltimore, New York, San Francisco, Palo Alto, in hotels, offices, coffee shops, airports, taxis and restaurants, I've been politely nosy. To notice, to ask.

I think I knew I was on to something on my first trip to the US after the pandemic when I got off a largely empty plane to be quizzed at JFK border control by an officer who asked me the customary question: "What are you doing here and what do you to do for a living?" I said, "I write about work." He talked at me animatedly for five minutes before saying, "Welcome to New York." I'm grateful to him, because he confirmed my instinct that the story of work is happening all around us, all the time. We're *in it*.

I've focused on the American story of work for a particular reason (although I would dearly love to gaze more globally in a subsequent book). The reason is not just that I know America a little bit, and "write what you know" is quite a good maxim, but that it's America's response to the post-Covid world of work which has set the tone for the rest of the world. This is partly because America is directly responsible for so much of what we use to work and indeed live: from the car to the corporation, from the credit card to the computer, from the MBA to globalized HR policies.

ABOUT THIS BOOK

America has famously worked come what may, and exported this agonized dedication through its art and culture. It has been always-on-and-always-in. There's a gripping scene in the final award-winning series of HBO's *Succession*, in which a hardworking consiglieri character, Geri, tries to calm nerves about a possible European takeover by reminding her colleagues, "we've been raised by wolves."

Edward Hopper's lonely paintings; Arthur Miller's plays; Billie Holiday's autobiography *Lady Sings the Blues*; and TV shows from *Cheers* to *Parks and Recreation*, from "Hello, this is Carlton your doorman", the most unseen worker in the history of TV entertainment to ever play a starring role,* to the Dilbert cartoons which ran from 1989–2023. All of this art and culture continuously reflects, almost unconsciously, that our work is critical to our identity and that work is as troubling and alienating as it is bonding and vital. The way we work is who we are.

I sometimes feel, watching American TV or the movies, that the world works inside an American set, reflecting back to all of us the story of our lives and that story includes how we make ends meet.

The American dream hinged on live to work, not work to live. You worked hard to be anyone, get anywhere, But the blush was falling from the rose on this for a long time with the uneven effects of outsourcing and the gig economy and automation bring-

---

* The US sit-com *Rhoda* was a hugely popular TV show in the 1970s. Such was the popularity of Carlton, that he briefly had his own spinoff show – and today has his own Wikipedia page.

ing disquiet. Covid-19 and the soaring inflation which followed immediately after began a process still unfolding: Americans no longer feel the same about work. If popular culture is any kind of guide then they are feeling existential angst, and disaffection. This flipping of priorities has been stark and broadly remains. By 2024 just under a third of paid days at work in America are WFH or "Work From Home";* the amount of unoccupied office space dropped from 20 percent approximately before 2019 to 50 percent average occupancy,† and polls consistently show that hybrid working remains firmly on the agenda of workers, despite strenuous efforts by some managers to persuade or force greater presenteeism.‡ America has fallen out of love with work – or at least it seems to have stopped believing in it quite so much.

It's worth emphasizing, of course, that the real-time story of work is evolving far faster than any serial or series can keep up with and you will have to forgive me for not being able to livestream this book (maybe AI will help us out here in future).

---

* Work From Home Research, February 2024, compiled by Jose Maria Barrero Nicholas Bloom, Shelby Buckman and Steven J Davids.
† Moody Analytics said that the national US office vacancy rate rose to a record-breaking 19.6 percent in the fourth quarter of 2023.
‡ From Gallup workplace analytics "Six Workplace Trends Leaders Should Look Out for in 2024", December 18, 2023.

ABOUT THIS BOOK

The United State Of Work

But the whole point is that it isn't just America affected by the changes in how we feel about work – and how work is for everyone. American culture just often expands this to a global audience: throughout this book are examples of where popular culture, originating in America, has reached a global audience with a message about work.

This book weaves together ideas I have written about the world of work, not only the American world of work, since 2022. Each one was triggered by topics or moments which on reflection are, I hope, still timely and do resonate globally. Of course there remain deeply specific cultural and national differences: Germany is considering the 4-day week in an attempt to reverse its productivity decline;* "The Right to Disconnect" is enshrined in some laws not others.

They are not reproduced in chronological order but according to themes. The six chapters here reflect the topics which I find myself consistently returning to when I write: jobs and skills, offices and the commute, wellbeing and culture and last but not least the amazing impact being differently experienced across generations. The final chapter, "The Amazing Age", explains why I think we have moved beyond the phase described in *The Nowhere Office*, with its uncertainty and liminal feel, into a new phase in which the evolution of work will be mediated by wonder and extraordinary opportunity.

A note on style: I tend to use American spelling over British ("labor" not "labour") but sometimes switch between. Equally "apartment" is American but "flat" is British. As the Americans say: go figure!

---

* "Germany launches major 4-day workweek trial amid labour shortage": *Euronews*, February 2024.

One more thing: I've made an executive decision to flaunt the trend of including hyperlinks which look indecipherable on the page. Instead, I'm going for more of a narrative explanation. You can, after all, look up more on Google, Perplexity, ChatGPT if you want…

I have been assisted in my thinking not only by interviews but by illustrations. In a nod to the times, and to test out the technology, you will see various black-and-white drawings done by my digital co-pilot DALL-E, Microsoft's visualization tool, which is astonishingly easy to use and terrifying in its ability to put illustrators out of a job. To offset this, I immediately commissioned my old friend, the award-winning graphic artist Nicola Streeten, to be the human in the loop and draw illustrations based on my words here (and my words, I should say, are, for good and ill, not "augmented" by AI).

Finally, some little word vignettes also illustrate the book. For an episode of *The Nowhere Office* podcast I commissioned the work historian Dr Andrew St George to write some short memories of old tech, things like typewriters and desk diaries, and they are kindly reproduced with his permission here. And Mr Gee, a brilliant poet and performer, has written a specially commissioned piece, "Where Do We Park Our Spaceships?" If that sounds futuristic, that's your working assumption. You'll find it at the end of chapter six.

INTRODUCTION

Some people make the working assumption that life and work neatly separate, but I don't think they do. Whether I watch *The Office* or *Homeland*; *Severance* or *Slow Horses*; Charlie Chaplin's comic conveyor belt struggle in *Modern Times* from the 1930s or Barack Obama's *Working* on Netflix; or listen to Beyoncé's "Break My Soul", the anthem of the "Great Resignation" of a century later, popular culture consistently tells us that work both defines and dominates our lives. From Walt Whitman to T.S. Eliot to Haruki Murakami, work's unfairness and inescapability is the story or soundtrack of our lives. Technology changes, times change, but this is a constant.

The narrative that work doesn't work, that work is a struggle, has been with us for over a hundred years. Can we ever change our assumption about it? Maybe we can. Maybe.

Towards the end of the exhausting, adrenalin-fueled terrorist drama *Homeland*, CIA agent character Saul says wearily: "Work: it's my Achilles' heel," and certainly every working person can be forgiven for feeling exhausted, burnt out, struggling to process the changes which have happened since the twin forces of Covid-19 and generative AI converged on working life in such quick succession. They created between them a kind of chaos theory of the workplace, by which I mean a butterfly flapping its wings in one corner of the world of work has huge impacts somewhere else.

Thus the massive shift to hybrid working has had equally vast knock-on effects on office space, and with it implications for team culture outside of offices and city design. Meanwhile, new schisms have opened up between hybrid-haves and hybrid have-nots – those who can't work remotely or perhaps never could.* The emergence of the metaverse and multiverse, virtual places rather than bricks and mortar ones, adds to the sense of chaos, or at the very least uncertainty. If you can put your hand up and say you even know what ChatGPT is, you're in a minority right now. If you know how to use it, you're part of an even smaller one. But by 2026 it's estimated that 80 percent† of workplaces will have what it can do embedded within them.

From bad management to pandemic ways of working to post-pandemic ways of working to… new ways of working. What does it all add up to? Work gets a bad rap in popular culture and in the media. The message? Work doesn't work.

Yet the more popular culture shows us work and continues to replace old shows with new ones where work remains a central leitmotif, the more it confirms how essential it is in our lives. We can't live with it, but we also can't live without it.

---

* I refer to "Hybrid Haves and Hybrid Have-Nots" in *The Nowhere Office: Reinventing Work and the Workplace of the Future*, Basic Books 2022.
† A report by Gartner shows that 80 percent of enterprises will have used generative AI APIs or models, or developed their own by 2026.

INTRODUCTION

Due to an ongoing eye condition I spend about half a day a month in Moorfields Eye Hospital in London. One fellow patient is an infrastructure engineer. He works twelve-hour night shifts under Klieg lights, sometimes seven days in a row. He then has four days off during which he "mostly sleeps – to recover". My work isn't anything like as physically demanding. Class, race and gender separate me from this bloke on the orange plastic chairs in the retinal therapy unit in EC1. But inside, we are not only united by our medical fate of an imminent eye injection. We're both taking time off work to be here, and we both understand each other perfectly. Neither of us want to *not* work. If anything, we grumble about the time our health takes *away* from it.

I'm an optimist in a pessimistic world. I am strenuously pro-work but I can see its stresses; I believe that to work is to be empowered, liberated, in control of your life, even with the caveat that much of work is unfair and unfit for purpose. I believe that we can only change work for the better by listening and seeing what is really happening and by challenging the assumptions we make about how work must work.

Especially now. Yes, the impact of generative AI and the large language processing model ChatGPT on the creative knowledge worker is profound, and has echoes of the turbulence wrought on the blue collar workers of the 1990s experiencing automation (after the outsourcing of the 1980s). But it's too early to say that we're entering a new phase that's bad for work. Assume nothing yet.

Everything Everywhere All At Once

When Covid-19 arrived all sorts of working assumptions about work fell by the wayside, seemingly overnight. That you had to work nine to five from an office; that a daily commute was the only model in town; that productivity was what could be seen and counted in situ; and that work felt valuable to people and was economically and socially worth their time and effort.

Then came ChatGPT, and more working assumptions came up: that white collar jobs would be at risk from automation like blue collar ones had always been; that generative AI would help us be more creative rather than just allow us to steal someone else's creativity; that artificial intelligence is going to create leisure time, and *that this is better than working.* The co-founder of Google's DeepMind, Mustafa Suleyman, wrote on X: "The goal of civilization is not to create full employment. It's to reduce suffering and increase happiness and health for everyone. That's the standard we should hold technology to, not its ability to create or replace work. The good news is, that's where we're headed."* To which I can only reply: discuss.

To use technological parlance: we're still processing all of this.

Yet it is not hyperbole to say that the scale of the disruption we're experiencing now has not been seen in the workplace for a hundred years. The impact on our lives and how we see them in relation to work has not been this vivid since the workplace moved from artisan homes and fields into factories and cities, or since the mass

---

* Post on X, October 30, 2023. In March 2024, Suleyman was announced as Microsoft's head of AI.

INTRODUCTION

migrations of the early twentieth century. Now, as then, people are moving to where work is and where they can afford to live. Now, as then, it's technology driving jobs. Now, as then, there's a new set of cultural norms emerging, new values, new stories.

The snowglobe I envisaged at the start of my last book, *The Nowhere Office*, is more accurately now a snowstorm we're just fighting our way blindly through.

Perhaps this sense of chaos explains why the Oscar-winning movie of 2023, arguably the first post-pandemic year, was *Everything Everywhere All at Once*. The fantasy/comedy/sci-fi/family drama set between a laundrette and a tax office brilliantly conveys family life, love, bureaucracy and a world buffeted by change, uncertainty, human frailty – all bookended by work. In the movie, technology transports us to a multiverse, exactly as work will increasingly do. And yet at the heart of the film is a very human story. As one of the lead characters says to another: "even though you have broken my heart yet again, I wanted to say, in another life, I would have really liked just doing laundry and taxes with you."

Like with all good movies, the audience always has to be wondering: what happens next? What is going to happen at work and how does it affect our lives?

> *We're in the curious position of looking forward with really unprecedented optimism through a lens of unprecedented gloom.*

WORKING ASSUMPTIONS

Living With Uncertainty

The world feels generally unsafe at the moment. There's post-pandemic anxiety and the effects of virus: 3 million people died directly from Covid-19 and a further 65 million people globally are experiencing long Covid.* Post pandemic there have been two significant conflicts, in Ukraine and Israel/Gaza, the second of which has unleashed culture wars of unprecedented scale and reach into society and workforces, especially university campuses and fashion brands.† Meanwhile the new technology of generative AI is currently in its fear phase: until people know how it works for them, they mistrust it. The perception right now is that jobs will be lost, and the robots are coming. There's also something else very new: a generation of young people who grew up and into the workplace during and post Covid.

This has brought entirely new challenges in terms of mindset, social skills, confidence, and a value shift which has been propelled forward in the last five years. "Purpose" over climate, identity and race which all had validity and made new Gen Z workers in particular very choosy about the jobs they wanted were joined by a new value shift post-Covid which I can only sum up as "why bother"?

Of course, some fiercely ambitious graduates remain, but so too does a disheartened cohort of graduates whose universities did

---

* The Lancet, "Long COVID: 3 Years in", March 11th, 2023.
† Claudine Gay resigned from her position as Harvard President in January 2023, ostensibly due to criticism of the University's response to the Hamas attack on Israel. The clothing retailer Zara removed an advertising campaign after criticism online.

nothing much for their pastoral care during the pandemic and which seem to have comprehensively lost control of the cultural safety barrier since the Middle East war which began in October 2023. This generation is scarred psychologically and politically by Covid and it is affecting their ability to work, and their approach to lifelong work.

Meanwhile many elders, Boomers and Gen X who have experienced a value shift of their own, want to work less, or more independently. Values are driving behavior. When you add to this the nightmarish inflationary cost of living crisis which has also happened in this period, in which studying and working have de facto become unaffordable, in which housing rents and prices have created mass internal migration patterns across countries like the UK and America in particular, it becomes increasingly difficult to imagine a return to a status quo.

All of which creates turbulence in the prevailing climate. This column probably best sums up the single biggest working assumption we should all make right now: that the future of work is going to be turbulent for the time being. It was published in the spring of 2023.

○

I once had a panic attack on a super bumpy flight across the Atlantic and am forever grateful to the flight attendant who appeared by my side, calmly handed me a paper bag and said kindly but loudly: "Breathe." My working assumption was always that I would land safely, but I needed help to get through the turbulence and, in fact, I needed a new skill. Artemis Aerospace now lists deep breathing as a way to overcome fear of flying.

WORKING ASSUMPTIONS

According to National Geographic, turbulence is caused by "chaotic and capricious eddies of air, disturbed from a calmer state by various forces." This seems an apt metaphor for the knock-on effects of an interconnected world coming to grips with competing headwinds ranging from inflation to climate change, from supply chains to talent mobility, from ageing to artificial intelligence.

Laura Tyson, former director of the White House National Economic Council and distinguished professor of Haas School of Business at the University of California Berkeley, told me: "There are two major things going on. One is the digitization of everything, and then AI, which is making all that digitization much more intelligent. Anything at all that is cognitive and routine in nature, the machine can do it better, faster, cheaper."

The fear of AI inevitably comes up, but so too the recognition that when AI complements rather than replaces humans it can transform economies. Singapore's track record in innovating was very much in evidence. Soon Joo Gog, chief skills officer at training business SkillsFuture, reminded us of the way in which robots have long been integrated in helping elderly workers: companies such as RoboCoach, robotic fitness instructors, have been in the marketplace for some time.

Speaking at the launch of the Future of Jobs 2023 Report, WEF Managing Director Saadia Zahidi talked about the scale of the turbulence in the global job market: 23 percent of all jobs will face disruption. "Overall the picture is yes, complex, yes, affected by many trends, but also something that seems manageable provided that we focus on the reskilling and upskilling of workers," she said.

INTRODUCTION

Klaus Schwab, the WEF's founder, coined the phrase "The Fourth Industrial Revolution" in 2016 to describe the technological and digital advances engulfing the world and bringing with them unprecedented challenges. I put it to him that thanks to generative AI people have already entered the Fifth Industrial Revolution – in which the interface between humans and machines is being tested afresh. He agreed, telling me that he had never seen the landscape around jobs, growth, technology and people this complex.

Finding the balance between the grandiose big-data-big-picture and the granular is what matters. As American strategist Maril MacDonald put it to me, there is no one size fits all: "Companies are trying to really address what employees want but they are not one monolithic group, they're individuals."

My key takeaway was that turbulence isn't transitory – it's here to stay. In fact, climate change is now thought to be exacerbating air turbulence itself. Grains of sand in a grandiose world. Keep breathing deeply.

[May 11, 2023]

> The new technology of generative AI is currently in its fear phase: until people know how it works for them, they mistrust it. The perception right now is that jobs will be lost, and the robots are coming. There's also something else very new: a generation of young people who grew up and into the workplace during and post Covid.

What's Next?

My sightline is not the usual five years away beloved of politicians and corporate boards, but much closer. I'm basing my working assumptions on changes which will be happening or have happened by 2026, which is an important year for work. It will be the centenary of Henry Ford's introduction of the five-day-forty-hour week, a landmark moment which changed the modern contract between worker and manager, and which overturned overnight the working assumption that the human at work could be treated like a machine.

Henry Ford's workers went on to be his biggest consumers: they worked to buy the cars they built in order to enjoy the leisure time he gave them. Mass consumerism, mass entertainment and mass marketing all stemmed from this moment when to work and live became entwined.

A new world of work is here. What if we embraced it rather than resisted it? What if, as Henry Ford did before he introduced the five-day week, we seek to understand the changes and then act on them? As Ford told an interviewer: "This decision to put into effect the short work week is not sudden. We have been going towards it for three or four years. We have been feeling our way."

What if instead of clinging to the quarterly report and the five-year plan and the KPI (key performance indicators) we said, something has changed and needs to change. Let's do it differently?

What if, like a movie, we made our own ending, or at least the next stage better than the last part of the story?

INTRODUCTION

There's a glorious if elegantly lurid "what if?" poem by the British poet Roger McGough about love written in the summer of love, 1967, in which he imagines what would happen if a normal bus trip instead became a wild lovemaking session among all the passengers.* There's a lovely line that reads: "That night, on the bus coming home, we were all a little embarrassed, especially me and the young lady in the green hat."

That poem thinks the unthinkable – what would happen if something extraordinary and out of character happened (in a good way)? But it also speaks to the idea that when sudden shifts do happen, someone always wants them to stop, to go back to the safety and measured tone of before.

The working assumption across all the chapters here is that we are at an inflexion point in two ways. Firstly, around how to identify and handle the undeniable changes already wrought. But secondly, around whether we want to be optimists or pessimists, and whether we want to jump into new territory or retreat to the old.

We are at a philosophical moment of great reflection which is almost spiritual. It's certainly cultural. In any event, dry data alone is insufficient to convey what is happening. Data, as Lynda Gratton who so generously wrote the preface to this book always says to me, "is only a record of the past".

So, in the context of the past and the present – on to the future.

---

* Roger McGough, "At Lunchtime, A Story of Love", 1967, first published in *The Mersea Sound*, Penguin Books.

> *A new world of work is here. But what if we embraced it rather than resisted it? What if, instead of clinging to the quarterly report and the five-year plan and the Key Performance Indicators we said, something has changed and needs to change: let's do it differently?*

THE NEW JOB COLLAR

"There will come a point where no job is needed – you can have a job if you want one for personal satisfaction but AI will do everything."

Elon Musk*

"I exaggerate everything, that is where I go wrong."

Fyodor Dostoevsky, Notes from Underground†

Let's begin with the richest man in the world, a man who employs over a hundred thousand people worldwide, and the human currently most associated with technology anywhere on the planet: Elon Musk. Is his working assumption, delivered in his famously direct way so beloved of journalists, correct – that the end of the job is nigh?

Well, to quote from Evelyn Waugh's *Scoop*, that 1938 magisterial parody of media barons, "up to a point, Lord Copper".

---

* Elon Musk speaking to UK Prime Minister Rishi Sunak, at the AI Safety Summit held at Bletchley Park, November 2023.
† Dostoevsky's novella was published in 1864.

WORKING ASSUMPTIONS

Or, if you prefer your references closer to historical home, here's the most unintentionally apt statement a politician may have ever made – US Secretary of State Donald Rumsfeld in 2002: "There are known knowns. These are things we know that we know. There are known unknowns. That is to say, there are things that we know we don't know. But there are also unknown unknowns. There are things we don't know we don't know."

Well, there are some things we do know and some which are no exaggeration. The future of work is more uncertain than at any point in a century. If you think about it, we are at a similar inflexion point to the 1920s. First, we're coming out of a pandemic (replace Spanish Flu with Covid-19); second, we are grappling with the impact of new technologies of unprecedented scale and speed (replace automation and mass assembly lines with generative AI, VR and robotics). Third, people are able to communicate extensively in new ways (replace the arrival of radio, television and the movies in the 1920s, a mass but passive consumption of media, with today's instantly interactive world of TikTok, YouTube, Facebook and X).

Bang in the middle of all of this turmoil are people. People who work. Nearly three and a half billion people work around the world.[*] The latest World Economic Forum's Future of Jobs report[†] suggests that roughly a quarter of jobs "will change" by 2028[‡] and that this includes not only jobs lost as a result of new technology, but gained through the creation of newly created "green jobs", while a 2023 LinkedIn study found that demand for skills which

---

[*] From Statistica Global Employment Figures, November 2023.
[†] The latest World Economic Forum "Future of Jobs" report is the 2023 report.
[‡] World Economic Forum, etc.

help with sustainability and energy transition outpace supply by a ratio of 2:1.*

When any seismic new technology comes along, there is anxiety and doomsaying. Six hundred years ago the Benedictine monk and scribe Filippo de Strata railed in his "polemic against printing" against the book, and not only the jobs at risk but the morality at risk:

> the damage which results from the printers' cunning. They shamelessly print, at a negligible price, material which may, alas, inflame impressionable youths, while a true writer dies of hunger. Cure (if you will) the plague which is doing away with the laws of all decency, and curb the printers. They persist in their sick vices, setting Tibullus in type, while a young girl reads Ovid to learn sinfulness. Through printing, tender boys and gentle girls, chaste without foul stain, take in whatever mars purity of mind or body; they encourage wantoness, and swallow up huge gain from it.†

So exaggerate risk at your peril. The truth tends to be slightly more squiggly than linear. Less obsolescence than metamorphosis. But with generative AI the real risk, and the one which has caught people's attention, is not just to jobs themselves but to a class of job and worker previously inured to the blows of new technology: the highly paid, highly educated "white collar" worker. The jobs

---

* According to the latest World Economic Forum "Future of Jobs" report, some 23 percent of jobs are expected to change by 2027, with 69 million new jobs created and 83 million new jobs eliminated.

† Jeremy Strong's website History of Information provides a summary on Filippo de Strata's "polemic against printing".

may not be lost so much as "reshaped".* As Henry Coutinho-Mason, an innovations expert, put it to me: "We're not going to lose our jobs so much as lose our job descriptions."†

> *In a movie the narrative arc tends to go through five phases: exposition, rising action, climax, falling action, and resolution. I would say that we're in a new "rising action" phase of work, in which fresh drama is unfolding and new characters are emerging to test the identity of everyone who wants a job or holds a job. We haven't yet reached the climax, but with the new generation of generative AI we might.*

---

* The Forrester 2023 Generative AI Jobs Impact survey is entitled "Generative AI will reshape more jobs than it eliminates".
† Henry's Coutinho-Mason co-authored *The Future Normal: How We Will Live, Work and Thrive in the Next Decade* (Ideapress Publishing, 9 May 2023) with Rohit Bhargava.

The Great Re-Evaluation

"Hybrid work is for everyone far stickier than most of us could ever have imagined at the start of the pandemic."

Emma Goldberg of *The New York Times*,
The Nowhere Office podcast, 2023

In a movie the narrative arc tends to go through five phases: exposition, rising action, climax, falling action, and resolution. I would say that we're in a new "rising action" phase of work, in which fresh drama is unfolding and new characters are emerging to test the identity of everyone who wants a job or holds a job. We haven't yet reached the climax, but with the new generation of generative AI we might.

Certainly every job of every kind is undergoing an identity shift of sorts. Pre-Covid work identity hinged a lot on the identity politics of sex, race and gender. That's likely to continue, but identity is taking on a new meaning. How an individual worker identifies in society at large will be accompanied by an emphasis on the identity of the nature of the work they are doing. Equally, the job description will matter less than the specific task at hand. Stackable skills will replace a single job, and in this way, identity at work will, in fact, multiply.

Back in 1851, William Mayhew interviewed a lot more "Punch and Judy Men" and "Mudlarks" than there are today for his volume *London Labour and London Poor*.* Some of the shifts in jobs come about through cultural change – prostitution hasn't gone

---

* William Mayhew, *London Labour and the London Poor*: a cyclopaedia of the condition and earnings of those that will work, those that cannot work, and those that will not work, 1851.

anywhere since Mayhew's time, but in December 2023 Amsterdam began clearing its famous red light window displays – but some have evolved through technology.

As the Oxford economists Carl Benedikt Frey and Michael Osborne point out:

> *attempts to assess whether a job is automatable by merely looking at the fraction of tasks that can be done by machines, as many economists have, will lead to flawed estimates: you will inevitably conclude that the work of lamplighters, farm labourers, elevator operators, car washers, switchboard operators, and truck drivers cannot be automated. Yet history has shown us that such occupations have indeed been automated.**

It's a valuable lesson: we can't live in a bubble of the present. The history of work and jobs is littered with disruption, change, and we live today as much with the relics of old ways of working as we do the moulds of new forms we are creating.

Disappearing jobs is not a new problem, and neither is dissatisfaction with work. I particularly love the only number-one single enjoyed by country singer Johnny Paycheck: his no-nonsense song "Take This Job and Shove It", released in 1977, "when we were in the middle of a mass technology consumer boom but five years out from double digit unemployment for the first time since 1940".† And who can forget Dolly Parton's "9 to 5", expressing her morning cup of coffee as "a cup of ambition"‡ in a sweetly packaged cry of outrage at the way women at work were treated.

---

* Carl Benedikt-Frey and Michael Osborne, "Generative AI and the Future of Automation: Brown Journal of World Affairs", January 2024.
† Historical US Unemployment Rate by Year, The Balance website.
‡ Dolly Parton's song "9-5" written for the comedy film of 1980 of the same name.

THE NEW JOB COLLAR

But today something is different. Jobs are dissolving into new forms in the areas which used to be insulated from disruption, namely among highly educated, white collar workers. People have more power than before to take the job and shove it in a labor market wildly disrupted by Covid, and the surprisingly strong gusts of inflationary wind which swept have through the world – surging to 7.5 percent in August 2022.*

Factor in too some other directly Covid-related effects: around the world, furlough disrupted the psychological contract many had with work.† The sense of carpe diem triggered by a pandemic instilling loss, fear and disruption into every single household had an impact on the record numbers of people who did not go back to work as before. Childcare plans changed. Commutes changed. Jobs which had been stopped restarted with a labor force somewhere else entirely than at the start of the pandemic. Young people locked down in their bedrooms or college rooms experienced work and life through a screen as never before.

Some say this new generation of young people is "Generation Glass" – they grew up with touch screens. They don't want to work like "we" did – "we" meaning Gen X or older. They don't have a lived experience of a job which is supposed to stick, so even well-educated college graduates are not rushing to pin down a job, preferring choice, preferring stop–start work. The phenomenon of the graduate barista isn't entirely due to work shortages anywhere else. It's becoming a lifestyle triggered by Covid.

---

* International Monetary Fund, "Here Comes the Change: The Role of Global and Domestic Factors in Post-Pandemic Inflation in Europe", December 9, 2022.
† BBC reported on global furlough rates, May 2020.

This was aided and abetted by a loose labor market, which thanks to the stop–start nature of lockdowns (and in Britain, Brexit causing many European workers to move away) experienced a recruitment and retention crisis. Certain sectors such as hospitality and care work were especially badly hit. Those who went back to work were cited as engaging in "quiet quitting"* – showing up, but not going the extra mile. The live-to-work ethic was becoming something else: work to live. All of it a sign of too much turbulence. Too much disruption. Too many new habits laid down across the world. This, coupled with an unprecedented global roll-out of remote technology such as teleconferencing which proved new ways to work, came together in a perfect tipping point.

People called this "the Great Resignation" but I think it was something else: the Great Re-evaluation. Nothing felt the same, just as nothing was the same. What then, was happening?

My first "Working Assumptions" column addressed jobs and was written in September 2022, a year before ChatGPT blew open the doors on the debate about the future of jobs once again.† I wanted to summarize the big trends in the round, the ones I thought would stick around. I began with a reference to my favorite modern artist, René Magritte, and in order to share it with you now I instructed ChatGPT's DALL-E to imagine a modern iteration of it.

---

* According to the *Los Angeles Times*, "quiet quitting" first hit the internet in March 2022 when Brian Creely posted a Tik Tok video about employees "coasting" at work.
† Julia Hobsbawm, "Hello to the Flexetariat, Empowered Employees Who Want a Change", Bloomberg, September 27, 2022.

THE NEW JOB COLLAR

Microsoft Bing's 2023 DALL-E's rendition of a modern take on Magritte's famous *Golconda* painting of 1953.

The future of work was foretold half a century ago, not in commerce but in art. In Belgian surrealist René Magritte's 1953 oil painting Golconda, *a throng of identically dressed men in trench coats and bowler hats fill the sky, framed only by buildings. They exist in tight, monotonous formation. Only on close inspection can you see any individuality on their faces. The suggestion of office life as surreal imprisonment is clear.*

In 2022, the prisoners have jumped the barricades. The air is full of the Great Resignation and quiet quitting. Nearly half of senior HR leaders surveyed by consulting firm Gartner Inc. are now concerned by "mass turnover events". Gone are the assumptions of an era the painting captured: capitalism's soaring post-war ambition, when professional and technical work quadrupled. When wearing the white collar of a suit and tie (versus the blue collar of manufacturing overalls) brought higher earnings and status. When conformity and a daily commute into gleaming city skyscrapers were a price worth paying for the promise of promotion.

Before the Covid-19 pandemic, 8 percent of professionals in knowledge work worked from home. By the second quarter of 2020, the International Labour Organization estimates that an average of 17.4 percent were working remotely. Statistically it takes sixty-six days to establish a habit: by spring of 2022, when a permanent return to working life looked possible in the majority of countries, 700 days had passed since the start of pandemic. New habits had been established in people's lives, new arrangements for childcare made as well as new relocations. And something else besides: re-evaluation.

Microsoft's Work Trend Index for 2022, which surveyed over 30,000 people in thirty countries, noted: "We're not the same people that went home to work early in 2020." The traumatic and unifying impact of Covid-19 itself made reassessing priorities mainstream and gave a new lease of life to the phrase carpe diem. People have indeed begun to "seize the day". A 2022 Gallup survey puts wellbeing and work–life balance almost neck-and-neck with pay as a priority.

The pandemic tipped a low rumbling about flexible working and work–life balance into a roar.

Clearly without the stop–start nature of lockdowns the shift to working from home and the surprise findings of productivity gains *would not have happened. To just "go back", which was the working assumption of most governments and business leaders, turned out to be wrong.*

Today we are at the beginning of a new era I call "The Nowhere Office", in which many of the old assumptions about where, when and how people work will continue to be shifted by new realities that dominate the people who seek knowledge work and those who manage and lead them.

I see three particular trends to note.

The Rising Demand for Flexible Working

The first is flexibility. The flexible workplace will win over the inflexible one, and the world has a new kind of worker: the Flexetariat. Today the unquestioning drudge, hemmed in by the commute, has been replaced by a highly assertive worker who puts freedom and flexibility at the center of their working identity.

McKinsey & Co.'s American Opportunity Survey shows that 87 percent of workers say that if offered flexibility they would take it. Some 58 percent of workers across both blue and white collar occupations already do – they're able to work from home at least one day a week. Data from recruitment firm Upwork Inc. shows that 78 percent of freelancers cite the ability to schedule flexibility as a key concern. The global freelance market is set to grow at a compound annual rate of 15 percent from 2021 to 2026.

The Flexetariat values their time as much as their freedom. Apple Inc. and Alphabet Inc. are among the companies that have all faced employee backlash against their presenteeism efforts, with Stanford University professor Nicholas Bloom, a key researcher on remote work trends, noting that noncompliance is as high as 40 percent in some companies trying to force return to office on staff.

Many leaders were – and some remain – skeptical of hybrid working (the post-pandemic way to describe flexible working) because it's hugely disruptive to implement and still very much a work in progress. These leaders continue to find it frustrating and disappointing that they can't either compel or cajole their office workers back. One of the most vocal has been Tesla Inc. chief executive officer Elon Musk, who has adopted a novel motivational leadership style by publicly berating workers who aren't in the office physically and suggesting "they should pretend to work somewhere else".

And yet smart leaders are beginning to loosen their presentation bias: a 2022 survey from Morning Consult, commissioned by Zoom, showed that 90 percent of senior leaders preferred a hybrid or remote working environment to full-time presenteeism. They understand that culture and cohesion can be built in new ways on new schedules.

Companies like Harman International Industries Inc., a Samsung Electronics Co.-owned audio technology producer of headphones and luxury in-car systems with about 30,000 employees around the world, has introduced Harman Flex and recently convened its senior global leaders in Miami to mandate them. It's expected to affect 40 percent of the company.

Four-day-week trials have happened and are underway throughout the world. Fujitsu Ltd. has embraced a flexible work policy dubbed #workyourway, making flexible working the norm, and some European banks now say flexibility is a competitive advantage. For better or worse, having a flexible working policy is going to become de rigueur.

Yet flexibility has its drawbacks. No one size fits all, which makes it very messy to manage. Plus, those who can work from home experience downsides, ranging from unwanted surveillance to longer hours and always-on culture. Also, those who can't work flexibly still outnumber those who can – and often tensions arise when they do so in the same workplace. In the future, the broker of many of these tensions will be trade unions, who are the focus of the second shift to watch: power.

The Employee–Employer Power Shift

Flexible working policies now feature in a raft of new legislation across the world. Ireland declared remote work a national strategy. Recent reform of EU employment law will affect 180 million workers and is designed to regularize an increasingly unpredictable labor market. The UK's "right to request" flexible working law is expected to be updated for the first time since 2014. A recent parliamentary recommendation stated the need to "continue to consider the rights of those who wish to work flexibly and develop a better understanding of what 'flexibility' means for the various groups that make up the workforce."

The admission that lawmakers must better understand their workers somewhat understates the power shift. The consulting firm PricewaterhouseCoopers LLP notes that "there is an opportunity for unions who wish to build a more prominent role to do so and to reassert their relevance in the modern workplace." While trade union membership continues to decline overall, 80 percent of countries were involved in union-led discussion during the pandemic, according to the International Labour Organization. Hitherto union-immune organizations – from Amazon.com

Inc. to Starbucks Corp. – have faced unprecedented activism and unwanted media attention.

White collar demands are becoming a contagion that may indirectly increase the power of frontline workers, too.

Part of the rebalancing of power is clearly connected to the historically tight labor market – making recruitment and retention, regarded in some industries as a headwind, every bit as significant as geopolitical instability or the energy crisis. But part of it is a failure of leaders to update their working assumptions.

The Australian psychologist and philosopher Elton Mayo, whose research in the 1920s and 1930s challenged assumptions about workers as mechanistic humans whose productivity could be improved only by extrinsic rewards like pay and who ushered in the human relations school of management, noted in The Social Problems of an Industrial Civilization *that "it is no longer possible for an industrial society to assume that the technical processes of manufacture will exist unchanged for long in any type of work."*

The Daily Commute Is Dead

Clearly, Mayo's "technical processes of manufacture" as it applies to modern knowledge workers is changing through technology, but so is the location of that process. On to the third shift: place.

The commute is now seen as a passion killer for workers. In the UK, towns like Watford, which is situated within an area known as "the golden triangle" between the universities in London, Cambridge and Oxford, are rising in fortune, while the recent billion-dollar deal by real estate agents Workspace Group Plc across fifty subur-

ban offices in the US shows a bet that the migration of offices to be near to where people live will continue.

Office life was changing at least a decade before the pandemic's tipping point. The internet, smartphone and teleconferencing ushered much of work into a new venue: cyberspace. WeWork Inc., the breakthrough pioneer of co-working spaces, was founded in 2010. Interestingly, property giant Cushman & Wakefield Plc invested $150 million in a strategic partnership with WeWork in 2021.

Back to Magritte's surreal masterpiece Golconda, depicting those samey humans in humdrum lockstep. It hangs in Houston, Texas, the state where the iconic I.M. Pei-designed Energy Plaza is being transformed into mixed-use workspace with apartments. Real estate analysis and investment firm CBRE notes that over half of companies want to reduce their office space "mostly to eliminate excess space they anticipate will be freed up by remote work and more efficient use."

Carpe diem plays its part in this shift. People don't want to waste time on travel that doesn't matter, or on being unproductive. Research by office outfitter Steelcase Inc. noted that in full occupancy times 87 percent of workers spent two to four hours away from their desk. (Not that the Flexetariat is without its contradictions: research by David Courpasson, a professor at France's Emlyon Business School and colleagues at the Louvain School of Management in Belgium also shows considerable resistance to hot desks because people want a fixed personal space, even if they don't want to have to use it every day.)

The office, historically, has both been a place to get the admin done, but also to bond and build culture. Spare a thought for the well-

intentioned CEO who wants growth to come the old-fashioned way: via the teamwork that comes from being face to face.

The biggest shift can be seen in the move from a property-based approach to a philosophical one. What will matter going forward isn't jettisoning the old assumptions of a large office space to house ranks of worker cubicles, but something else entirely: a place to give people meaning and the new assumption that this isn't all day, every day, in one place.

Sandy Pentland at MIT and colleagues in the human gymnastics lab interpret the "social physics" philosophy of the nineteenth century into real-world innovation in how people move around space to work their best. To gossip and huddle and innovate before springing apart again to their lives.

The leader who wishes to get colleagues back to the office more will have to invest in a socially scientific understanding of dynamics around networks, collaboration and innovation. Simply plumping up the cushions and installing better showers and coffee isn't going to move the needle.

It turns out that the definition of what productive work is and how work culture can be successfully fostered needs to be radically revised. No, it isn't the end of the water cooler, and no, it isn't the end of growth, and no, it isn't even the end of the office.

But it's the beginning of a new time in which place, identity, culture, purpose, wellbeing and productivity occur against a new set of working conditions.

It's the beginning of a new time when the worker being is understood to be the human being, shorn of their job title or uniform (or bowler hat) and replaced instead by a group of individuals who still need to work – but differently from before.

[September 27, 2022]

How did these initial working assumptions hold up? Well enough, as anyone who doesn't have commercial skin in the game perpetuating the old model can have. Chapter two deals with the power shift and chapter three with the commute. In December 2023 I was asked for my single prediction for 2024, and I cited "the Flexetariat",* because it has become clear that it's the "roar" over flexible working which has stuck most as the biggest single shift in workplace practices before ChatGPT came along.

Flexible working, hybrid working (the terms matter and it's a little messy how they are used, which needs to change) has come to represent the real and existential crisis facing work and the workplace. Although over half of jobs cannot be done remotely or even hybrid, the universal desire to have flexibility as an option has become emblematic of the dissatisfaction across all sectors of work, and the shift from one old order to a new, as yet incomplete one.

---

* Quoted in "The Flex Report: 2024 Predictions", published by Flex Index (December 2023).

WORKING ASSUMPTIONS

Shirking from Home

"Sighed Mayzie, a lazy bird hatching an egg: 'I'm tired and I'm bored And I've kinks in my leg from sitting, just sitting here day after day. It's work! How I hate it! I'd much rather play!'"

Dr Seuss, *Horton Hatches the Egg* (1940)

As a child I was quite an avid reader. I ate up all the Laura Ingalls Wilder *Little House on the Prairie* books and the Enid Blyton series *Mallory Towers, Secret Seven* and *Famous Five*, but no matter how old I got there was one battered book I would pull down again and again: *Horton Hatches the Egg* by Dr Seuss.

I was gripped by the story of hard-working Horton, an elephant who ambles by a tree where Mayzie the lazy bird persuades Horton to (he imagines) briefly take over her job sitting on her egg, only to fly off and plan on not returning. The conceit of this story was incredible to me. A bad mother bird, so bad that a big fat boy elephant was better than her! And Horton was the most loyal, principled elephant. "I meant what I said and I said what I meant… An elephant's faithful, one hundred percent," he says, through wind and rain.

Horton is rewarded: the egg hatches, not as a bird but an ele-bird with wings and also a trunk "just like his"! It is enchanting, but it's also subversive: it imagines a world of job role-play, rather presciently. And it takes a pop, as you might expect from an American of Dr Seuss' generation, at the idea of a working mother: in his other very famous book *The Cat in the Hat*, children are left alone all day to play, all sorts of havoc ensues, and the returning mother is characterized by a single image – half a silhouette in impeccable stilettoes, hat and coat, marching purposefully home after neglectfully *not* working at home.

The working assumption that women's place is in the home has been replaced by a more widespread hostility to working *from* home, whoever is doing it. The culture war around the future of hybrid work and flexibility has become the main narrative arc to date of the story of post-pandemic work. LinkedIn, the social network for professionals which is proving to be a reliable source of opinion and data on a rolling basis, is alive with argument, counterpoint and datasets.

When I wrote my last book, *The Nowhere Office*, it was never an argument for no office – nor was it to forget that the majority of the world's workers are not white collar at all. But it did point out that work was changing fundamentally whether people liked it or not, due to a coalescence of factors which had been bubbling up at work since the end of the Second World War. Covid was the proverbial tipping point, and hybrid working using the latest technology the manifestation of a desire to not "go back" to old ways of living and working.

That working assumption has broadly held. At least among employees. But out of it has come a battle about presenteeism which continues unabated. One of the most memorable phrases of the Covid pandemic was the one made by Goldman Sachs chief David Solomon in 2020 that working from home was "an aberration",* a sentiment which by 2023 had morphed into "shirking from home",† a phrase used by the British newspaper columnist

---

* Speaking at Credit Suisse's annual virtual financial services, April 2019.
† Richard Littlejohn is a *Daily Mail* columnist.

Richard Littlejohn (who, as I understand it, files his copy remotely). Phrases such as "get your butt into the office" or entreaties to stop being "lazy gits" have also been bandied about.* Nearly four years later, you do not have to scratch the surface hard to find these views prevail, especially among male leaders of a certain generation. One utterly charming captain of industry told me at an awards dinner at Claridge's, London, in the winter of 2023 that "as soon as the economy shrinks, people will stop all this stuff about wanting to work flexibly".

Well, it's the economy, stupid. Maybe he is right. Maybe this is the modern boss's dream rather than dilemma, to force workers to scuttle back to old *modus vivendi* in order to prove they were right all along. Enlightenment? More like entrenchment. Assumptions based on fear, bias or ignorance and enforced by diktat seldom end well or as intended, but, of course, mud sticks.

And it continues to stick to women.

As economics professor Claudia Goldin, who became the first female economist to win the Nobel Prize in 2023, has shown, women reached heights of employment, but a pay gap has persisted, as have the effects of what is now known as the "motherhood penalty".† I attended a conference entitled "The Implications of Remote Work" at Stanford University in the autumn of 2023 and one of the most memorable papers showed that a bias against women persists not only when they work but

---

* Negative comments on working from home by MillerKnoll CEO Andi Owen and Sir Alan Sugar.
† Claudia Goldin won a Nobel Prize for her research on female employment, which showed that employment among married women decreased in the 1800s, as the economy moved away from agriculture and towards industry.

> *The working assumption that women's place is in the home has been replaced by a more widespread hostility to working from home, whoever is doing it. The culture war around the future of hybrid work and flexibility has become the main narrative arc to date of the story of post-pandemic work.*

when they work flexibly.* Show someone an apparently empty office and say it belongs to a man and they make a very different working assumption (he's out at a meeting) than if you assign said office to a woman (she's not working because she's not in). At the end of 2023, when it was clear that the arguments over flexible and hybrid working were not abating, Erin Grau of workplace consultancy Charter wrote an article in *Fortune* headlined "Flexible work is feminist – and women won't return to a system that hasn't served them well to spare the feelings of powerful men".†

It's clear that the assumption that women who work and have children are inconveniencing their co-workers or bosses is being weaponized by arguments that flexible work is somehow selfish or inefficient or both; and that the real beneficiaries of those who can afford to return to old models of presenteeism are unlikely to

---

* Claire Daviss, Emma Williams-Baron, Erin Macke, "Hiring the Ideal Remote Worker: The Gendered Implications of the Rise of Remote Work", Stanford Institute of Economic Policy Research.
† Erin Grau, "Flexible work is feminist–and women won't return to a system that hasn't served them well to spare the feelings of powerful men", Fortune, May 14, 2023.

have caring roles, with their inherent limits on old model "always in" flexibility.

This isn't to say that flexibility doesn't have drawbacks and inequalities. But the argument that every woman who wants to work flexibly is de facto a modern-day Mayzie the lazy bird is to be resisted.

> *There is no longer one size fits all when it comes to managing workforces. I think this is amazingly exciting and important, but I can see how it throws a spanner in the works of an entire generation of leaders brought up on a globalized standard – from the MBA to off-the-shelf solutions with names like "Agile". If I sound sneery it's because I am. There is nothing wrong with creating models or applying them, but that only goes so far. Emerging challenges require innovation, reaction, responsibility.*

Think Global, Act Local

Dr Seuss had one thing right in *Horton Hatches the Egg*: he painted a picture of a world of global travel (at one point Horton is hauled across oceans to become an exhibit showing a man-elephant minding a she-bird's nest).

Jobs have never been more transient or more transportable than now. "Talent Mobility" has become a buzzword within companies, with research showing that a third of global CEOs want to "reimagine their global rotations".* What this means is that the corporate world, and American corporations are some of the world's largest employers outside of America, are constantly moving teams around the world. Those teams of course are in different time zones, which has given rise to the wonderful phrase "time zone adjacency".† What does this mean in practice? Even if you are in your office, you might be in a meeting with someone halfway around the world. At least some of you will be attending remotely, even if you technically work from an office.

Ironically, the globalized model of managing jobs, of managing HR, of managing how hybrid works out has increasingly come to require local, iterative, customized solutions. There is no longer one size fits all when it comes to managing workforces. I think this is amazingly exciting and important, but I can see how it throws a spanner in the works of an entire generation of leaders brought up on a globalized standard – from the MBA to off-the-shelf

---

* "Navigating the increasing complexities of talent mobility", Mercer.
† Arpit Gupta Vrinda Mittal Stijn Van Nieuwerburgh, "Work from Home and the Office Real Estate Apocalypse", National Bureau of Economic Research, September 8, 2022.

solutions with names like "Agile".* If I sound sneery it's because I am. There is nothing wrong with creating models or applying them, but that only goes so far. Emerging challenges require innovation, reaction, responsibility.

There are plenty of good leaders doing this, by the way. Companies from Atlassian to Salesforce, from Patagonia to Panasonic are embracing true flexibility. In Japan they call their flexibility policy "Work Your Way".† My friend and mentor Charles Handy, author of many business bestsellers with glorious titles like *The Empty Raincoat*, says, "We are all prisoners of our past. It is hard to think of things except in the way we have always thought of them. But that solves no problems and seldom changes anything."‡

The reality is that everyone serious and reasonable in leadership is doing their level best to iterate as they should, workplace by workplace, industry by industry, and not to try and impose a top-down model which is in itself an outdated working assumption about what success looks like. The corporate world is littered with the corpses of leaders who did not listen on all sorts of things. The BlackBerry, Blockbuster and Kodak are all examples of twentieth-century companies which rode huge technology waves and then did not embrace new times.

---

* Ken Schwaber and Jeff Sutherland are the creators of the Agile project management methodology.
† "Work Your Way" is Fujitsu's flexible work approach.
‡ Charles Handy is an Irish author/philosopher specializing in organizational behavior and management whose books garnered a cult following in the 1980s and 1990s. This is from *The Elephant and the Flea: Reflections of a Reluctant Capitalist*, published in 2003 by Harvard Business Press.

The leader who keeps failing to read the room on workforce flexibility looks Luddite. It's as simple as that.

This battle between those who believe that flexible working is a combination of disloyalty, inefficiency or lack of work ethic, and those who believe that a new adaptive way of working has presented itself which should be taken advantage of is a particular shock to the American way of work, which has always been always on, and which has flipped since the pandemic from a live to work ethic to the precise opposite: work to live.

It is possible to have a foot in both camps. There are people who recognize that flexibility is about personalization by workplace, by team requirement, by deadline, by *job*. Nevertheless, the hostility to the notion of working flexibly remains, usually with men of a certain age in a certain kind of industry. Not all men, it should be said: the viral video of 2023 was the speech Andi Owen, CEO of MillerKnoll, gave to her executives telling them to leave "pity city" and "just get the damn $26 million" target.*

> *We may not have 20:20 vision but we all have a vision post 2020 about how things were, how they are, and how they can be.*

---

* MillerKnoll CEO Andi Owen's video tirade to her employees about not asking for bonuses went viral in April 2023.

The Presenteeism Premium

To be fair, hybrid work is hard to handle, and causes a headache for managers precisely because it is not one size fits all. At every corporate gig or party a CEO will come up and grumble about how hard it is to implement. They have a point.

While white and blue collar jobs used to feel separate, with different uniforms, types of work and working hours, the new hybrid workplace has created class divisions within a single workplace like never before. Presenteeism is political – a penalty for some, a choice for others.

I sat on a London tube train in the summer of 2023 and eavesdropped on striking primary school teachers on their way to march over pay and conditions. "My flatmate works from home three days a week," one said. "That doesn't feel fair." You can hear the butterfly wings of chaos theory flapping here. Teachers are not normally counted as remote or flexible workers, but that was before the pandemic, when day-to-day classroom teaching in schools was done in person, not remotely. Ditto medical help. Yes, you could provide video conferencing to far-flung places which could not be accessed, but as a mainstream activity? These were jobs where you "had" to be in person.

The online learning platform Coursera now has 136 million users, aka students online, and is seeing a steady rise since the pandemic.* What is also interesting is that this company now specializes in online certificated learning for some of the world's biggest

---

* Dhawal Shah, "Coursera Consumer Revenues Nearing $100M, Driven by Industry Content", The Report, October 21, 2023.

THE NEW JOB COLLAR

FIRST THEY COME FOR THE BLUE COLLAR
THEN THEY COME FOR THE KNOWLEDGE WORKER

companies, among them Google, IBM and Microsoft. I myself have joined the books of an online corporate learning business called Teamraderie* to teach classes to "students" in adjacent time zones all over the US.

This has completely changed. There now *has to* be a reason to be in person, a reason which everyone agrees with on both sides of the table, manager and worker alike. And increasingly, a premium for doing so. My working assumption is that presenteeism is going to play a far more vivid role in negotiations, just as it is in recruitment: LinkedIn saw a 52.4 percent rise in hybrid role postings in August 2023, according to their annual Workforce Report.†

---

* Teamraderie.com
† LinkedIn's Workforce Report (WFR), hybrid jobs saw a 52.4 percent year-on-year (YoY) increase and accounted for 20.1 percent of the postings in August 2023.

Flex Index is a new quarterly measurement of flexible working in the United States. Its data showed that far from rising post pandemic, the number of companies with full-time presenteeism in the office dropped from 49 percent post pandemic to 42 percent in the second quarter of 2023.* But the most startling fact is that flexible working policy is prevalent in companies founded after 2000. Over 80 percent of these companies offer "work location flexibility".

In future employers will need to acknowledge the location and hours of workers and even offer a presenteeism premium when they want their workers – public or private sector – to work from a fixed base, on a rigid schedule.†

You cannot put the genie of flexibility back in the bottle, and the working assumption that you can will prove one of the biggest management errors of the post-pandemic economy.

> *The corporate world is littered with the corpses of leaders who did not listen to all sorts of things. The Blackberry, Blockbuster and Kodak are all examples of twentieth century companies which rode huge technology waves and then did not embrace new times.*

---

* Rob Sadow is the CEO of Scoop Technologies and mastermind behind the Flex Index which unveils fresh research on Fortune 500 hybrid work trends.
† Tom Rees, "Want a Pay Raise? Work Five Days a Week in the Office", Bloomberg, January 27, 2023.

Inputs 'n' Outputs

The poster-man for flexible working, or at least the person who has consistently said that hybrid working is here to stay, is the British-born academic Professor Nicholas Bloom, the William D. Eberle Professor of Economics at Stanford University whose research* is updated monthly. I interviewed him late in 2023 for a series of short Bloomberg Originals video interviews and asked for his take on what he has described as the biggest mass social experiment since the Second World War:

> *I think most people agree the shift to hybrid working is permanent, but there's still some debate. To give you a rough overview of where we are, 60 percent of Americans and Northern Europeans can't work from home at all. So I think of people that work in McDonald's, you know, or hospital security, etc. They just have to come in every day. Plenty do. The majority of workers do.*
>
> *There's another 30 percent that are hybrid that typically work from home two days a week. And then there's the remaining 10 percent that are fully remote. And they're working from home every day, day in, day out, week in, week out. If you look in the data, employees typically want to work from home about three days a week. But while professionals and graduates want something like two days a week working from home, if you interview senior managers, they want more like one. So you have almost like haggling happening!*

---

* See wfhresearch.com for monthly data compiled by Professor Bloom and his colleagues around the world.

WORKING ASSUMPTIONS

> *The most surprising thing of all is actually that work from home has worked so much. I did a study back in 2010, 2012 that showed this enormous positive productivity impact on work from home. And certainly, if you had asked me if there was global pandemic and forced working from home, what will happen, I would have probably said it would be chaos, the economy will collapse. I would have said then, you can't do it.*
>
> *Then we did have a pandemic. Then forced working from home did happen. And as it's happened, it's worked out surprisingly well. And actually by 2023, we're probably better off. I think productivity is a bit higher from some folks being hybrid. So I've just been amazed about how well it's worked and it makes you think, what else is out there we should change?!*
>
> *I mean, there's other things no one would have thought that work from home would have been successful. Maybe long summer holidays, maybe a five-day week, maybe, you know, organizational structures and firms. Some or all of this stuff could change and we'll discover we're much better off.*

For some, this argument is a red rag to a bull. This is partly because there is no doubt that implementing hybrid working has been hard and adds a layer of complexity. How to measure people who aren't toiling away in front of you requires a leap of faith and imagination, and the ability to trust on a task-based not time-based measurement of productivity.

And productivity has become the political football of the whole hybrid debate.

It's important to remember that not every job can be flexible or location agnostic, and that labor markets are not all the same.

THE NEW JOB COLLAR

Microsoft DALL-E's AI-generated image of a manager monitoring productivity (note that no gender was specified so it selected one automatically based on the information it's drawing on).

The debate about where and when people work is as variable as the vast global standard classification which stretches over ten core areas and thousands of sub-divided jobs.*

Flexible working and how productive it is or isn't can become weaponized or contextualized. For instance: *The Economist* ran

---

* International Labor Organization, classification of jobs.

a piece in July 2023 headlined "The fight for working from home goes global",* citing two pieces of research which showed that productivity in some data entry work which was fully remote in India dipped by as much as 18 percent, and an Asian IT firm was 19 percent less productive at home compared to the office. *The Economist* is often "against" working remotely or hybrid.

I broached the topic of productivity in a Bloomberg Work Shift column in October 2023. It was headlined "Productivity Matters, But Not as a Political Football for Remote Work":

◇

I have been toiling away on your behalf thinking about the future of work and being, if I may say so, rather productive. I mean "productive" in the driest economic sense, which is that my "inputs" have included attending two conferences on work in the US recently – "The Implications of Remote Work" conference on the West Coast, hosted by the Hoover Institution at Stanford University, and "Going to Work" on the East, hosted by Bloomberg Beta in Baltimore – and my "outputs" include this column.

Productivity is a hot topic now. The working assumption that productivity matters has been turbocharged by a combination of recent technological and social changes at work. Much faith is being placed on how generative AI will only increase this elusive elixir.

But in order to make progress we need to do two things. We must re-examine how we measure it and we must go beyond the weaponizing of productivity in relation to remote work. Productivity has definitely become something of a political football in

---

* *The Economist*, "The fight for working from home goes global", July 2023.

the culture wars post-Covid when it comes to whether working from home helps or hinders output. The context, as academics are wont to say, is "heterogeneous", which translates as every workplace and workers' circumstances being different in some way from each other.

For example, one recent working paper cites lower productivity in some working-from-home situations while a paper presented at the Stanford conference shows the opposite. Nevertheless, according to Nicholas Bloom, a professor at Stanford and co-convener of the remote work conference, there is growing evidence of "the triumph of the post-2020 US productivity acceleration."

This doesn't stop those who remain wedded to permanent presenteeism from including it as a measurement of productivity and to commandeer surveillance software to do so: 37 percent of employers are using live feeds to monitor their remote-working employees, according to one survey.

Is productivity all about presenteeism anyway? Obviously not. What about other metrics? How about the output side? I asked Carl Benedikt Frey, a professor at the Oxford Internet Institute whose joint paper was presented at Stanford's remote work conference. He told me when we talk about productivity we need to talk about quality, not just quantity.

"Long-run productivity depends on innovation and innovation requires time to think and reflect, potentially reducing productivity in the short run," he said. "Metrics can at times even be counterproductive. Take China, where incentives are provided to file as many patents as possible. The result has been plenty of weak patents rather than a few strong ones, leading to patent inflation."

So showing up or producing more isn't always the right measurement. There's more bad news for those wedded to dry measurement of output and that comes with research cited by the World Economic Forum, which shows that napping at work can significantly increase productivity. Shock! Horror! Clearly, we need to rethink productivity, and a clue comes from something economists devoted to data may not feel that comfortable with: feelings.

In a paper published in 2006, around the time that the idea of measuring wellbeing alongside gross domestic product was surfacing, the psychologists Daniel Kahneman and Alan Krueger proposed "the U-index, a misery index of sorts, which measures the proportion of time that people spend in an unpleasant state."

In other words, you can measure all you like, but you might be measuring misery. Plus, not all work is knowledge work. Some work can be measured more easily than others. Take Bethlehem Steel, once one of the largest steel producers in the world. Its mill in Maryland, which closed in 2012, was in the same state where my second work conference took place and also happened to be at the epicenter of early experiments on productivity a century ago. Frederick Winslow Taylor memorably conducted his "pig iron" studies to forensically break down worker tasks and productivity in time and motion measurements.

Can this column be measured like pig iron, or by how little or how much sleep I had crossing continents to write it? I can tell you I enjoyed myself in the production process. Readers will have their own metrics of productivity, but like academic papers on the topic, no two measurements will be exactly the same.

[October 20, 2023]

Just as you can't measure a column like pig iron, you cannot generalize about all jobs beyond pointing out that this is a moment when all jobs, in their infinite variety, are being affected at the same time by similar forces: global economic headwinds, from inflation to war. All jobs are affected by the knock-on effects of a pandemic which has impacted public health in the short, medium and probably long term, has disrupted supply chains, and has created fissures between different kinds of work down in the same workplace. And the exponential speeding up of technology to impact jobs, annihilate others, and create new ones in an intense burst not seen for a century. All jobs are experiencing turbulence, *everything everywhere all at once*.

> We're all in a new state of work – I call it the United State of Work. The global workforce is more united than at any point in its history. Common challenges render differences narrower than at any time in the last century. Jobs which are dominated by class, by educational difference, are all facing the same challenges and a blurring of roles within those jobs. We can see this now.

WORKING ASSUMPTIONS

Redrawing Work's Boundaries

The addition of generative AI, specifically ChatGPT, arriving as it did, as Hemingway might have said, gradually then suddenly, in October 2022 might have seemed by some to be divine intervention and by others to be the mother of all headaches. But it once again underscored the universal upheaval of jobs.

It seems absurd to ask a computer to draw an illustration from scratch "in the style of Vincent Van Gogh, imagining a traditional blue collar worker and a traditional white collar worker", but this is what I did at Christmas 2023 and this is the result… in less than thirty seconds. It took longer to label it and upload it than to get it done in the first place.

Why this seems more extraordinary than a Google search, or a Word doc, or a typewriter is debatable, but by late 2023 it was clear that ChatGPT was a gamechanger for the world of white collar work in a similar way to automation and outsourcing had been decades earlier for the blue collars of the world. Generative AI had definitely replaced remote and hybrid in my mind as the dominant issue, not because the question of work location isn't live and connected to wider issues about productivity and presenteeism, but because the way in which a new technology burst so *quickly and comprehensively* on to the scene made us all sit up.

Overnight the cultural chatter flipped like a channel. What was AI anyway? What did ChatGPT mean? And specifically, what did it mean for humans? I wrote this piece on the eve of the first anniversary of OpenAI's creation joining Google's search, Apple's iPhone

THE NEW JOB COLLAR

I thought it would be fun to ask DALL-E to draw me a black and white line drawing of a white and blue collar worker as imagined by Vincent Van Gogh.

and App Store and, going further back, the typewriter and the telephone as tools at work which would be transformative. The arrival of ChatGPT turbocharged our understanding of how fast work is changing and ushered in an identity crisis we are only just beginning to comprehend.

WORKING ASSUMPTIONS

As autumn leaves start to fall, I'm shedding some of the working assumptions I made a year ago when I began writing this column. While we have all been having endless arguments about flexible working and what has been rudely mocked as "shirking from home", that chapter has been written. Hybrid working has persisted despite efforts by large companies to lure workers back to the office. The dominant story about the present and future of work is about a different kind of hybrid: how ordinary workers co-exist with digital co-workers.

Work's main issue is no longer the future of the inanimate bricks and mortar of offices – significant economically though this is to city centers, commutes and the real-estate industry. Nor is it about the alternative "space" of the much-vaunted metaverse, which Wired *magazine describes as so vague that if you replace it with cyberspace "ninety percent of the time, the meaning won't substantially change."*

Instead, the next chapter of work concerns the gamechanger of ChatGPT, which arrived in November 2022. It took everyone by surprise, gaining about 1 million users in five days. OpenAI's conversational chatbot not only blew open the doors on the idea that computers could generate ideas and de facto mimic humans, but it heralded a new era in which white collar professional workers were directly threatened.

This group's job security had previously been inoculated against the arrival of new technology. Now articles with titles like "How to Save Your Job from ChatGPT" are aimed squarely at such workers and it's a shock to the system. The promise is that AI will save time, save work, allow humans to be their best creative selves, but the risk is the exact opposite.

By way of illustration, I typed this article on a very fast new laptop. It was definitely quicker than a typewriter or old-fashioned pen and paper, so I'm not complaining and I'm not naive. But if I tell you that the AI-assisted tools have made my task significantly slower due to all the pop-ups and "intuitive" suggestions you might smile indulgently at my technophobia. You might also nod in recognition: this isn't generative AI but its sibling, predictive AI. For the first time my "knowledge work", as the great management guru Peter Drucker called it, is constantly being interrupted by a noisy digital "co-worker" trying to being "useful".

Replacement Anxiety

The authors of a new book, The Coming Wave: Technology, Power and the Twenty First Century's Greatest Dilemma, *identify a new kind of human creature who they call "homo technologicus – the technological animal".*

This may sound like a cute soundbite, but it has the ring of truth. Thanks to generative AI and in particular ChatGPT, the porous line between human and machine is becoming confused. So much so that the central issue facing people in the workplace can be summed up in one word: authenticity.

I asked Alice Sherwood, visiting senior fellow at the Policy Institute at King's College London and author of Authenticity: Reclaiming Reality in a Counterfeit Culture, *what an age of generative AI means for worker identity. The concept of being true to yourself originated in the 1960s with the British psychoanalyst Donald Winnicott, but more recently took a workplace setting when Harvard Professor Bill George wrote the best-selling* Authentic Leadership: Rediscovering the Secrets to Creating Lasting Value. *The authentic self at work has come to mean a shorthand for showing your true self as someone who is therefore more trustworthy. But Sherwood notes that authenticity has become complicated by a new fear: replacement anxiety.*

While AI can already do many jobs better than humans, such as form-filling, blurb writing, assessing X-rays and developing new drugs, it can't make human connections with colleagues and clients – but that may be about to change, Sherwood said. *An employer can already use generative AI to make plausible, deepfake videos of their employees. If they add in a voice imitator that offers "ultra-realistic text-to-speech fakery" they can script staff to speak the company's words in their own voices.*

"No wonder employees are uneasy. When there's a deepfake that looks like you, sounds like you, never gets tired, never goes on holiday, and can even phone your mother why wouldn't they get the job instead of you?" Sherwood said. *"But replacement anxiety is about more than a loss of jobs, it's about a loss of identity. Who has the right to your digital self, your facial features, your voiceprint, and who can put words into your mouth, is set to become one of the hottest legal and employment issues."*

Recent research from the Wharton School of the University of Pennsylvania echoed Sherwood's view on replacement anxiety, noting that "LLM technology in the form of ChatGPT4, a technology available for just a few months at the time of our experiments, is already significantly better at generating new product ideas than motivated, trained engineering and business students at a highly selective university."

History Books

Let's look at this moment in the context of the history of work and of new technology. It's almost always the case that the new bits spook us. The arrival of the printing press was met in fifteenth-century Venice with the polemic against printing from the Benedictine monk and scribe Filippo de Strata. Indeed, the path of Mr Gutenberg and his bible wasn't smooth.

A leap forward to the middle of the twentieth century takes us to when Moore's Law first articulated the increase in computing power, a limit AI has arguably breached. Then with the dawn of the internet at the end of the twentieth century – AI after all is about digital operations – we can begin to see what speed and scale can do.

But perhaps the best comparison is Henry Ford's first assembly line in 1913. The transformative element here wasn't a large language model, but a production line which moved – literally. The innovation was to introduce physical movement into production at scale and in a sequence human workers slotted into, not vice versa. The rest, as they say, is history: within a year Ford was mass producing more cars with fewer people, more "efficiently" than any competitor.

Unsurprisingly, generative AI is projected to become a $1.3 trillion market by 2032.

Skin in the Game

Just as unsurprisingly, there's a lot of anxiety and it's beyond jobs. It's about human agency and autonomy as well as authenticity. There are distinct whiffs of Mary Shelley's Frankenstein *abounding: we worry we've created a monster. I especially worry when those with most to gain commercially show this nervousness. That's exactly what has happened with ChatGPT. Within six months of its launch, more than 1,000 technology leaders including Elon Musk and Steve Wozniak, co-founder of Apple Inc., signed an open letter warning that things were getting "out of control".*

Disquiet is catching. Prominent writers corralled by the Authors Guild wrote to AI industry leaders to "compensate us for using our writings, without which AI would be banal and extremely limited." Recently a central feature of the bitter artist strike in Hollywood hinged on the replacement of humans by AI-generated images and at the very least a lowering of pay as a result.

Regeneration – and Regulation

Clearly this moment calls for regulation. In a recent presentation to the UK Parliament, Oxford University Law Professor Jeremias Adams-Prassl noted: "If someone tells you that they can sell you an algorithm, then watch a two-minute video and then give you an exact score of your teamworking capabilities, that's what we call snake-oil AI."

This moment also calls for prioritization. Adams-Prassl has argued that privacy, information access and keeping the management with the humans will be pivotal to determining whether we rise to this occasion.

Interestingly, the American word for autumn is fall. It's easy to think we may be falling into a bleak future of work, in which humans don't regenerate as fast as their technological opposite numbers. But like all moments in history, humans learn to work with the machines.

THE NEW JOB COLLAR

I'm an optimistic pessimist. I see leaves coming away from trees and fluttering to the ground in an endless cycle of endings and beginnings.

[September 25, 2023]

Alice Sherwood was definitely on the money. "Authenticity" became Merriam-Webster's word of the year in 2023.* As the blurb went, "with the rise of artificial intelligence – and its impact on deepfake videos, actors' contracts, academic honesty, and a vast number of other topics – the line between 'real' and 'fake' has become increasingly blurred."

Not knowing where work begins and ends, not knowing if you value your job any more, not knowing if your job is safe. All of this has been happening at speed and scale. You can no longer delineate between white collar workers and blue collar workers in the same way. This isn't to say that shelf stacking or twelve-hour shifts as an engineer on an infrastructure project aren't differently stressful (not to say paid) than the job of a teacher or someone working in media, but Covid and ChatGPT have united the world of work rather strangely. Everyone is in transition, experiencing turbulence.

This is good and bad news. It's good news in that the less atomized and isolated workers feel the more they may recognize each other's concerns, voices and experiences to push for better change for everyone. I'm not some Pollyanna here, but let's not forget that before Covid the World Health Organization declared stress, and

---

* Merriam Webster Dictionary, Word of the Year 2023.

workplace stress, as a major contributory factor to disease.* All was not well with work then and it still isn't now.

The sense of status previously held by knowledge workers has been replaced by exhaustion and insecurity. At the start of 2023 IBM, which had kickstarted the AI revolution with its data analytics processor Watson in 2010, laid off 1.5 percent of its workforce due to inflation and AI; just a few months later Bloomberg ran a piece headlined "Half a Million Job Cuts Could Be Just the Start", with the subheading "ChatGPT could reap what Zoom has sowed"† – and by Christmas the "big four" consulting firms PWC, Deloitte, EY and KPMG had slashed 15 percent more of their workforce compared to the year before: in the UK Deloitte's planned cuts put 3 percent of its 27,000-strong workforce "at risk" (reported by *Financial News*).

So what has changed is job stability and security. Here's Nicholas Bloom on this:

> If you are hybrid, you're coming into the office, let's say three days a week. AI probably helps you out. It makes you more productive. It helps you design and write stuff. So for hybrid workers, I don't see in the near term that it's really a threat. If anything, it's maybe supporting that job. It's very different if you're fully remote. AI potentially – particularly if you're doing a repetitive, relatively basic job – could replace your job. If you think of AI, the software side of it or the visual side or

---

* World Health Organization, "Occupational health: Stress at the workplace", October 19, 2020.
† Bloomberg, "Half a Million Job Cuts Could Be Just the Start", Lionel Laurent on Bloomberg Opinion, (on white collar tech downsizing) April 4, 2023.

voice side is really pretty good. If this was a Zoom call, I could almost just about be AI. After I didn't respond very well, you may figure it out. If I was in person, the robot that replaces me is vastly clunky and it's just never going to work. If you think of data entry, call centers, HR, payroll – this kind of thing that's fully remote – a lot of this may be replaced by AI in five to ten years.*

THE NOWHERE OFFICE GENERATION

---

* Julia Hobsbawm, "Five minutes with Nicholas Bloom on how the working from home revolution continues to unfold", Bloomberg, December 8, 2023.

WORKING ASSUMPTIONS

Making Your Own Luck

The shift and gig worker associated with factory floors or even Uber driving seats have been equalled by the contract work in universities, consultancies, and all add up to a more singular workforce, the all-collar worker, who is the more entrepreneurial partner of the Flexetariat, what you might call the Flexetariat with the side hustle: the "solopreneur".

Here's a piece I wrote when I discovered that someone I thought was a music critic and radio host turned out to be behind a new breakfast cereal which he marketed with a pop start like a pop record. My mind blown, I thought, as I often do: "There's a column in this" – and here it is. It speaks to the new kind of jobs we do – side-by-side side hustles with whatever else we do – or did when times were more predictable.

◌

I'm going to tell you a story about breakfast cereal, pop records and career change. It will, I hope, challenge the working assumption that you have to stick to one career for your whole working life. (Hint: you don't.)

But first, let's talk about career identity. Are you "in finance" or "in HR" or "in marketing?" We often get stuck in a mindset that what we trained for, or ended up in, defines us. Our work becomes our working identity. This would be all well and good if there were job security in it. However, this is far from the case these days.

From waves of corporate layoffs to geopolitical instability to "quiet cutting" – when an employer doesn't fire you but reassigns you to a job you may not like – it all points to a realization that reinvention may be the order of the day when it comes to managing your career.

Enter the "solopreneur", which literally means solo entrepreneur. I view them more broadly, though, as "freelance or part time", and really anyone for whom dropping in and out of a fixed place on a fixed schedule matters less.

Perhaps this explains the 500 million skills LinkedIn members are adding to their profiles across the world from Australia, Brazil, India, UK and US, equating to a 56 percent year-on-year increase. At the launch of a new edition of her classic book Working Identity: Unconventional Strategies for Reinventing Your Career *Herminia Ibarra, a professor at London Business School, asked 200 of us in the audience to put up our hands if either we or someone we knew had transitioned careers, or was thinking about it. About 80 percent of us did so.*

What can you do if you're in this situation? As Ibarra writes in her book: "By far the biggest mistake people make when trying to change careers is to delay taking the first step until they have settled on a destination." *Her strategies for reinvention include working your networks. In another book,* Act Like a Leader, Think Like a Leader, *she writes of activating your "dormant ties" – an echo of the research by sociologist Mark Granovetter in the 1970s – to what she calls experimenting with "possible selves", in which you challenge the assumptions of your old, fixed job boxes, and experiment.*

That brings me to breakfast cereal. Specifically muesli: the oats, seeds, nuts and fruit cereal with a surprisingly large market. Global sales of packaged muesli are estimated to rise to $29.5 billion by

2033, up from $18.3 billion in 2023, according to research group Fact.MR.

What does this have to do with solopreneurship? Let me tell you.

Pete Paphides, a music journalist and record producer, has combined his original passion with an entirely new side hustle creating and marketing a brand of muesli preferred by one of his favorite artists, Robert Forster of a band called The Go-Betweens. Paphides noticed Forster brought his own muesli to hotels when he was on tour and suggested approaching a manufacturer to produce exactly the right mix and then marketing it like a record. The result, called Spring Grain, is a clever reference to one of the band's songs, "Spring Rain".

Is this muesli better than the others? Well, the nuts are ground, and it's vegan friendly with no added sugar. Like pop music, muesli is all a matter of taste. But what is interesting is how a music journalist like Paphides ever decided to get into something as different as manufacturing and food retail. As a side hustle to his main gig as a music critic and producer, it was strangely complementary in terms of his skill set – branding, design and selling a product – but also completely different.

As he wrote of the breakfast launch in The Times*: "We had to send out the launch party invites twice," he said, because everyone thought the 9:30 a.m. start time "was a typo".*

An estimated 10 percent of Americans have a side hustle. The solopreneur – whether operating literally solo or in new types of partnerships – knows these gigs are only partly about income generation; they're also about being happy. Roughly three in four US independent workers are "highly satisfied" with their work and their work–life balance. Now this job satisfaction speaks to the power of reinventing working identity. Why not sprinkle a little variety in your career? Muesli and musicians? Sounds delicious. And good for you, too.

[November 17, 2023]

◯

My own career ended up accidentally being solopreneur a long time ago. Although it has been spent in the rarefied knowledge worker office-rich worlds of media, consulting, full of business lunches, launches, conferences and travel, I don't have a university degree (which has always been an anomaly). Through the happenstance of what I call being born with a silver networking spoon in my mouth, to parents who were big social hosts across a polytopic world of culture, politics and history, mine is actually a generational story of luck at work which lasted from the 1980s to the hard stop of 2020 and Covid-19. Just as it was possible for a wide range of social backgrounds to go to college in the first place during this period, rising at one point to over 50 percent in the UK,* it was also possible to work your way up through word-of-mouth networks.

In the 1980s and 1990s, in my twenties and thirties, before I officially became a solopreneur and started my own small businesses, I enjoyed an informal form of white collar apprenticeship which doesn't exist now. Everything is done by process, algorithm, and while there are of course good arguments about meritocracy the formalization of work has created impenetrable bottlenecks for many. Plus, the power of networks has always mattered in all

---

* Figures from the Department for Education, for 2017–18, show 50.2 percent of people going into higher education for the first time.

jobs and denying its power and validity has always struck me as pointless. The most famous academic paper of all for me is Mark Granovetter's 1973 paper "The Strength of Weak Ties",* which shows precisely how people really get jobs: through word of mouth, through luck, through an open system of recommendation, trust and social networks.

For blue collar workers word of mouth has often meant getting in line and queuing. No one had any hang-ups about that. For the white collar worker it became more and more a thing to be chosen, and to be chosen by your education establishment, your MBA, your CV, and your ability to virtue signal that you belonged.

The white collar world always operated on the working assumption that qualifications from university secured a job for life and were combined with aspiration to continuously rise up the ranks. It did not factor in disengagement, at scale, both physically and emotionally, simultaneously, as happened in 2020. Nor did it imagine that new technology would disrupt its world as comprehensively as outsourcing and offshoring had the blue collar community thirty years earlier.

I find it interesting that Billy Joel, one of America's great singer-songwriters, sang "Allentown" on his world tour in 2022, thirty years after he wrote it, about the closing factories and the failed promise of a college degree and the graduations displayed on walls which "never really helped us at all". We're somewhere we've been before with jobs, only different.

---

* Mark S Granovetter, "The Strength of Weak Ties", *American Journal of Sociology*, Volume 78, May 1973.

2

TASK FORCES

 Every job is a dance between human and machine.

Working is about many things: money, identity, camaraderie. But it's fundamentally about doing tasks with varying degrees of skill using technology of one kind or another.

I'm classed as a "knowledge worker", by which I mean I use my head more than my body to complete my tasks. But I use tools just like someone operating a stove or a lathe does. Even though who I know and what I know accounts for much in what I do, when something goes wrong with my "kit" which stops me communicating any of this content, I realize, oh: I can't work. My own production line grinds to a halt.

The typewriter was my first workplace tool and remains so despite having morphed over time into an electronic keyboard. I type in the self-taught way of motivated writers the world over, which is: badly but sufficiently. My hands move in a quick but illogical way, like a bad piano player. The left and right fingers sometimes clash with each other like they are playing "Chopsticks" rather than Chopin. Let's just say I could never dance as deftly on the keyboard as Fred Astaire and Ginger Rogers did in the 1930s film *Shall We Dance*, which is one of the glorious to revisit on YouTube.

Unlike my mother, who learned to touch-type at secretarial college in the 1950s – a common "profession" for young middle-class women who were not deemed as capable of the other kind of "university" college as men – I learned by copying her as a young girl in the 1970s in our living room at home in London. Her fingers flew over her smart teal Olivetti Studio 45 portable typewriter. Although she later became a "solopreneur", a self-starting music teacher, she was also a continuous administrative muse to my father, a successful writer, for half a century. Her technology became the recorder, but it began, as did mine, with the typewriter.

Whatever the job, some kind of technology is everyone's middleman and skills are everyone's killer app. The story of how we qualify to work and adapt to learn and use technology at work is changing. This isn't new, but some of the underlying working assumptions are. Such as: you only need to learn one kind of technology once. Or this one: technology always improves things and makes things easier.

I discussed this with a young man in a tourist shop in Baltimore. I stopped off on my way the Museum of Industry, a beautifully curated warehouse of all the obsolete or evolved technology which the workplace of today was built on: garment machinery, an original drugstore, cars, canning tools, and media and communications – each has a room dedicated to the obsolete or now replaced (including typewriters).

The young man was processing my purchases – a tin of Old Bay Seasoning for one son and a T-shirt with famous Baltimore crabs on it for my grandson. We had time to talk as he fiddled with what is nowadays called a "POS retail system", i.e. a till (we don't call tills "cash registers" much now because cash is being phased out in retail). This one looked especially complicated – more like a computer with a keyboard attached. Like if you pulled the electricity it wouldn't open at all. Had he been trained on it, I asked? Not really, came the sheepish reply. Just have to learn on the job.

Half a mile away one of the old original cash registers, a 1912 Esskay Market National Cash Register, is on display. Not much more than a keyboard, a bell and a drawer.

AI image rendered by Microsoft's DALL-E of old and new office equipment in a black & white drawing.

A SHORT HISTORY OF THE TYPEWRITER

© Dr Andrew St George, 2021 for The Nowhere Office podcast

Think of a typewriter and call to mind the litany of names that came and went from the time of its invention in 1868 to its demise in the late twentieth century.

Royal, Olivetti, Olympia, Adler, Smith Corona, and Remington. Remington was an early manufacturer, also a gunmaker, proof of the close relation between moveable type and moveable gun parts. The New York company made its first typewriters with floral patterns, as it assumed users would be women taking dictation.

Well, soon enough they were, in large numbers, in typing pools. And what was an individual machine became co-opted into a collective effort from the 1880s onwards. Typing pools filled by ranks of emancipated and well-educated working women, accurate and speedy, at a hundred words per minute. Mark Twain was the first author to submit a typescript rather than a manuscript. That was in 1874. Jack Kerouac, son of a printing family, wrote On the Road in 1951 on ten-foot rolls of teleprinter paper, a way of staying in the flow and not changing paper. Another Jack, Jack Nicholson in The Shining, never got beyond that first single line, typed out repeatedly on a ream of paper. All work and no play makes Jack a dull boy.

Some places still use typewriters for form filling, certificates, and work too secret to risk being hacked. That means government agencies, courts, defense, prisons, whose inmates are not allowed internet access, but are allowed transparent typewriters, made by Swintec in New Jersey.

> *And there's money in other kinds of correction, too. Bette Nesmith Graham invented correction fluid in the 1950s and sold her company, Liquid Paper, to Gillette for $48 million in 1979. I love the raffish side of the typewriter. It means freedom and style to write what you want. And you can still buy that Olivetti, just not in the modish Ferrari red model called Valentine, created by its inventor to use any place but the office.*
>
> *To keep amateur poets company on quiet Sundays. So all the way from Johannes Gutenberg in the fifteenth century, a printing press on your desk. To write what, when, and how long you like.*

Technology confounding us is not a new phenomenon. There's a wonderful *New Yorker* article by E.B. White (author of *Charlotte's Web*) written in 1936 about the most pervasive piece of technology ever owned at scale other than the telephone, TV, and the computer: the car. In particular, the Ford Model T, of which 15 million were made and sold and which defined not just leisure but work – think of the travelling salesman, the migrating worker, the commuter on America's highways.

> *Mechanically uncanny, it was like nothing that had ever come to the world before. Flourishing industries rose and fell with it. As a vehicle, it was hard-working, commonplace, heroic; the car, possessed of only two forward speeds, catapulted directly into high with a series of ugly jerks and was off on its glorious errand.**

---

* E. B. White, "Farewell, My Lovely!" *The New Yorker*, May 8, 1936.

Ugly jerks. Well, I could be rude, and say I've met some people like this. But sticking to the tech, I like this reminder that technology is messy and must be learned, because I think it puts us in good stead for what's coming. We've had the car, we've had the computer. We have, after the steam engine and the combustion engine and automation, the digital era breaking into software, and that fluffy cloud, now AI.

What's changed? The complexity. The software. The large language processing models. The limitless possibility. The asymmetry with someone else's hardware or software, or skill set. Oh, we use paper. Oh, that's in the cloud. Oh, we haven't backed that up yet. Oh, that's in storage. And now: oh, we're developing a prompt library. To you and me, that's teaching us how to ask like Google once taught us how to digitally search. Same old, new old.

All of this symbolizes advance, progress. But it also complicates the way we work, because constant training and learning is needed. Try using generative AI six months from now and you will need fresh skills. Which is why I wrote a column about AI and skills at the end of 2023, just as the penny was fully dropping (for me anyway) that ChatGPT in particular had already infiltrated the workplace in a way which was doing for the white collar office what the production line and the factory floor had done a century earlier and, more recently, digital automation had done for warehousing.

A day after publication came the news that *The New York Times* was suing Microsoft and ChatGPT, in which it holds a huge stake, for copyright infringement "over the unauthorized use of published work to train artificial intelligence technologies".*

---

* Michael M. Grynbaum and Ryan Mac, "*The Times* Sues OpenAI and Microsoft Over AI Use of Copyrighted Work", *New York Times*, December 27, 2023.

It all adds up to this: the white collar toolkit just got a whole lot more complicated.

○

Every end-of-year working assumption is the same: next year will be different. This is the eternal optimism of business and the neverending story of innovation. But this time it's true, certainly when it comes to workplace technology. All sorts of incredible things will be possible at your desk (wherever your desk is), but it will come with a price: possibly the steepest learning curve in knowledge work since the word processor way back in the analog age of the 1970s.

ChatGPT's arrival a year ago has captured the collective imagination, with 100 million users per week, according to its creator, OpenAI. Workers got a taste of what it's like to ask AI tools to write their emails and summarize documents for them, but in the year ahead these tools will only get more sophisticated and be able to respond to images, voice commands, and potentially carry out more complex tasks with limited human intervention. That has the potential to radically change the day-to-day experience of work.

But, as Roy Bahat, head of Bloomberg Beta, which has invested in artificial intelligence since 2014, told a recent conference, "it's pretty confusing". That said, he's adamant that AI tools are a career necessity, telling me on my podcast that "Just like when computers were first introduced, skills went on a resume. Saying today you are proficient in AI is a skill."

AI Dividend

Humans do learn how to use technology, and amazingly fast when you think about it. But AI brings a new turn on the tech wheel, *and we have to learn it, too. Why? Because the impact of AI on how we work and the jobs we do is as revolutionary as the internet. According to research from McKinsey Global Institute, the earnings boost for some banks is as high as $340 billion, or a 9 to 15 percent increase in operating profits.*

As Peter Miscovich, global future of work leader at real estate firm JLL put it: "Generative AI has risen to become an equal and increasing priority for global organizations in comparison to the enterprise priorities of hybrid working and providing flexible work environments." *But the corporate sector is on the same steep learning curve as you and me. JLL found in a recent survey that while generative AI comes in third in a ranking of impact on their industry (clean energy solutions is number one), it ranks lowest for* "level of knowledge."

The real estate sector isn't alone in recognizing the knowledge gap. Wipro, an Indian IT company, has committed $1 billion to training its 250,000 workers, both to help them understand generative AI but also to integrate it into its product offerings. Wipro's own webpage on AI shows a bewildering technical array of terms. Just as new acronyms define the flexible working era take your pick from GPU (graphics processing unit), NLP (natural language processing), ML (machine learning), LLM (large language model).

I sought the advice of Henry Coutinho-Mason, co-author of The Future Normal, *to explain what's what in the ever-expanding lexicon of AI.* "The next frontier of interactive and query-able chatbots is going to be voice activated not text-led," *he said.* "Either way, there are plenty of new things to get your head around such as the correct 'prompt' to give generational AI which will only be as good as the information it already stores and receives – just like Google search was back in the day."

He also explained (patiently) that chatbots are only part of the AI equation, albeit a big one. Did you know that by this time next year you may have one of your own, an infinitely customizable way of creating and using any information you choose in an app with your name or brand on it? Or, if you know how, it might only take you an afternoon to create your own personalized bot.

Immersive Metaverse

I've written about the importance of authenticity in the debates about generative AI, and authentic has been named by Merriam-Webster as word of the year for 2023. I predict that "immersive" may be a contender in the years to come.

Meta Platforms Inc. has bet big on representing the metaverse as a place for workplace training and brainstorming. This is all part of the education dividend in an "augmented" world being promised by Meta, as Nick Clegg, president of global affairs, outlined in a LinkedIn post earlier this year.

Sondre Kvam, co-founder and chief executive officer of Naer, a mixed reality workplace app which was selected to be part of the launch of Meta's Quest 3 virtual headset, told me that "Avatar technologies seem to be frog-leaping each other every other week. Mixed reality workplaces have the potential to foster greater productivity than their hybrid and single location counterparts." And the global virtual reality market is projected to grow from $19 billion in 2022 to $166 billion by 2030, according to Fortune Business Insights.

At the heart of any investment in workplace technology is the desire to improve productivity. Naer shows how AI producers are pitching their products on a continuing rise in hybrid, remote or "mixed *reality" workplaces. They are suggesting that in future you will be able to visit your office as an avatar just as you use teleconferencing, but that it will be far more engaging. This could be a significant antidote to "Zoom fatigue" – or it could be another version of the same old new technology promises.*

We don't yet know. And I realize I'm a contrarian here. The metaverse has been slow to take hold and Meta's embrace of it – to the point of changing its name from Facebook – so far has drawn more critics than supporters. But I, for one, see it as a longer-term gamble worth taking as generations brought up on touch screens and gaming enter the workplace.

Super Screeners

AI is poised to have a particularly big impact around talent acquisition and job searches. Interestingly, the apprenticeship group Multiverse founded by Euan Blair, son of former British Prime Minister Tony Blair, is all about this new realm of digital possibility. From chatbots to the metaverse and Slack channels to LinkedIn, it all has to be navigated and negotiated.

And not just by white collar workers. The most interesting of all the startups I have come across is Upwage, an employment platform for America's hourly wage workers. "We care about two things: wage and commute," co-founder Diana Tsai told me. "Our obsession was always to disrupt a very outdated and inefficient job search and application process for hourly workers, but also how amazing it would be if we could build an AI interviewer that skipped the entire application process and enabled workers to instantly interview with employers. When GPT came we had the opportunity to combine our search-based engine with the employer side product." Upwage's "Super Screener", launched in December, aims to save companies $336,000 a year while also providing candidate-convenient 24/7 screening.

"We'd be talking to hourly workers who don't have time to interview except for on the weekends. When recruiters aren't working on the weekend, the Super Screener is," says Tsai.

A caveat here, too: there are very real concerns that using AI to automate recruiting and hiring will effectively automate bias. It's a complex problem, but the technology is only progress if that doesn't happen.

In the end, business loves nothing better than a new market, and AI is packed to the rafters with possibility. But, yes, it's complicated. Humans need to learn to use the technology which might, in fact, make their jobs obsolete – at least that's according to Elon Musk. "There will come a point where no job is needed. You can have a job if you want a job," he told UK Prime Minister Rishi Sunak.

I'm betting that Roy Bahat is right. We will get proficient at AI. And humans at work are not done yet.

[December 27, 2023]

Liquid Paper

*"ChatGPT can make mistakes.
Consider checking important information."*

Disclaimer, ChatGPT4

Beware the working assumption that technology will get things right – or help you to. From ChatGPT to Google's Gemini, their early years have been mired in inaccuracy-related problems. Why? It's simple. The internet data it draws on to give you answers just may be wrong. In other words, your "co-pilot" may be taking you off-course. I find this a lot with voice recognition, which is much vaunted as the way ahead for white collars: all you have to do is ask your "co-pilot" a question.

Take the issue of transcription. This is a profession very much under threat from generative AI. Why pay a human to sit with headphones and translate at their pace, and their hourly rate, when you can have a transcription for a fraction of the cost and time? Those of us in the podcast business know these temptations, and I'm sorry to say the tech is a clear winner. Except. Writing about "queenagers", the middle-aged demographic (see chapter six), I get "Queen Asias". Or the company MindGym, whose founder Octavius Black I interviewed, comes back as "Mind Jim". In AI the airy excuse of "hallucinations" came up, as if the technology has ingested something designed for recreation, not work.

It isn't just voice recognition. As the techno-ethicist philosopher Alice Thwaite pointed out to me on an episode of my podcast *The Nowhere Office* looking at the safety of AI:

> One of the examples I like to give is, you know, there's a lot of talk around self-driving cars, for instance, which use AI quite significantly. A lot of the facial recognition cameras and image recognition cameras do not tend to be very good at picking up black skin and black bodies. That, for me, is an existential risk for a human. You know, there's other existential risks for the people who are caught up in the kind of surveillance systems, which might enable them to go to prison and be wrongly convicted.*

Mistakes. We all make them. But when we put blind faith in technology and regard it as infallible, this can amplify and magnify the mistakes, not minimize them. Perhaps the most egregious example isn't about AI but plain old software. In the UK the Post Office, the nationalized postal service, installed an IT system called "Horizon" with faulty accounting software which led to the wrongful conviction and imprisonment of hundreds of innocent post office operators.† To date, no director or manager of the Post Office has been convicted, had a fine or been imprisoned. Some mistakes, as George Orwell might have said, are less equal than others.

What about intentional harm by IT, or by humans using it? Cyberattacks are on the increase. Blackberry Cybersecurity (remember that Blackberry? Well, it's now dedicated more or less entirely to malware) put out a report showing they had thwarted over three million cyberattacks over one single quarter in 2023, an increase of 70 percent. The British Library, one of the world's

---

* *The Nowhere Office* Podcast, AI special in association with PwC: Programme 1.
† BBC News, "Post Office scandal explained: What the Horizon saga is all about", January 17, 2024.

great cultural institutions suffered a catastrophic cyberattack at the end of 2023 in which over half a million files were leaked online. The cause was not a mistake but an attack with a ransom demand the British Library wisely – but expensively – ignored from a group called Rhysida. Somewhat incredibly, so prevalent are cyberattacks that this operation has a job description: RaaS – Ransomware-as-a-service.

Then there are the harmless workaday mistakes. Back in my day I liked correcting my typing errors in my first secretarial job (watching my mother came in handy) as I could type well using something called Tippex to correct mistakes on the page, which later became obsolete with the arrival of autocorrect on a computer. An American woman called Bette Nesmith Graham discovered "liquid paper" in the 1950s which she later sold to Gillette for a handsome $47.5 million – not bad for technology of the day. I like this story not least because it was a manual technology you could use to overlay the error caused by a machine. There's something about the control at your fingertips which matters.

We all know that our desktops, then laptops, now smartphones contain more computing power than it took to put a human on the moon. But they often need "updates" which get tangled and malfunction. For some of us a malfunction is a frustrating bore. For others, it's a matter of life and death or injury. Instances of industrial accidents dropped substantially between the wars* as health and safety legislation improved, but there's been a clear pickup as automation and robotics arrive.†

In 2015 a twenty-year-old car factory worker called Regina Elsea died in an industrial accident, crushed by an injury from "Robot 23" on a Mercedes-Benz production line in Tuscaloosa, Alabama.‡ Reports have emerged of robots malfunctioning at the Tesla plant

---

* Staysafeapp.com. The introduction of the Health and Safety at Work Act 1974 saw a 73 percent reduction in the number of workplace fatalities between 1974 and 2007. Non-fatal injuries also fell by 70 percent.
† Strategic Organizing Centre, Primed for Pain: Amazon's epidemic of work place injuries report found that in 2019, the last year of injury data available prior to the COVID-19 pandemic, Amazon's sortable facilities with robotic technology had a serious injury rate of 7.9 per 100 workers, more than 54 percent higher than the serious injury rate at non-robotic sortable facilities in the same year. As reported in the *Washington Post*, June 2021.
‡ Peter Waldman, Bloomberg, "Inside Alabama's Auto Jobs Boom: Cheap Wages, Little Training, Crushed Limbs", March 23, 2017.

in Texas, injuring a worker. When your working assumption is that technology is safe, and that humans can speed up as a result, accidents are more likely to happen. Humans and machines working together always has the potential to be fatal. Take the dreadful example in March 2024, when the container ship Dali lost power and crashed into the Francis Scott Key Bridge across the Baltimore harbor. All we know for sure is that the ship malfunctioned. Up to eight lives of construction workers were lost and the biggest global supply chain disruption since Covid took place on the northeastern seaboard of America.

Accidents happen, of course. And not all mistakes can be erased with Tippex. But the point is that vigilance about technology is always preferable to blind faith in it, because the room for error in the end is always small.

> *I have a theory that culturally something shifted in the white-collar mindset after the pandemic, perhaps during. We could see the frontline workers toiling away, without breaks, often without protection, and we could see they had to go back to their tasks without the flexibility of hybrid working. And we willed them on. There is a greater appetite for fairness now and a greater desire to call things out.*

Clean and Dirty

Turbulence throws up disturbance in the atmosphere. The job market has churned significantly with changing behaviors coinciding with changing jobs after the "break" – and with it, a change in tasks and roles. Talk of "reskilling" was everywhere and filled in the gaps of "the Great Resignation".

In the US a "hole" of 3 million workers emerged.* Many economists were baffled. A significant number were older workers, a problem the UK encountered with its own hole of half a million in this demographic. The reasons were partly a jolt into retirement, or ill health – long Covid being chief among them. But another reason is that the transition to "green" jobs† in renewable energy such as electric vehicle manufacturing was beneficial to educated younger white collar workers with sales and software skills. Jobs in the so-called "dirty" industry – carbon and fossil-fuel intensive manufacturing – were still there, but a study by the National Bureau of Economic Research showed that possibly only 1 percent of workers would transition to green and that the proportion of those being older was less.‡

---

* Michael Sasso, "Millions of US Workers Are Still Missing After the Pandemic. Where Did They Go", Bloomberg, February 24, 2023.
† Nina Lakhani, "Transition from 'dirty' to green US jobs rises, leaving older workers behind", the *Guardian*, August 14, 2023.
‡ National Bureau of Economic Research, "Workers and the Green-Energy Transition: Evidence from 300 Million Job Transitions", August 2023.

Penguins Don't Like Peanuts

Do you want to reskill at forty-five as much as you did at twenty-five? And what is the incentive if it isn't even a job you can make ends meet from (something the inflation crisis which began in 2021 has made significantly worse)? Back to the Great Re-evaluation, as I call it. "Quiet quitting" and "The Great Resignation" are manifestations of rebellion and resistance. But there has also been an uptick in trade union activism since the pandemic, with previously non-unionized corporate workplaces like Amazon and Starbucks bowing to the power of campaigns to have unions at all.

The undercover practice of "salting" – to organize from within – reminded me that I've been on a unionized strike, once.* Here's the story. The first big job I got, in 1985, aged twenty-one (I didn't go to college, so I started work early and worked my way up in a small publishing house as a secretary) was at Penguin Books.

Looking back on it, these were glory days to be in publishing. I was as green around the ears as they come, and as a young publicist all I had to do was write paperback press releases and nip round the corner to the famous La Famiglia restaurant on the nearby King's Road with hugely interesting authors – and put it on expenses!

But publishing then – and now – wasn't well paid. I was well-heeled, I'd just managed to get a mortgage with a small loan from my parents which was beyond most people's reach. Plenty around me were in the gilded cage of an enviable brand name job but

---

* Josh Eidelson, "The Undercover Organizers Behind America's Union Wins", Bloomberg, April 3, 2023.

weren't making a decent wage. I wanted to prove my worth, and I joined the union. They wanted to strike – a prospect which I confess utterly terrified me, goody-two-shoes that I was (and still am). But I could see they had a point.

My contribution wasn't just to join them on the picket line – which I did, nervously, for a single day, having apologized profusely to my manager in advance (deeply uncool, I know) – but it was to come up with a neat catchphrase they put on campaign T-shirts: *Penguins Don't Like Peanuts.* Not quite as salty as an undercover Starbucks organizer, but still.

It isn't just that trade union organizing has become extremely good, or that it is necessary – the Amazon and Starbucks campaigns to have the right to unionise are for a good reason, not a bad one: worker protection and pay.

I have a theory that culturally something shifted in the white collar mindset after the pandemic, perhaps during. We could see the frontline workers toiling away, without breaks, often without protection, and we could see they had to go back to their tasks without the flexibility of hybrid working. And we willed them on. There is a greater appetite for fairness now and a greater desire to call things out.

The 2020s feel very different from the 1980s or 1990s. No one says "greed is good", the catchphrase from the 1987 movie *Wall Street*, and gets away with it anymore. The mood has shifted. Hence the widespread support in 2023 for the striking Hollywood writers of WGA-West and SAG-AFTRA, who were rightly concerned that their human skills would be copied and replicated without fair pay by generational AI-generated images and voice.

The view is not that the workers are new generation Luddites, resisting technology without good reason, but that the leaders who fail to pick up the signals and implement sufficient protections are. Back to Alice Thwaite, the millennial techno ethicist philosopher I spoke to:

> *I love innovation. I think that people and humans are capable of doing crazy, amazing things. There are a ton of problems that need solving right now. There is so much stuff that we can do. Do I feel that AI has a place in all of this? I do not personally believe that companies like Meta, Microsoft, are going to be able to guide AI in a way that's going to help 8 billion people get out of poverty, solve the climate crisis, get better at everything that they're doing. So it's like this, is there potential there? Yes. But it is only a very narrow idea of what intelligence is.*

> *The 2020s feel very different from the 1980s or 1990s. No one says "greed is good", the catchphrase from the 1987 movie* Wall Street, *and gets away with it anymore. The mood has shifted.*

Followership Force

It's definitely a failure of intelligence these days to underestimate the power workers have, even if they aren't in an official trade union.

The hottest technological company of the day – OpenAI – got into incredible hot water just as they were on the cusp of realizing a valuation of $86 billion, just over a year since ChatGPT burst into the world – and the workspace. This was my observation at the time:

I don't know about you, but I'm longing for the latest episode of a new soap opera I'm calling Succession: Silicon Valley. *I am not the only one who has been transfixed by the saga of OpenAI's boardroom coup-turned-volte-face, which saw arguably the biggest AI unicorn in history cast aside the working assumption that what happens inside the corridors of tech power stays well hidden from view.*

Famous boardroom coups have happened before, but not as publicly or in real time. When Steve Jobs was ousted from Apple in 1985, it wasn't until Walter Isaacson's biography in 2011 that we got anything like the inside story from the horse's mouth, recreated in the 2015 Aaron Sorkin script for the eponymous movie.

No dramatized account was required for OpenAI in 2023. This has been a simply jaw-dropping corporate infotainment of the highest order. For one, the principals themselves were singing like canaries.

The action was unfolding in real time on X, formerly Twitter. Sam Altman, for example, posted a whimsical image of himself holding a visitor's pass with the caption "first and last time I wear one of these" in between his ousting and reinstatement. He also retweeted – complete with three bright red hearts no less – an agonized post by his former friend and mentor Ilya Sutskever saying, "I deeply regret my participation in the board's actions… I will do everything I can to reunite the company."

Whatever happened seems to boil down to one of two theories: money or ethics.

On the former, Bloomberg's Matt Levine put it well: "OpenAI's board members are not venture capitalists, don't own equity at all, are not motivated by hopes of a trillion-dollar valuation, and were in fact adverse to its venture capitalist investors… They took a very long and grandiose view of the importance of their product and its ability to change the world, while the employees would like to see some cash now."

As for the second – ethics – I asked Richard Straub of the Global Peter Drucker Forum, the management conference, a simple question: what would the management guru Peter Drucker say about what has happened at OpenAI?

"Drucker would have been critical about the confusion between for-profit goals and the nonprofit mission as we see it at OpenAI," Straub said. "Drucker wouldn't reject the development or the use of Artificial General Intelligence (AGI)… He would support its usefulness as long as humans stay in charge."

The precise definition of AGI remains a topic of debate but is considered to be some version of AI that surpasses humans' intellectual abilities.

But the third and most important issue is board governance and leadership.

Barbara Kellerman, a fellow at the Harvard Kennedy School's Center for Public Leadership, has identified seven types of bad leadership: incompetent, intemperate, callous, rigid, corrupt, insular and evil.

"The board of OpenAI definitely fell into the categories of being incompetent, intemperate and insular: they failed completely to take into account the AI superhero status of Sam Altman or the power of their biggest client Microsoft CEO Satya Nadella," she told me. "But above all, the drama was driven by the approximately 700 (out of 770) OpenAI employees who threatened to walk unless Altman came back."

Above all then, Kellerman said, this was a story about "follower power", in which "people without obvious sources of power" exert it at scale.

In all of this, what has surfaced is a story of how boards work – or should work – in the face of balancing risks in industries with high-stakes ethical issues where they try to do the right thing against that age-old lure: the charismatic founder deemed to be indispensable.

The last time we saw charisma get in the way of governance publicly was with Sam Bankman-Fried, now convicted of epic fraud at FTX, who managed to hoodwink the good and great. The case prompted me to call for a "chief critical officer" to join boards that might be dazzled by founders.

Boards don't yet have CCOs, but they do have clear responsibilities. History will judge whether the actions of OpenAI were more than clumsiness. Of the key mandates of any board, "one is to provide oversight of strategy, the second is to hire, and in some cases, fire the CEO," Dambisa Moyo, who sits on the board of Chevron Corp., told me recently.

87

WORKING ASSUMPTIONS

What she didn't know at the time was that in OpenAI's case they rehired Altman. The next questions are what the new strategy will be and whether it can create profit without drama.

Next episode please!

[December 5, 2023]

> The dance at work is of course not only between humans and machines but between humans and each other. This dance has different names. Communication. Collaboration. Management. You cannot have one without the other, and cooperation cannot only be delivered with technology.

The Chief Critical Officer

The dance at work is of course not only between humans and machines but between humans and each other. That's the one with the real drama to rival anything we can watch on *Succession* or any number of cop shows (from *Kojak* to *Bosch* the narrative arc usually is the same: a hero thwarting a bad, arrogant boss).

This dance has different names. Communication. Collaboration. Management. You cannot have one without the other, and co-operation cannot only be delivered with technology.

It isn't only employees or trade unions which have to take management to task, however. The working assumption that boards should is correct – but we're seeing time and time again that this isn't often happening. I wrote about this during the infamous FTX cryptocurrency collapse of 2022.

◇

After Enron filed for bankruptcy twenty-one years ago, history is repeating itself.

The irony can't be lost on anyone that John J. Ray III, the man hired to oversee Enron's liquidation, is doing the same again in 2022 for FTX, the failed cryptocurrency exchange. My working assumption is that it's time to focus less on the charisma of entrepreneurs and corporate leaders and show more healthy cynicism and criticism if such scandals as Enron, FTX and Theranos Inc. are to be avoided in the future.

Let's start with charisma. At the time of their downfall, Kenneth Lay of Enron, Sam Bankman-Fried of FTX and Elizabeth Holmes of Theranos – who was recently sentenced to eleven years in prison for fraud – were all celebrities in their own right.

Holmes attracted a range of heavy-hitting investors, including the family of former Education Secretary Betsy DeVos, Alice Walton, an heir to the Walmart Inc. fortune, and News Corp. Chairman Rupert Murdoch. Holmes' pitch that she had discovered a revolutionary way to analyze blood, using a machine with the name "Edison", relied entirely on what might be called chutzpah. But it worked.

Sam Bankman-Fried's youth, demeanor and confidence put him alongside Tony Blair and Bill Clinton earlier this year at a crypto conference in the Bahamas.

In an article entitled "Charismatic Leadership and Corporate Cultism at Enron", published in the Journal of the International Cultic Studies Association in 2006, authors Dennis Tourish and Naheed Vatcha address "the dark side of charismatic leadership" and note that charismatic leaders surround themselves with a group which operates in a bubble. No critique gets in.

The question of why is certainly interesting, because a charismatic leader needs followers. It's a mix of FOMO – fear of missing out – and what the marketing psychologist Robert Cialdini calls social proof, or in other words, persuasion through influence. Some investors do appear to be more immune than others: one of Warren Buffet's legendary aphorisms is that the five most dangerous words in business may be: "Everybody else is doing it."

Another question is how in this day and age such lack of corporate oversight still happens.

One reason, according to Dambisa Moyo, a board member at Chevron Corp., 3M Co. and Condé Nast International Inc., and author of the book How Boards Work, *is that corporate boards haven't changed sufficiently since their inception in the 1600s and are badly in need of an upgrade. She told the Man Institute podcast: "boards have a three-pronged mandate, oversight of the strategy of the companies in which they serve, they are responsible for hiring... and they are also responsible more and more for the oversight of the cultural norms." She believes a focus on ethics plays an increasing role in this oversight.*

Of course not all CEOs are corrupt, foolish, or playing fast and loose with other people's money. And not all boards fail to independently scrutinize the decisions from top management.

But too many of them are packed with good intentions, enablers – people who end up being complicit in the crimes and misdemeanors of their CEOs.

Of FTX, Ray said, "Never in my career have I seen such a complete failure of corporate controls and such a complete absence of trustworthy financial information." That says a lot coming from the person who unwound the Enron mess. It's unclear what role boards played at the exchange.

If the cult of charisma were replaced by a culture of critique and criticism, history would look very different. Who might be a good role model? I recommend Empress Maria Theresa, the eighteenth-century ruler of the Habsburg Empire, who took over the reigns of power as sovereign at the age of twenty-three when her father died suddenly. A big job if ever there was one. She faced constant battles and undermining incursions on her leadership, not least from Frederick the Great.

According to historian Nancy Goldstone in her book In the Shadow of the Empress, *"the Queen of Hungary and Bohemia surprised everyone by appointing an official whose sole task consisted of critiquing her behavior and job performance with brutal honesty." The man given this job, a Portuguese nobleman twice her age, Count Emanuel da Silva-Tarouca, had no need to be nervous. Both flourished under the arrangement.*

At a time when the C-suite of the future is in flux, with new roles like chief people officers, chief sustainability officers and even metaverse heads, let's take a lesson from Maria Theresa. Add "chief critical officers" or the like with a mandate to cut through the charisma and avoid the next governance disaster.

[November 30, 2022]

○

We all need to be our own chief critical officer, of course, and check our own bias when it comes to the way we think workplaces *ought* to work, rather than the way they actually *do*.

Wasn't this the big takeaway from the pandemic? That when the entire working world stopped at the same time and restarted under different conditions, things were revealed which can't be unseen, un-felt, unheard. Much of what we do and how we do it isn't going to change with technology because we will stay the same: we feel things, we corrupt easily but also have moral cores, and these two human states will always have to co-exist.

Time Marches On

I'm returning to Henry Ford. He did two seemingly contradictory things. He introduced mass automation with the assembly line, ushering in repetitive factory work for 25,000 workers at the turn of the century, keeping turnover low by introducing the $5 dollar a day payment. But then he did something else remarkable. He introduced the five-day week in 1926, declaring:

> We found long ago, however, that it does not pay to put men at work, excepting in continuous operations, from midnight until morning. As a part of low cost production – and only low cost production can pay high wages – one must have a big investment in machinery and power plants. Expensive tools cannot remain idle. They ought to work twenty-four hours a day, but here the human element comes in, for although many men like to work all night and have part of their day free, they do not work so well and hence it is not economical, or at least that is our experience, to go through the full twenty-four hours. But a modern factory has to work more than eight hours a day. It cannot be idle two thirds of the time, else it will be costly. This decision to put into effect the short work week is not sudden. We have been going towards it for three or four years. We have been feeling our way. We have during much of this time operated on a five-day basis. But we have paid only for five days and not for six. And whenever a department was especially rushed it went back to six days – to forty-eight hours. Now we know from our experience in changing from six to five days and back again that we can get at least as great production in five days as we can in six, and we shall probably

> *get a greater, for the pressure will bring better methods. A full week's wage for a short week's work will pay.**

In the teeth of a technological revolution which transformed the modern economy and society, Henry Ford understood that humans are not machines – they just use them. And he understood that we value autonomy over tasks and time only slightly higher than we value pay.† Before Henry Ford it was Welsh utopian socialist Robert Owen who first called, in the nineteenth century, for "eight hours work, eight hours recreation, eight hours rest".

Then there's the harmless workaday mistakes. We have managed to get ourselves very tangled up when it comes to distinguishing between what different kinds of flexible work mean. In Germany *Gleitzeit* means flexitime in which workers choose their hours. That's very different from part-time work or shift work, or indeed hybrid work. But time and our control over it remains at the heart of jobs, as it has done since the introduction of standard time in railways at the dawn of industrialization.

We clock in and we clock out. The big delineation between blue collar manual workers and white collar professionals used to be measured by time, and our control over it. One of the most successful corporate classes I have ever given focused on a single simple task: "Treat your schedule like your body, and don't

---

* Henry Ford, "Why I favor Five Days' Work With Six Days Pay", Interview with Simon Crowther in "World's Work", October 1926.

† Henry Ford believed – correctly – that there would be a productivity boost in paying workers the same amount for less work. Debate rages today about whether this calculation can apply across all industries and sectors with the new push for a four-day week. The global campaign 4dayweek.com focuses on leisure and "aims to create a million new years of free time". At time of writing it's created just over 2,000 years.

TASK FORCES

DALL-E's rendition of timepieces old and new.

let anyone put anything in it without permission." It turns out that the number-one thing which irks people is their inability to control meetings they don't want or need, as much as where those meetings take place.

Managing your time has become a holy grail issue, and it underpins the unresolved state between employers and employees over flexible working. The roots of the modern movement of working less, and in particular the dropping of a day per week's work, lie very much with Henry Ford: as I wrote in the introduction, 2026 will be the centenary of the introduction of the five-day week. This ushered in an era in which working hours began steadily dropping. There have been exceptions. The industrialist Kellogg famously introduced a six-hour day in 1930, no doubt inspired by Ford, but it was stopped by modern managers in 1985, despite having been transformative for work–life balance, and particularly for male employees.

Everyone is trying to find a fit, a compromise. For many it is the four-day week, which has become a very vocal campaign. I am probably in the "supportively skeptical" camp, because I think it imposes more rigidity than flexibility, as I wrote in early 2023 – much to the annoyance of its growing group of supporters.

The business world badly wants a silver bullet to solve the existential crisis engulfing white collar work as productivity falls.

A working assumption is that the silver bullet in question is the four-day week. It follows much fanfare about the success of trials around the world, and now a bill that would amend the definition of the work week in federal law has been relaunched by Democrat Congressman Mark Takano.

"Workers across the nation are collectively reimagining their relationship to labor," Takano said in a statement.

So what's not to like? Certainly, there is a systemic problem with work, one which I and many others debate and chronicle.

When the Takano bill first came in a year ago, I drew comparisons with Henry Ford's five-day week, and went back further to the early trade union movements including the Welsh socialist pioneer Robert

Owen and his 1817 slogan a century earlier: "Eight hours' labor, eight hours' recreation, eight hours' rest." Ideas around less work and more leisure regained traction a decade ago with an influential book, Utopia for Realists by Dutch social thinker Rutger Bregman. He devoted a chapter to the fifteen-hour week – revisiting the famous 1930 essay of economist John Maynard Keynes – and argued that automation and AI would shorten the working hours anyway.

But in reality this is proving to be significantly messier than anticipated.

Lynda Gratton, a professor of management practice at the London Business School, lays bare the complex struggles leaders have had in the past three years to find models of hybrid that work. Only 42 percent of companies and executives she surveyed globally had settled on "final hybrid-work design," she wrote in the Harvard Business Review.

The ambition to codify new working norms into a single system like a 20 percent reduction in working hours for 100 percent of pay is laudable, but I don't think is workable. <u>The F should be for flexibility, not four days.</u>

In its recent report "Working Time and Work Life Balance Around the World", the International Labour Organization acknowledged that "mismatches between workers' actual hours of work and their preferred hours of work exist for a substantial portion of the global workforce", namely "workers would prefer to work longer hours to increase their earnings but are unable to do so."

The labor market today simply cannot be compared like-for-like to that of a century ago, which is the inspiration for the four-day week campaign. The use of new technology is pervasive and not *confined to the factory floor. The white collar worker and the blue collar worker are strangely united by both the pressures of separating work and leisure and increasingly the economics of doing so.*

What's more, many who are experimenting with the so-called four-day week itself are structuring their programs not on a stringent four-day schedule but flexible arrangements that suit the needs of the individual workers and companies, such as two half days instead of one full day off. Research in the UK showed that most people prefer flexible hours over the rigidity of a four-day week. In Australia, which is facing an acute labor shortage, the share of job postings citing a four-day week is rising dramatically, but it still represents a fraction of overall jobs.

Christy Hoffman, general secretary of UNI Global Union, which represents 20 million workers in 150 countries, pointed out in a session on the four-day week at Davos that "flexibility is what everybody wants. Some people would rather have a five-day work week and then have six weeks off."

And Rob Sadow of Scoop, an office time scheduling tool, who publishes an index of flexible job openings, told me: "Most people started bringing their work home with them anyway as soon as email made it onto the phone. I expect in a few years' time we'll see a lot less focus on when exactly an employee is working, and more focus on the outcomes that employee is generating for the business."

Here's hoping. In the meantime, I caution against the silver bullet theory of work resting on a four-day week or any other fixed model. The panacea is something far more nuanced.

[April 11, 2023]

Time marches on differently in different time zones and in economies developing at a different pace. The "Global North" countries may be rejecting old working norms, citing burnout and new values and the progress of working less, but this is not the case with more emerging economies in the "Global South". It was interesting that just as the UK introduced flexible working laws,* Narayana Murthy, the father-in-law of UK Prime Minister Rishi Sunak and head of Infosys, was arguing for India to impose a seventy-hour working week: "Unless we improve our work productivity… we will not be able to compete with those countries that have made tremendous progress. So, therefore, my request is that our youngsters must say, 'This is my country. I'd like to work seventy hours a week.'"†

But context is all, and here is more on the end of the globalized norms and more on the no-one-size-fits all. The economist Juliet B. Schor, a keen advocate of the four-day working week campaign,‡ told me for my podcast how the US healthcare system is an integral reason why long hours work culture has failed Americans:§

> *Health insurance is an accident that was never corrected, and it's a real tragedy because it led to this major sort of dysfunctionality in the US labor market, especially because the US health care system became so dysfunctional and expensive. It created a huge tax on every employee, which led companies to want fewer employees working longer hours.*

---

* The UK government announced that the new flexible working regulations will come into effect on April 6, 2024, giving employees the right to request flexible working arrangements from day one of employment.
† Meryl Sebastian, NR Narayana Murthy: "Why Indians are debating a 70-hour work week", BBC, Kochi, November 1st, 2023.
‡ 4 Day Week Global – 4 Day Week is a reduced-hour working model campaign.
§ *The Nowhere Office* podcast, Work Rebellion, Juliet B Schor.

WORKING ASSUMPTIONS

America's dysfunctional healthcare system in which you have to keep working in order to keep up with the health insurance that goes with your job clearly is neither something to emulate anyway, nor can it be replicated as a global norm elsewhere. But does this apply uniformly to a shoe factory in England or a healthcare facility in Singapore?

Arguments say yes, but I still disagree.

Whose working assumption will prevail? That's one for the history books. My working assumption is that the four-day week will join the campaign for universal basic income and remain an active niche which will not become universal but which will contribute to the burgeoning demand for actual flexibility across all jobs. Experimentation with different models should continue, from the "sprint" of a project under deadline to the idea that different generations in jobs might need to work more intensively and immersively, say at the onset of a career.

One of the key points at which audiences of mine have "leaned in" regarding flexibility is when I have acknowledged that one size doesn't fit all generations of work when it comes to flexibility. I put it like this: babies need nine months to get ready in the womb for the outside world. Coming out any earlier is always a bit of a problem. But staying in too long is too.

Why not create longer immersive "incubation" periods for new team members, on some kind of temporary shift, similar to blue collar shifts, which ease up after say nine weeks or nine months?

Let's use our new-found awareness of flexibility to innovate, to keep everything on the table and to not be afraid to experiment.

TASK FORCES

The University of Work Life

"I think what MBAs should do right now is focus on a lot of digital transformation, because that's what all CEOs are struggling with today. I don't want to be cynical, but I think it needs to drastically change to become more relevant and more attractive. We believe that there is no such thing today as a single major degree, we really believe that some topics need to be intertwined, completely interdisciplinary."

His Excellency Ahmad Belhoul Al Falasi, Minister of Education, United Arab Emirates, speaking to me on *The Nowhere Office* podcast at Davos*

There is one final aspect to tasks, skills and technology which is confounding the working assumptions which have been in place for a century or so, and this is the education piece. Specifically that the "best" universities and the MBA in particular will reign supreme. The MBA, or Masters of Business Administration, is over a hundred years old, sharing its history with that of the Ivy league universities such as Harvard (where the MBA began in 1908). It has come to symbolize the management class more than any other qualification, to delineate between the barista and the boss, between the factory floor and those flying business class.

Even before Harvard University became engulfed in a culture war row in the winter of 2023 along with many other universities as a result of their paper policies on tolerance clashing horribly with irresponsible student behavior which they seemed powerless to manage, the blush was beginning, subtly, to fall from the rose

---
* *The Nowhere Office* podcast from Davos, January 2023.

of the MBA. I heard the US Labor Secretary, Marty Walsh, wax lyrical about apprenticeships at Davos at precisely the time that the UAE's Minister of Education, a former engineer, stunned a panel by admitting that it no longer funded students to do American MBAs.*

Now, anyone who has walked along the snowy promenade of Davos, in the rugged Rhaetian Swiss Alps, and taken advantage of one of the plush branded "Haus" hospitality houses for coffee or schnapps or snacks knows that for the five days of the meeting, there are probably more MBAs per square inch there than anywhere in the world.

But the old way of thinking about singular, siloed qualifications needs to adapt to become multi-faceted, and of course primarily digital. You can see business schools beginning to pivot away from long courses to short, intensive "burst" ones, with that all-important "reskilling" agenda.

Another interviewee on *The Nowhere Office* podcast, Dave Eisenberg of the venture capital firm Zigg, told me that while he thought the American economy would remain pre-eminent, precisely because of the tech industry and AI being so Silicon-Valley heavy, it was nevertheless noticeable that "in the United States, if you needed a super high-precision tooling, engineers or mechanical workers, maybe you could fill a large conference room. In China, you can fill many, many football fields over and over again."†

---

* US Secretary of Labor Marty Walsh at Davos 2023, visited one of Europe's foremost job training centers in Zurich, and learnt more about apprenticeship programs in Austria as recorded in the US Department of Labor.
† *The Nowhere Office* podcast.

It is not just technical skills which must be learned in this brave new world, however. Soft skills, the humanities, a literacy which spans continents and history must co-exist alongside a workforce which can build, operate and produce what civilization needs. The question is really whether the managerial class is learning the right lessons, in the right places.

The learning gap at work is not the skills themselves – whoever builds the technology knows how it works or is capable of working, even generational AI – but harnessing this at work and the interface with people is the tricky part. Can all managers be sent back to school, not to do an MBA but a new kind of qualification, fit for the times? I'm assuming not. But I can't help wondering if it wouldn't be a good idea.

Education is a big guardrail for leaders – 40 percent of top Forbes leaders have an MBA on their CV – and the working assumption that leaders of tomorrow will have it rather than, say, a rolling array of technical skills remains to be seen.*

The next big shibboleth which is changing, after jobs themselves and after the way we regard skills and power at work, is of course the workplace itself. Because the jobs and tasks are changing but as the old advertising adage goes, it's still all about location, location, location.

---

* "Nearly 40 percent of Fortune 500 CEOs have an MBA on their resume", US News & World Report.

> *Ever since global "stay at home" notices were issued around the world in March 2020, the working assumption that the majority of people must commute to work daily ended. The city, the office, the home: this is the new trio of locations battling to be the workplace for anywhere the technology allows.*

3

COMMUTER TRIANGLE

> *"As a vehicle, it was hard-working, commonplace, heroic;*
> *To get under way, you simply hooked the third finger of the*
> *right hand around a lever on the steering column, pulled*
> *down hard, and shoved your left foot forcibly against the*
> *low-speed pedal. These were simple, positive motions;*
> *the car responded by lunging forward with a roar."*
>
> E.B. White on the Ford Model T, *The New Yorker* (1936)

Times change. A century ago 15 million Model-T Ford cars released consumers and workers alike to a freedom which in turn released the American Dream: to be mobile in a changing world and to move with the times. Never mind that it was clunky: it *moved*.

The singer-songwriter Tracy Chapman became an overnight sensation in the late 1980s with her song "Fast Car". The lyrics are a pure distillation of the desire and hope to get a better life through work. Henry Ford's affordable motor car spawned a million pop songs. To work in a city and belong. To be at the wheel of your own destiny. Mickey Haller, the bestselling creation of writer Michael Connelly, is "the Lincoln Lawyer" – the Lincoln being his car. His workplace? The freeways. The office has been everywhere and nowhere for some time – but people go and move to where work and fulfilment lie.

In my own way, the car has always been my commute. In Camden, North London, in the 1970s I used to gaze longingly out of the plate glass window during assembly at the cars and lorries trundling up the trunk road. Most of my peers went to university but I went to work – in my car. For my twenty-first birthday my elderly cousin Gretl gave me a silver Toyota Corolla which I used to drive around London in – to my first big office job at Penguin Books in the King's Road, then to the BBC not so far away. I belonged less in my workplace, which changed, than in the car itself. I worked from a desk in both places, but the connecting tissue was what got me there and what happened in between. The office was a static place, with its filing cabinets, corded telephones and piles of paper. But the car? That was the exciting way I knew I was entering the grown-up world of work.

Times change. All of the offices I have ever worked in have. The BBC White City HQ, which used to be called "Television Centre", has become a vast Soho House. Penguin Books became, I think, a block of apartments, what the British call "flats". The idea of driving a car to an office in a city has changed too, and is as politically off limits as smoking now, partly because of climate change and pro-cycling city politics, partly because public transportation systems have grown, and partly because of Covid's impact on the commute.

The car is a symbol of what gets outdated – and updated. Cars are changing massively, from petrol to electric to driverless. The car, the commute, the city – it's all connected, and it's all changing. The traditional forces upon which a commute was based – a daily

COMMUTER TRIANGLE

I think it's very revealing how unconsciously biased ChatGPT currently is towards sexism, given the image it produced when I invited it to imagine a modern city worker in a Ford Model T car in a contemporary cityscape. Strappy heels and a straining shirt? I think not. But of course it isn't unconscious bias. It's evidence-based knowledge-gathering from the existing way women are portrayed. Is AI and ChatGPT nature or nurture? A question for later.

journey to a nine to five job in a single central building in a city or town center, which millions upon millions of people did, no questions asked, for nearly a century – are being upended by a different kind of motion: the desire for personal mobility.

WORKING ASSUMPTIONS

The game was up as soon as mobile phones and the internet arrived. When outsourcing and globalization arrived, migration for work became internal: a million Americans have moved from north to south already, and an Upwork study predicted up to 10 percent of the entire workforce will ultimately move physically as the remote work revolution gains traction.* Flexibility is here. Mobility goes hand in hand with it. The Uber driver has come to represent this too: cities work well now with Ubers, and they simply work less well without. Uber is, however, a good example of how it takes time to settle in to new systems, especially where technology collides with work practices. It's not only that it took Uber a while to wake up and smell the coffee that they needed to treat workers properly, with certain rights and protections. In London it mightily disrupted the famous black cab taxi drivers, who now have to handle card and cashless transactions as a matter of law. This was expensive, and my goodness, they grumbled. But it works better now.

Perhaps we know what we don't want rather than what we do at the moment. One thing we do know is that the commute has come to represent everything people hate, namely a time-suck on someone else's rules. And we know that there is a direct correlation between the drop in office occupancy of the cities, where getting in and out takes over an hour.†

We also know that the commute isn't just unpopular but unhealthy. And although in the UK car trips account more for

---

* Upwork study 2022, The New Geography of Remote Work.
† Sarah Green Carmichael, "CEO'S can't fix our biggest problem with return to office awful commutes", Bloomberg, September 23, 2022.

shopping and leisure than commuting,* not so elsewhere in the world: three quarters of Americans still prefer to use their cars to travel between home and work.† A recent study shows that switching to remote work can minimize carbon emissions by 58 percent.‡ Climate change of course is affecting where people live and work from anyway: shrinking property insurance associated with climate risks accounts for a staggering 17 percent of GDP in the US.§

> "I think some people think of work from home as this luxury, which it certainly is for a lot of people; that they can have the flexibility to sit and do their jobs on their couches and then more easily manage throwing in a load of laundry or picking their kids up. But the fact is that if they decide to do that, if a worker decides to stay on their couch, that has ramifications for, you know, the coffee shops that they used to patronize or the subways that they used to ride or, you know, every part of the economy that they used to and still do interact with."
>
> – Emma Goldberg of the *New York Times*, interviewed on *The Nowhere Office* podcast, September 2023¶

---

* Valentine Quino, "Does working from home cut carbon emissions? Not necessarily – in fact, it can have the opposite effect". LSE, September 21, 2021.
† Felix Richter, "Cars Still Dominate the American Commute", Statista, May 18, 2023.
‡ Yanqui Toa, Longqi Yang, Sonia Jaffe and Fengqi You, "Climate Migration Potential of teleworking are sensitive to changes in lifestyle and workplace rather than ICT usage", PNAS, September 2023.
§ Alice C. Hill, "Climate Change and U.S. Property Insurance: A Stormy Mix", August 17, 2023.
¶ *The Nowhere Office* podcast.

The central story around the commute hinges on how people move into and across the city, from where they live to where they work. Ever since global "stay at home" notices were issued around the world in March 2020, the working assumption that the majority of people must commute to work daily ended. The city, the office, the home: this is the new trio of locations battling to be the workplace for anywhere the technology allows.

People are ultimately place-agnostic and person-centered about the workplace, but not about how they live and work. They want three things now: 1) better work–life balance; 2) for work to comfortably cover the cost of living; and 3) good tech which works wherever and whenever they work. Commuter towns will grow in locations in which housing and childcare is affordable and plentiful, which are safe from climate change, and increasingly, within a reachable radius of HQ.

This was my first column on the topic, in late February 2023 – a time when the working assumption of "going back" to normal office occupancy still prevailed among much corporate real estate.

The new frontier of work hinges on a move from the city to the suburb and a redefinition of the central business district.

To paraphrase Karl Marx, all workers of the world are uniting. They seek change, and in tight labor markets white collar workers are increasingly getting it. The number-one trend for human resource departments globally, according to Mercer, is "improving the employee experience for key retention populations". That translates roughly to "the balance of power has shifted". My working

COMMUTER TRIANGLE

I wanted to ask Chat GPT to re-imagine Edward Hopper's beautiful 1953 painting "Office in a Small City", but it replied to me *I'm unable to generate images in the style of Edward Hopper's "Office in a Small City" due to our content policy. However, I can create an image inspired by the general themes or elements characteristic of early 20th-century office scenes. Let me know if you would like me to create something along these lines.* So I fed it some more lines and got this instead. The Metropolitan Museum of Art in New York acquired the original, immaculate painting which the artist's wife described as "the man in concrete wall".

assumption: the power struggle isn't just around people but place, and specifically the city has a renewed competitor – the suburb.

The draining of revenue for Manhattan is just the latest alarm bell tolling the end of the central business district, the area most associated with offices as we know them. In Australia, so-called e-changers have moved from cities to regional and coastal areas but kept their city jobs. In London – a city defined by its six-fold growth in a decade at the beginning of the industrial revolution – the collapse in commuter-based revenues and rise of anti-commute habits is such that Govia Thameslink Railway, the UK's largest railway network, is offering discounted tickets on Mondays and Fridays.

The city as we know it is less than 10,000 years old and has always been about three things: population, trade and growth.

The trajectory of growth is set to continue: by 2050, it's projected that nearly two-thirds of all people will live in urban areas. Yet what happens in cities is changing profoundly. A century ago, Carl Sandburg's poem "Skyscraper" captured the proto-industrial age commute so well: "By day the skyscraper looms in the smoke and sun and has a soul. Prairie and valley, streets of the city, pour people into it and they mingle among its twenty floors and are poured out again back to the streets, prairies and valleys."

Today the buzz is less of the skyscraper than of the fifteen-minute city, popularized in Paris by Mayor Anne Hidalgo and now seen as a model across the world – although times are shortening. Seoul is aiming for a ten-minute city. These concepts imply having all necessary amenities within a short walk, bike ride, or public transit trip from one's home, for convenience, community and to reduce reliance on cars for climate-related reasons.

Not everyone is happy about this shift. In England, Oxford has become a hotbed of conspiracy theories around its plans to limit private vehicles, and has attracted international attention as a result of the rising tensions.

Nevertheless, you can clearly see the influence of the fifteen-minute city concept both locally in towns and suburbs and in the adaptations of city centers to what's called "mixed use", or repurposing central business districts for business, residential and public space. This is being done to either attract new models of tenancy or to create new income streams on evenings and weekends if offices themselves are going to remain under-occupied. But it also reflects the live/work culture of the moment.

The Age, a daily newspaper in Melbourne, reported on Mad March, an upcoming month of city-based festivals and other attractions that draw people to the city. Meanwhile in Saudi Arabia, the Royal Commission for Riyadh City has predicated its entire Downtown Riyadh Development Program to be in essence mixed use for residents, tourists and business. In Lithuania, Zaha Hadid Architects have won the contract to redevelop 24,000 square meters of mixed-use space in the business district of Vilnius.

The speed of change has taken some people by surprise. At the end of his influential 2017 book Scale: The Universal Laws of Growth, Innovation, Sustainability, and the Pace of Life in Organisms, Cities, Economies, and Companies, *the physicist Geoffrey West noted "the vast majority of people who could in principle de-urbanize and yet remain connected to the center choose not to. I know of no high-tech geeks who are operating from high up in the mountain ranges of the California Sierra."*

But in The Momentous, Uneventful Day: A Requiem For the Office, *published in 2020, Gideon Haigh reminds us of what lies at the heart of the switch away from purely office-centered cities: "The convenience of working in a domestic setting." He notes that "The White House, 10 Downing Street, the Palais de l'Elysee, Zhongnanhai, Sori Daijin Kantei: all have combined their functions as headquarters of government leadership with residences for senior officialdom."*

The ordinary white collar worker has a home life as well as a work life. They clearly want the benefit of their education and skills to play out in where they work and play. Technology affords many more opportunities to unite what the worker wants with what they can now get: work–life balance. It isn't the end of the city, but potentially the beginning of it. Or, as Marx might put it: the redistribution of it.

Those wishing to re-energize their workforces and stay more capitalist than socialist have their work cut out, but they should also take heart: the maxim to "think globally, act locally", coined by the Scottish planner and conservationist Patrick Geddes, has been rolled out successfully by large companies like McDonald's Corp. Yes, offices will perhaps need to relocate or fragment into smaller regional franchise hubs. But is that such a bad thing?

[February 22, 2023]

⬡

This moment has many more questions than answers. My working assumptions are influenced by what I see happening in London, where I live, and New York, which is something of a home from home, from where I work several times a year. Someone who helps me make sense of the overall trends is a New Yorker, Peter Miscovich, who is the Global Future of Work Lead for Consulting at JLL, one of the world's leading commercial real estate advisory firms.

Peter, who has been in the real estate and work transformation space one way or another for well over a quarter of a century, has the rare gift of being deeply commercially savvy, corporate to his fingertips (some of the biggest brand names in the world are current or former clients of his), and yet wonderfully candid. Peter is a realist who sees things in the round. He was one of the first people to confirm my suspicion that the world of corporate real estate was being changed forever by the pandemic at a time when plenty were flatly denying it.

I met Peter in a rooftop restaurant overlooking Central Park on top of the Museum of Arts and Design on Columbus Circle called Robert (very New York).

Having a conversation about the future of commercial real estate with Peter in New York, which has been more heavily affected by the Nowhere Office era than most, from this location seemed apt: looking over a park which is an iconic unchanged landscape at first glance but which of course, like all of nature, restlessly iterates all the time.

JH: *The first point I'd love to just ask, Peter, is, how long have you been in the corporate real estate business? And how much has it changed in the last five years?*

PM: *Well, I'll begin with a bit of career history, having long launched early workplace transformation practices at Accenture and then at PricewaterhouseCoopers and then coming to JLL.*

WORKING ASSUMPTIONS

I've been in the real estate and workplace transformation sector for over twenty-five years. In many ways the pandemic was like a time machine, or an accelerated time portal, where it pushed us all forward in terms of the accelerated scaled adoption of hybrid work, workplace transformation, and commercial real estate transformation. In two and a half years, we experienced seven to ten years of accelerated transformation.

In my career, also having a background in operational resilience, workplace continuity, business continuity and disaster recovery, we were actually anticipating a pandemic-like event as we have been preparing for such crisis events over the past twenty years. And this was not my first pandemic, having lived through the AIDS crisis, the SARS crisis, multiple disaster recovery events, including earthquakes in California. After Superstorm Sandy, we had twelve clients impacted who were forced to relocate to other facilities. We also lived through 9/11 in New York whereby all of my clients in lower Manhattan were significantly impacted by the terrorist events of that day. We understand crisis management and how to enable operational resilience in response to these incredibly disruptive crisis events.

So, when that pandemic hit in early 2020, from a mindset perspective, our teams were fully prepared to address the challenges of remote work in response to the COVID pandemic crisis. We mobilized very quickly in March 2020, as we witnessed 3 billion people who all went remote and mobile in a matter of three to four weeks. It was an incredible accelerated response to the pandemic crisis at a global scale that we have not experienced in recent history. For those of us who have been in the hybrid work, hybrid workplace, remote work, workplace transformation and operational resiliency sectors, we were prepared for what was happening in early 2020.

However, I think in retrospect the world at large wasn't fully prepared for the significant elongation of the COVID pandemic. As the pandemic became more prolonged, we saw that a major structural shift was occurring within the commercial real estate sector with the scaled adoption of these new ways of working. I think this major shift is still ongoing today during 2024, whereby the elements of innovative hybrid work experimentation and experiential workplace design have all sped up considerably.

Corporate real estate is the infrastructure and physical envelope that houses knowledge work, knowledge workers, and the enterprise workforce, and there's a supply and demand component to it, whereby the supply is provided by developers and landlords in terms of the buildings that are built, and then there is the "occupier" demand component. We at JLL Work Dynamics are focused upon the occupier demand component for corporate enterprise entities.

The complexity of all of this is now accelerating. If I look back to the late eighties and early nineties, the ecosystem "balance" between supply and demand was actually quite stable – predictable, even. Twenty years ago, we would develop a corporate real estate strategy for a major client [Peter worked in his early career with the likes of AT&T, IBM and Citigroup] and would typically develop a five- to ten-year global real estate strategy; it was a very stable approach to corporate real estate long-term strategic planning and execution.

WORKING ASSUMPTIONS

THE FIFTY-YEAR LENS

But what's occurred over the last fifteen or twenty years has set the scene for what is happening now – accelerated advances in technology, disruptions in the workforce, globalization, and corporate "digital" re-engineering, as well as the acceleration of mobile working at scale, with the advent of the iPhone, iPad, then 3G, 4G, 5G, soon to be 6G Wi-Fi, pervasive wireless connectivity, and finally the global scaling of powerful social mobile networks. Then we saw the huge co-working uplift that occurred with the experiential campuses of Silicon Valley that were developed during the 2010s through 2020. All that change permanently transformed the real estate demand and supply ecosystem in a significant and structural way.

And then we had the pandemic hitting in early 2020.

I tend to look at corporate real estate and the real estate industry sector with a thirty- to fifty-year-lens, and there was really almost thirty to forty years of transformation that is now accelerating even faster with more disruption and with more complexity. And with this comes an interesting emergent paradox around supply and demand, with a new focus upon cost management in parallel with enhanced human experience, integration of new disruptive technologies enabling new ways of working in parallel to massive workforce demographic shifts – all these influencing factors are impacting the corporate real estate simultaneously at scale today.

So, the paradoxical complexity of the corporate real estate landscape has really increased dramatically over the last five years. We're now working with several global clients and looking at 2030 strategies, and we're looking at those strategies in -year tranches – from 2024 to 2027, and then from 2027 to 2030. The real challenge is to be able to forecast how people might be working in coming years of 2027 and 2030 and how these corporate occupiers will need to orchestrate these physical aspects with continuously changing work modalities which as we all know, as physical envelopes and buildings are not so easily fungible, malleable, or flexible. The challenge is to create inherent long-term flexibility as these accelerated changes continue, as we move from 2024 into 2027 and then onward to 2030 and beyond.

JH: What are the fundamental trends for the next three years in the demand occupied space?

PM: *We see the next three years of continuous innovation and experimentation. And when I say experimentation, we'll see further development of hybrid and even new types of remote work with gen AI enablement combined with spatial computing and immersive computing, the evolution and adoption of generative AI use cases at scale in parallel with the adoption of new distributed workforce strategies.*

EXPERIMENT, EXPERIMENT, EXPERIMENT

We'll be in a "continuously emergent and experimental state" over the next three to six to seven years, whereby we will be continuously responding to the novel issues, challenges and environments arising out of these emergent and disruptive technologies in combination with continuous disruptive workforce changes. We believe there will be stronger emphasis not only on making greater technology investments in perhaps fewer physical locations and sites and those fewer sites and locations will have greater levels of technology investment which will enable those essential and critical "peak human workplace experiences".

We do see that with the Gen Z and Gen Alpha workforce cohorts – these growing workforce cohorts will be demanding greater "human experience" in terms of health and wellness for the office environment, all closely aligned to ESG and sustainability-leading practices. Unfortunately, as we witness the continued acceleration of climate change – and these generational cohorts now entering the workforce will continue to grow in size, scale and societal influence – they're very concerned about how their employers behave as global "citizen" organizations, how their employers occupy space and how these organizations utilize energy.

So, a much stronger focus upon technology investment and advanced converging technologies, including Gen AI, immersive spatial computing, and distributed computing, all will be influenced by these generational and demographic shifts that are occurring in terms of these new workforce cohorts.

The Gen Z and Gen Alpha workforce cohorts will be focused very much on human experience, wellness, wellbeing, life–work integration, and for their life priorities to come before their work priorities. And then the social impacts, if you will, the societal ramifications of equity, inclusion and fairness; most of our more progressive corporate clients are starting to address all of these issues in concert, as we look forward to 2027. Equity and Inclusion will matter more and more in the coming years than ever before for the next generation workforce.

JH: I just want to come back specifically on the point you made about fewer sites, but more tech enabled. I mean, how does a

business make money if it's selling less product? Is it that the commercial real estate business is moving more into an advisory role and helping clients imagine how to use their workspaces? Is that what makes up the shortfall?

PM: Yes, I would say that the entire sector, and JLL in particular, has been pivoting and will continue to pivot into more advisory services with the reimagination of real estate with a focus upon experiential, commercial real estate. And if we think about retail, the retail Armageddon that started fifteen, even twenty years ago – here in the US, we were probably twenty times over supplied in terms of retail shopping malls.

In 2023, experiential retail was doing quite well, and omni-channel retail today is doing quite well. The transformation of the retail sector was perhaps a precursor to the commercial office sector with the flight to quality, technology-enabled amenitized "experiential" buildings. We have corporate occupier clients today that are asking the landlords and the developers to provide the amenitized services versus providing it for themselves, so the entire corporate real estate ecosystem is shifting in the flight towards greater quality of building product as well as the continued migration towards more desirable building locations and higher quality of building products/infrastructure. All commercial real estate will become technology enabled, and soon all buildings will be fully Gen AI-enabled – with the additional ability to flex with intelligence, and, if you will to easily transform "in real time" the entire real estate infrastructure and associated building envelopes.

I have one client with twenty global corporate campuses, and we're looking at flexible spaces across all twenty campuses *because of the many corporate occupier variables and unknowns that we're discussing today.*

JH: *In some ways, you're the bearer of bad news, aren't you? Or at the least you are telling powerful senior clients in the C-suite that they must rethink strategy and pivot and not plan anything like as predictably as previously?*

THE PROPHET IN THE DESERT

PM: *You know, I've been a prophet in the desert for twenty-five years and am very accustomed to being not only misunderstood but often ignored and denied in my points of view! There is divergence across corporate leadership today and there is a generational bias to various historical ways of working. As an example, we saw in the advent of the internet that even some of the most prophetic technology founders at the time of the launch of the internet thought that it would never be used for business and that the internet would be used only for consumer exchanges. So, we need to remember something: it's very difficult to forecast the future.*

That said, we do know that change is inevitable, and that, in navigating change, resistance is often part of that change journey. There is more progress for clients who are embracing change, embracing new ways of working, and navigating with our support through an often complex and paradoxical journey. And this is part of the new era of complexity and paradox that we're all living through.

I was at the MIT Media Lab doing early social network analysis during the 1999 to 2003 timeframe, and if we think about the nature of work prior to the year 2007, as I find that 2007 was a very pivotal year in history with the launch of the iPhone, as well as the growing popularity of social media. In retrospect, many thought that Watson AI in 2010 was going to be the big AI breakthrough – that AI in 2010 was going to transform health care, transform work, transform the enterprise, and transform society. In a matter of two to three years, all that momentum dissipated. Things often emerge, then subside, and then only re-emerge several years later. We have been involved in the metaverse and immersive computing and have been for twenty-plus years. People may think the metaverse began with Facebook rebranding itself as "Meta" in October 2021, but it was mid-way through the long-term journey to integrate virtual reality and mixed reality and immersive computing within the work environment. We will see a similar journey for generative AI and multi-modal AI: AI may have multiple peaks and troughs over the next several years, but it doesn't go away, and, ultimately, the next evolution of Multi-model AI will change the business operating landscape and everything that goes with it.

ZONING IN AND NOT OUT

JH: Can I switch the subject to the bricks and mortar of office and corporate buildings, and talk about zoning? I have a theory that you might start to see almost like a campus feel for singular office block buildings whereby they start to get rezoning permission and make bedrooms, fitness centers, so that there can be a more immersive reality for people coming to the office two or three days a week or coming in bursts for two or three weeks and then going away again. Do you see that happening? Or have I just imagined that could happen – a kind of radical rezoning so that certain office blocks and buildings get really properly repurposed for the first time in a generation?

WORKING ASSUMPTIONS

PM: You know, it's fascinating. If we compare and contrast between, let's say, San Francisco, New York and London, New York comprises probably seven to ten innovation districts as the diverse ecosystem districts that comprise the greater New York metropolitan region that, even during the course of the pandemic, New York remained quite vibrant across many of these diverse innovation districts. Whereas San Francisco has this core financial center downtown zoned only for office. I'll use my experience with lower Manhattan as another contrast: post 9/11, the prediction was no one would ever want to occupy an office building in lower Manhattan near the World Trade Center again. Fast forward... it took almost twenty years but over 30 million square feet of infrastructure and building envelope was transformed and repurposed in lower Manhattan, which today is a vibrant, innovative, multi-use, diverse district.

And I think New York has survived well, during the pandemic and post pandemic, because of this diverse ecosystem and vibrancy of diverse sectors and diverse lifestyles that New York fully supports at scale. Diversity breeds prosperity. I do not discount San Francisco; San Francisco has been challenged, but it may yet re-emerge. I think London is another great example of this diversity of lifestyles and behaviors. New York and London will continue to thrive over the coming decades because of their inherent vibrancy, diversity and resilience – regardless of how many waves of change may impact these two global cities.

Whether rezoning or alternative, urban resilience requires a public will and a public sense of leadership and governance. I've been a believer in the fifteen-minute city, the twenty-minute city. You look at what Paris is trying to do, and Singapore is a great exam-

ple of this new type of urban regeneration. So, I do think you need the public will, leadership, the governance, and, yes, rezoning, but it is much more of a societal fabric approach required to achieve urban regeneration success. We need to embrace urban resilience and urban regeneration in completely new ways in order for all global cities to fully thrive moving forward.

PEAK WORKPLACE EXPERIENCE

JH: Am I right that offices were pretty much only occupied 80 percent pre-pandemic anyway, and that post pandemic, the net occupancy is going down to roughly 50 percent? And therefore it's not just how much office space is let, but what happens in that office space so that people can live and work in different bursts.

PM: Absolutely. As I say, we've been a believer for twenty years in "the peak workplace experience". Even if you're in the office one day a month, three days a week, two days a quarter, four days a week, or six days a week, there's an experiential value proposal that needs to be there that is consistently presented and fully enabled for the office occupiers, and, without a doubt, office technology needs to be superior to the home technology. This issue of commuting; the elongation of commute is a major inhibitor of office engagement and office attendance, so we need much more of an ecosystem approach to provide the peak workplace experience and how to enable that peak experience consistently from a worker perspective. This is the biggest paradoxical challenge for the coming years.

PEAK EMPLOYEE POWER

During my early career certain things were just expected of you because management could mandate everything, and the workers had to succumb and follow all of the management mandates – there was this workplace dynamic whereby management ruled the workers. Well, that dynamic has shifted during the past fifteen to twenty years. This shift in the power from management ruling everyone to employees having greater agency and authority over their work experience – this societal shift has occurred during my career, during my lifetime. As I do think that this is a significant societal shift combined with a major societal shift to become more human centric, more worker centric, with an experiential preference which will continue to create this growing management to employee societal tension and conflict that we'll continue to see between now and 2027 and perhaps even beyond to 2030.

THE PINBALLING EFFECT

That paradoxical tension and conflict between management and employees – this management versus workforce challenge will require a great deal of experimentation, innovation and change leadership. It will also require data, it will require experimentation, and it will require the courage for continuous trial and error and the willingness to accept the failure outcomes that go along with continuous experimentation. I think we're starting to see that now with what I call this pinballing effect of various hybrid work and return-to-office policies and practices across multiple organizations, many of which are my clients, who are navigating through how best to evolve towards the next future state of the workplace.

Consequently, there may need to be a management generational shift. The millennials will be in charge by 2027 and 2030, as the Boomers and the Gen X folks move out of key leadership roles, and we'll probably see a very different management structure, new management cultures, and more effective leadership styles.

JH: You've given me an idea that in it's not just about corporate real estate, helping and advising the redefinition of what the workspace and workplace is for, but it's also that maybe you can get involved in making the commute more workplace friendly. If you think about the great train repurposing for luxury travel during the Orient Express era with sleeper trains and the idea that you would have peak experience, at the moment, most trains do offer laptops for business and certain amount of Wi Fi connectivity and charger stations, but they don't offer a really immersive place in which you could book a room to have a comfortable call on a train, for example. So, my question is, do you think that the idea of space and real estate could in theory be extended to planes, trains, automobiles?

THERE'S A TIME AND A PLACE FOR HYBRID WORKING

PM: *Absolutely! I would add autonomous vehicles, as the ability to have very low-cost, autonomous mobility, whether it's a train, a bus, or a personal vehicle or whether it's autonomous aerial transport. We are beginning to think about what that next generation mobility journey map really looks like, and this of course may include your point about rezoning and provision for corporate on-campus overnight accommodations. The corporate campus may take on a much more dynamic "hospitality" orientation in the future to provide the full peak experience for the next generation of AI-enabled knowledge workers.*

JH: One final point, on the global nature of all of this. We're sitting in New York, but you're dealing with clients in multiple geographies. What is the impact of all of this on operating globally?

PM: *I was a globalist for years, fully in favor of centralization, and I've seen this shift over the last five years moving further and further away from globalization towards a much more regional, localized and diverse set of strategies within a given single organization. That's yet another interesting societal shift that we believe will influence the future of work during the coming years.*

> The corporate campus may take on a much more dynamic "hospitality" orientation in the future to provide the full peak experience for the next generation of AI-enabled knowledge workers.

You Say POTATO, I Say P.O.T.A.T.O.

The fifty-year lens. Peak worker experience. Rezoning. This is all new language for new times. It reminds me of the slew of acronyms which have emerged recently, sufficient to make an entire column out of: which, reader, I did.

◇

When it comes to flexible working are you – and please excuse my language – a TW*T or even, by contrast, a POTATO?

Let me explain. One stands for "Tuesdays, Wednesdays and Thursdays" in the office. By contrast POTATO means "possibly on Tuesdays and Thursdays only."

I love that P for "possibly". I also love the reference to the potato, last made popular in Toy Story 2's *famous scene when Mrs Potato Head tells her husband she has packed his shoes "and your angry eyes" for a trip.*

Both phrases originated in Britain, home of Monty Python humor, and confirm the widespread working assumption that flexibility is here to stay.

They also confirm that deploying humor may be a good strategy in the face of the increasingly heated debate about flexible work: Amazon.com Inc.'s chief executive Andy Jassy is the latest big corporate boss to turn up the heat on the company's RTO policy.

TW*T made it early into the lexicon of work in January 2019 by the Ogilvy Group Inc. advertising executive Rory Sutherland. In an article in The Spectator *headlined "The TW*T Revolution"* he remarked that "Friday and Monday is spent at home, and dedicated to business activities which are location-independent: email, video calls, phone calls and so forth." It's a bit of wordplay off the common British slang for a stupid or obnoxious person. Pretty prescient, given it was a full year before Covid-19 reared its head.

The POTATO neologism was coined mid-way through the lockdowns by the networking entrepreneur Oli Barrett, who wrote a LinkedIn post in 2021 saying "I'm coming back as a potato… coming into town Probably on Tuesdays and Thursdays Only. A variant on the 2:3 formula."

Do these acronyms soften the blow for bosses of large companies who have clearly struggled with the idea that their people have a new-found desire for flexibility and are getting their way? After all, flexible working jobs in the US are being filled at a faster rate than more rigid presenteeism roles.

Words matter. They direct the traffic of our minds. And the lingo around flexible work is short, sharp and witty. The compact acronym is by definition shorthand: RTO of course, for return to office. It's as if the hurried, condensed time schedules we are seeing are being reflected back in the language. And the shorter and snappier, the more things stick.

With words, less is often more. But so, too, is humor. We've had a lot of wry, brief catchphrases, haven't we? Quiet quitting and so forth are all symptomatic of the times and perhaps the increasingly dominant young workers: the Gen Z and TikTok generations.

But that same pithy humor is also biting the leaders who can't accept the new flexible world. David Solomon of Goldman Sachs Group Inc. may regret calling working from home "an aberration".

I doubt that New York Magazine *would have run a profile quite as disparaging as this recent one, headlined, "Is David Solomon Too Big a Jerk to Run Goldman Sachs?" if he had not made that remark. Solomon told CNBC last week that the "personal attacks" weren't "fun", adding that "I don't recognize the caricature that's been painted of me."*

This is because a tide has turned. Even blue collar workers are going flexible where they can: General Electric Co. may be too polite to call their model anything other than "flexible" but they have in fact been experimenting with a TW*T model since 2020 in all but name.

William Shakespeare, who combined sublime comedy with seriousness, wrote in his play Hamlet *that "words without thoughts never to heaven go." The language of work right now is sending to heaven those whose words are helping to conjure up new working norms. And it's consigning those who push back against the tide of these new ideas to ridicule, or at least to silence.*

The joke about calling your work life a POTATO or calling yourself a TW*T is this: it makes light of a struggle. All we can do is work through this moment, pack away our angry eyes – and have a bit of fun while we do.

[September 15, 2023]

> The leader who keeps failing to read the room on workforce flexibility looks Luddite. It's as simple as that.

Urban Doom Loops and the Nike Swoosh

The language matters, and the language of post-pandemic working is becoming something of a fashion reflecting two things: the drama and dynamism of the moment, and the transitional nature of what matters when. Especially relevant to commercial real estate now is the "doom loop" and "urban apocalypse" predicted by the economist Arpit Gupta,* who reminded me not only that cities have evolved continuously around the available technology (or lack of it) – e.g. New York's theater district evolved around the nearby garment district – but that there is a simple cost equation now which just isn't adding up for many office tenants:

> *Our dollars and cents number, our estimate was something like, for a typical white collar firm, real estate rental accounts for about $15k per employee. It's a substantial lineup on your expense book. Put yourself in the shoes of an entrepreneur, someone who's starting out. When I talk to people that are creating their own companies and starting from scratch these days, one thing that is very clear, in their heads is, well, you know, I knew as a startup founder that I had investors but I didn't realize that a silent partner at the time was my landlord, who was taking, you know, that much, which is, from the founder's perspective, that's their equity.†*

---

* Professor Arpit Gupta and co-authors Vrinda Mittal and Stijn Van Nieuwerburgh analyze the impact that remote work has had on the New York City commercial office space sector in "Work From Home and the Office Real Estate Apocalypse".
† Interviewed in New York, December 2023.

> Whereas if I'm founder of a new company, it is essentially my own money. So they're making very different decisions because it's their money. Something like 65 percent I think is raw people cost.

The death knell for the commute and the doom loop gives rise to something else: the Nike swoosh.*

Professor Nicholas Bloom of Stanford University, a high-profile academic predicting remote and hybrid working, wrote a guest piece in *The Economist* in August 2023 predicting that "Remote work is set to undergo a Nike swoosh, with an initial post-pandemic drop, followed by its current stabilization and a future long-run surge."

I spoke to him about a month later in California, when I attended the second "Implications of Remote Work" conference he hosted at Stanford's Hoover Institution with his colleagues fellow professors Steven J. Davis and Jose Maria Barrero, who co-author the research on working from home which "drops" monthly like an eagerly awaited podcast episode for fellow work nerds.

He told me then:

> To be honest, I think two days a week outside of the office is about where it's roughly right. So you think about a typical week Monday, Friday at home: I'm saving the commute and it's quiet. I recharge. I have time to do email reading, writing. Tuesday, Wednesday, Thursday I'm in the office. A lot of mentoring meetings, presentations.

---

* The Future of WFH, "Nicholas Bloom predicts a working-from-home Nike swoosh", *The Economist*, August 29, 2023.

WORKING ASSUMPTIONS

> *So that seems to roughly work. You know, that's where things are settling out.*
>
> *If you look at folks working from home, they certainly feel happier to work from home. In the data, what we see is typically if you're working from home maybe three days a week, that we see the maximum happiness and work satisfaction and kind of life satisfaction scores.*
>
> *I honestly don't think there's been anything this big and this fast, probably since the Second World War. So what we saw is millions of men went off to fight. Millions of women were called in to work in factories, shops, governments. And, you know, society discovered what seems obvious now, but it wasn't obvious back then that, look, women can do these jobs just as well as men, in many cases better.*
>
> *And so that kind of stuck. So the men came back, the female labor force participation jumped. And it's been rising ever since. The only other thing that's similar because the pandemic just generated this massive jump that everyone kind of turned around and said, wow, this work from home, look, it isn't perfect, but, you know, we should be doing a lot more of it than we used to.*

There is of course, the new mass-produced technology – not the car, not the computer, but generative AI. I asked him what this means for jobs.

> *AI has a really big intersection with work from home. If you are a hybrid, you're coming into the office, let's say three days a week. AI probably helps you out. It makes you more productive as a co-pilot for coding. It helps you design and write stuff.*

So the hybrid work, as I don't see in the near term, it's really a threat. I think if anything, it's maybe supporting that job.

However, it's very different if you're fully remote. If you're fully remote, AI potentially, and particularly if you're doing a repetitive, relatively basic job, could replace your job because the software side of AI and the visual side and the voice side in particular is already really pretty good.

If this was a Zoom call, I could almost just about be AI: you know, if I didn't respond very well you may figure it out if I was in person, or if the robot that replaced me is fast and clunky that's just not going to work in that setting. But if you think of data entry call centers, HR payroll, this kind of thing that's fully remote, well, a lot of this may be replaced actually by AI in five to ten years.*

> *The smart money is on making offices attractive for a return on a social basis, a part-time basis, and different basis – but not the same basis as before.*

---

* Nicholas Bloom, "Hybrid Working is Here to Stay Post-Pandemic", Bloomberg Originals, December 30, 2020.

The Great Refurb

So the inevitability of a changed landscape of work is clear, all that remains is how workplaces themselves will change. Peter Miscovich is right about the flight to quality. And I think I'm right that transportation will become offices on the move. But what of the bricks and mortar? How will that change?

Here's a column from early in 2023, when optimism still abounded that old occupancy norms would return in a matter of months:

◇

Seismic changes have been triggered in worldwide corporate real estate, office design and management systems over the last three years in a shift as profound as the Great Resignation: let's call it the Great Refurb.

The working assumption that offices will return to the old five-day-nine-to-five week way has turned out to be wrong. Equally off was the idea that remote working would replace the office wherever possible. The reality lies somewhere in the middle, mirroring the halfway mark reached for office occupancy in key US cities. The focus is now moving from purely organizing patterns of working time to the design of the workplace itself.

In the Great Refurb, three key issues dominate the way offices look and feel: safety, sustainability and social space.

Safety first: offices remain targets for attack. More than half of US mass attacks occur at businesses, including the places "where we eat, shop, work, heal, or receive services." That means that we are stuck with anything from airport-style bag X-rays to long waits *on arrival in central lobbies. Unwelcome visitors also pose a threat to cyber security: the global market is forecast to increase from $197 billion in 2021 to $657 billion by 2030, according to Next Move Strategy Consulting, a market research and consulting firm.*

This isn't entirely new. Although safety is a perennial preoccupation of those in the business of running workspaces, the new priority is to protect workers and visitors from airborne disease. Not since the clean tiled lines of Le Corbusier following the flu pandemic of the early twentieth century have we seen such a burst of safety-related innovation in office design. Today these developments range from far-reaching UV technology to foot-pulls on doors to minimize handle touching to anti-microbial paint.

I recently had a hard hat tour of the new London headquarters of Google – dubbed "Platform G" and set to open in 2024. The architects have capitalized on the trend for fresh air by making the roof, normally a place for equipment, an extension of the office, with trees to provide canopied cover. Inside, Google has adapted a separate safety feature, the emergency exit staircase, to become an integrated part of the way people move daily through the building. More stairs and less elevator use are also more germ avoidant.

Next, there is the issue of sustainability – literally in terms of saving the planet. In a global Ipsos survey from November, 68 percent of respondents said they want stricter climate change policies.

Then, there's the social setting. This is the mother lode for leaders who want to future-proof their organization. How can you design a workplace that's attractive enough to retain and build loyalty, cohesion, productivity – and sustain it? The modern equivalent of William Blake's famous "dark Satanic mills" of nineteenth-century industrialization isn't physical exploitation, but the ennui driving quiet quitting, career cushioning and all the other white collar rebellions and rejections of post-pandemic working life.

This is pointless presenteeism, which triggers the listlessness people feel when they're in an office for no reason doing work they can do elsewhere. I'm reminded of Joshua Ferris' novel of corporate existentialism, Then We Came to the End*: "We loved killing time and had perfected several ways of doing so. We wandered the hallways carrying papers that indicated some mission of business when in reality we were in search of free candy."*

Pointless presenteeism can be offset (possibly like carbon can) by the creation of fresh, immersive offices which put social experience at the heart of what they do. In a new report by the workplace research firm WORKTECH Academy, the group identifies the shift towards creating meaningful experiences for employees, from being honest in some cases that the office is better regarded as an offsite than a daily stop-off, to storyboarding a worker's experience from entrance to exit, rather like they do in the movies for those who wish people to enter and not feel like they have to wander corridors in search of free candy.

The Great Refurb is a throwback to a hundred years ago when cities sprang up and the world began a new moment in which old norms were swept away. They all hinged on place, where people put themselves in real time. As a 1926 ad in the Chicago Tribune *wisely said: in the end, it's all about location, location, location – nowadays that's inside and out.*

[February 8, 2023]

What's happening right now is a very unequally distributed return to the office, with very uneven results. When WeWork went bankrupt at the end of 2023 it marked the end of an era in which the working assumption office life would last forever proved to be an expensive mistake. WeWork's rise and fall serves as a metaphor for the end of the office, even though it was only actually the end of WeWork. Nevertheless, the global market in office space dropped by a good twenty per cent after 2020, and the influential Conference Board report of January 2024 showed that global CEOs have come to regard attracting talent as "high focus" but getting them back to the office as "low focus".* All proof that the smart money is on making offices attractive for a return on a social basis, a part-time basis, and different basis – but not the same basis as before.

Although the WeWork model and its imitators was marketed as a drop-in-freelance-worker model, it made its bread and butter from sub-letting to larger companies who either ran out of space or wanted to look hip. Until they didn't. By the time it closed, WeWork's million or so workstations were empty in nearly 800 locations in forty-odd countries around the world. The only thing left of WeWork now, other than its signs over partially empty buildings all over the world, is its fictional rendition on Apple+ in *WeCrashed*, starring Jared Leto and Anne Hathaway.

One trend I've noticed, and possibly I'm biased as a big coffee drinker, is that significant effort has gone into the simplest drink of all: coffee. So much so that after a trip to New York shortly after I wrote the refurb piece, I dedicated one entirely to the significance of this odd little bean:

---

* The Conference Board, "Leading for Tomorrow", C-Suite Outlook 2024.

WORKING ASSUMPTIONS

Data show workers are staying in the office for coffee and here's why it may be part of return to office strategies

I was in New York for in-person work meetings a few weeks ago. While there were the requisite lunches and cocktails at my favorite haunts, one thing stood out: coffee. My working assumption that coffee is an unremarkable and often undrinkable aspect of working life changed when I realized that it's playing a central role in rebuilding corporate office culture in the new hybrid era.

For employees returning to offices on a hybrid basis, on average three days a week, having a coffee with someone is the perfect way to rebuild relationships with people they haven't seen in possibly three years. As I wrote in this column recently, offices break the isolation and monotony of working from home, and yet company leaders have to work hard at offsetting the drag of the commute, especially given the fact that the pandemic showed remote workers could be successful.

I took my anecdotal observations to the research firm Ipsos, which analyzed location data from nearly 10 million mobile phones in over 5,000 coffee shops in the New York City area for me. It showed that only 12 percent of visits occur during working hours, but outside lunch hours. It's hard to argue with the appeal of free coffee in the office given surging inflation.

I saw the benefits of coffee in reviving office camaraderie first hand on a tour of the Park Avenue offices of corporate real estate consultants Savills Plc. Vice Chairman Gabe Marans showed me a plethora of newly refurbished work spaces, from small, soundproofed booths to open-plan cubicles and some offices complete with their own sofas and tables forming a corner office look with privacy for

DALL-E's response to my prompt to create "an anthropomorphic rabbit in an office energetically holding a pot of coffee, surrounded by colleagues".

senior executives. But the pride of the renovation is a vast kitchen/ hangout area called "the Happy Room".

The coffee break and its role in bringing people together socially isn't new. In the seventeenth and eighteenth centuries, coffee became a competitor to tea as the beverage of choice for both elites and workers. In his book A History of the World in 6 Glasses, *the writer*

WORKING ASSUMPTIONS

Tom Standage describes European coffee houses as "the internet of the Age of Reason". Today the coffee break is widely understood as much in a work context as anything, with the "Fika" break in Sweden, "Elevenses" in the UK or even "Smoko" in Australia or the frequently seen canned coffee in Japan, normally the home of tea. Although the US is the largest coffee machine market, the fastest-growing is Asia.

What's new today is the way the office is aiming to emulate the coffee house in-house. Coffee consumption is rising while office use has halved in cities like New York compared to before the pandemic. Global green bean exports in November 2022 totaled 9.2 million bags, up 10.8 percent from the same month of the previous year, according to the International Coffee Organization. On the ground, media magnate Sir Martin Sorrell told me that despite reducing his office space to factor in a three-days-in norm, he agrees "totally" that redefining offices around social space has become indispensable for clients and teams alike.

That's especially true now that many workers don't have assigned desks. "When the time came to reopen our London office, we switched to hot-desking. A more flexible use of office space ensures you always have room to grow your team if your revenue does," said Drew Benvie, chief executive officer of communications agency Battenhall. Expanding the social space when people are coming in at unpredictable times is a way to mitigate there being nowhere for employees to sit. Battenhall recently posted "a day in the office" on TikTok to underscore that the hot desk life is fun, though the practice remains a topic of debate.

Now to the issue of quality. Gone are the stewed pots of tasteless water. It was notable on my recent trip that I was offered not even the pod-brewed coffee supplied by Starbucks, but the specialist, expensive espresso variety administered from top-of-the-range machines. But the one which got me most was delivered on tap: nitro coffee (reader: it's punchy).

Obviously, social life and office life have combined before, but the emphasis used to be on out-of-office bonding – happy hours and beers on Friday kind of stuff. These days, no one is in the office on a Friday if they can help it. So what happens during working hours to keep people connected matters a lot – and coffee is rising to the challenge.

[March 27, 2023]

◌

But it's not completely enough. The fact is that office occupancy rates have continued to plummet in relation to their pre-pandemic rates, as Professor Bloom observed. What matters is not that Zoom announced in 2023 that it would be asking some people back to the office, or that many major corporates followed suit, to screaming headlines about U-turns and gleeful predictions that hybrid and remote working was over. What matters is that they are only doing so on a hybrid basis, *maximum three days a week*. This is not the same as before, not at all.

On LinkedIn, where some of the keenest debate about the future of work happens, you cannot fail to understand the shift happening towards remote, hybrid, flexible and/or four-day week working when you follow contributors such as Dr Gleb Tsipursky, Brian Elliott, Christine Armstrong, Ollie Henderson, Dave Cairns, Heejung Chung, Rob Sadow, Herminia Ibarra, Prithwiraj Choudhury, Annie Dean, Debbie Lovich, Nicholas Bloom, Andy Lake, Gemma Dale, Flex Index to name but a few. Read collectively, and

I hope I can count myself among them, there's a movement emerging, a movement of people passionate about work, about working, and equally passionate that work has to up its game.

No matter how painful and transitional this phase is, I firmly believe it's for the best. The risks are real – from whether jobs are lost, or skills and training available, or the cost of living affordable. The risks are real about AI not just taking jobs but taking souls by destroying our trust in human authenticity. All of this is real and some might happen some of the time.

But to be clear: it couldn't carry on as before. Humans are driving the change just as much as the tech. Humans are in the driving seat, still.

> *There's a movement emerging, a movement of people passionate about work, about working, and equally passionate that work has to up its game. No matter how painful and transitional this phase is, I firmly believe it's for the best.*

How to Stay in the Office
And Go Out at the Same Time

Back to the more pedestrian idea of offices, and whether all the nitro coffee in the world isn't enough. It may contribute to a peak experience, but it won't have people come back or in more than they want to.

Another trend following hot on the heels of office refurbishment is that people are in theory going back to the office – only to go back out again to conferences. Or to meetings. Or to other offices. Business travel is up, with an inevitably optimistic outlook from the Global Business Travel Association that it will top $1.78 trillion by 2027.*

But the conference, or what it represents, is part of the story of how we're finding workarounds to go back but hold on to that new-found appetite for mobility. Which is why, just a couple of months after writing about office refurbishment, and several business trips later, I wrote specifically about it.

◇

The urge to do business again is being amplified by a desire to do so offsite and is bringing innovation to the conference genre

Forget for a moment the ongoing debates about hybrid working and haggling over how many days need to be spent back in the office.

Yes, anchor days (when a whole team is mandated to be onsite) are useful, and of course salaries approaching $1 million make five

---

* Mary Schlangenstein, "Business Travel Spending Will Top Pre-Covid Level in 2024", Bloomberg, August 14, 2023.

days a week back in the office more appealing (call it a presenteeism premium). These office hours arguments are predicated on the working assumption that wherever you work you need to be indoors for a prolonged period of time, say eight hours.

An interesting workaround is being quietly adopted, which still looks like presenteeism, but it's in fact about being out of the office – just with your boss's approval. The conference – that tried and tested way to sell, network, learn and be away from your desk – is making a comeback.

The market in trade fairs and conferences is returning post pandemic. Deloitte reports the biggest drivers of the expected increase in corporate travel are the growth of live events and easing of restrictions. Meanwhile, Informa, the B2B trade show company, which just spent $940 million to acquire events business Tarsus, cites "growth and momentum in Live and On-Demand B2B events."

It's definitely the case that there's a point to conferences in their own right. They are more than tactics to evade office tedium or an extension of what British journalist Richard Littlejohn, one critic of hybrid working, calls "shirking from home". In many cases, they provide the only opportunity to seal the deal, directly sell and also develop networks and relationships. When I attended the World Economic Forum in Davos earlier this year, the conference hall was often half empty, but the bars and parties were packed. This is partly because everyone can watch or catch up online, including delegates, and partly because the parties are often where the interesting information is exchanged. Conferences are about building trust and exchanging information: As Joseph Nye memorably said: "Smart power is neither hard nor soft. It is both."

Conferences are a good way to get out of what's a clear drawback of unbroken office life: the monotony and the politics. The film industry has been entertaining us for years with depictions of offices you just want to get out of. Particular favorites of mine range from Billy Wilder's 1960 Oscar-winner The Apartment *to the 1992 adaption of David Mamet's Pulitzer Prize-winning play* Glengarry Glen Ross, *about the brutal business of real estate sales.*

Of course, not all conferences involve directly sealing a deal as per book rights fests like the London Book Fair. They are being transformed by technology and the use of network apps in a market set to be worth over $2.5 billion by 2028, according to research group The Insight Partners. The smaller end of the conference market, that isn't the transactional trade shows but those focused on team-building, or knowledge sharing, such as senior leadership gatherings or independent investor gatherings, are the ones undergoing the most change. These are increasingly shaped by a desire to swap a cavernous conference center to get out into nature. Take Voyagers, the "community of impact-driven people", which uses hiking and outdoor retreats to generate ideas and do business.

The trend towards congregating outdoors for business and pleasure took off during the pandemic and has continued beyond it. This is the backdrop for two other trends. The first is general getting-away-from-it-all-while-you-work services. Over fifty "digital nomad" visas are being offered around the world and new co-working start-ups set in nature are sprouting up. Ashore, a platform for finding remote work properties, has launched with the slogan "Escape your office. Explore the UK."

In her book Enchantment: Reawakening Wonder in an Exhausted Age, *Katherine May describes the way being outside in nature is a good corrective to the fog engulfing so many technology-bound stressed workers, replacing it with "something to set free in all this billowing air."*

For all of these, the second isn't so much a backdrop as a backpack, which has become a corporate status symbol. A recent Kickstarter campaign for a backpack branded W.F.A (Work from Anywhere) was 100 percent funded in fifteen minutes and oversubscribed to 1,000 percent in five days, according the company that makes it. Its promotional video says: "Work has always been a thing to do, not a place to go."

That said, working generally still requires a room. And conferences are a way to combine our desire to preserve the time outdoors many came to appreciate during the pandemic and the practical needs of getting work done and spending time together. As Stephen Carter, CEO of Informa, put it to me: "As the world's supply chains need refilling, you can't do industrial business development or market access remotely." That's a rather technical way of putting it. I think we know, though, what he means: you need to be face to face and get out and about, but now you have considerably more choice about how to go about it.

[April 24, 2023]

◯

In the end, we will still live and work in buildings – if we're lucky. But the pattern of movement will change, and movement will remain a defining quality of how people live and work. A final word on space. The truth is we just need less of it. Here's a snippet from a column I wrote on leadership culture and taking tough decisions on what this meant for office space:

Employee office experience has changed forever, and leaders need to figure out what that means for corporate real estate.

Denis McGowan, former global head of real estate at Standard Chartered, who looked after 85,000 people in 1,500 locations, led the strategy to downsize space from 16 million square feet at its peak to 11 million by the end of 2022. The property team he managed coined the phrase "twice the experience, half the space" to reflect the ambition to make remaining offices a hub for experience. He told me that "we put collaboration, connection and collision spaces into the portfolio as we knew it was about activating spaces for the community of colleagues, not just providing desks."

The lesson from this for me is twofold. First, that no one in corporate real estate now thinks office space will continue at the same size or configuration as before. And second, that the leaders in C-suite roles, such as facilities chiefs and property portfolio managers, are beginning to play a central role in redesigning work in 2023 and beyond.

[March 10, 2023]

⬡

One way or another we're on the move again between home and work. The stay-at-home notices have been lifted. So many of us are back, or half back, or differently back and – what then? Then the hard work of cultural cohesion begins afresh. That's next.

DALL-E creates "a modern reimagining of the iconic 'Lunch Atop a Skyscraper' photograph featuring a mix of people. Some are dressed in contemporary office attire" (time taken to reproduce: thirty seconds).

4

CULTURE CLUBS AND CLASHES

What did it feel like, 850 feet high above the city of New York, sitting atop a single beam in your overalls and worker boots, in 1932? Well, you can find out. Because the Rockefeller Center, New York's iconic skyscraper, now offers a digitally recreated experience as part of the tourist trail. Yes, today you can buy a ticket for an experience which (don't ask me how) puts you in that lineup at the top of "The Rock" to rotate above Central Park, sixty-nine floors below.

The iconic photograph, originally called "Builders of the City Enjoy Luncheon", captures ironworkers in an image conveying industry, camaraderie, risk and shared endeavour.* It wasn't in fact wholly authentic – it was a staged publicity shot to promote the building (like the Hollywood Sign was originally erected as a piece of real estate PR). It took ChatGPT less than a minute to follow my "prompt" to produce a modern rendition of the famous photo.

---

* rockefellercenter.com, *The Center Magazine* featuring the 'Lunch atop the skyscraper" story.

This fakeness seems timely: AI is known to "hallucinate", and indeed the image I asked it to recreate added considerably more people than the original, stacking the beam. Some bit of language in the large language model has overlooked not only the accuracy of the number of people but the symbolism that eleven is the ultimate team number, represented in soccer/football, hockey and cricket. In other words, that photograph is a symbol of the ultimate work team – but AI so far has misunderstood.

The apex of anxiety around AI hinges on its ability to recreate reality in false ways. The creative industries themselves are the canary in the mine when it comes to seeing the extraordinary capability and risk alike of a newly rendered reality. But the real anxiety is this: in an increasingly digital world, where we work in unreal worlds, recreated worlds of metaverse and multiverse worlds in which we remain real people, what happens to culture itself?

> *"Viewed from the standpoint of social science, society is composed of individuals organized in occupational groups, each group fulfilling some function of the society. Taking this fact into account, psychology – the science of human nature and human consciousness – is able to make at least one general assertion as to the form a given society must take if it is to persist as a society. It must be possible for the individual as he works to see that his work is socially necessary; he must be able to see beyond his group to the society."*
>
> **Elton Mayo, Democracy and Society 2019**

It's over a hundred years since we have begun to think seriously at work about the impact of what we feel about belonging, and how individuals and groups interact, and increasingly this is defined by a single word with multiple interpretations: culture. Edgar Schein, the influential MIT management scholar, believed culture at work to hinge on values and belief. At work the tasks we do used to be thought of as devoid of culture, i.e. devoid of humanity or human engagement. The turning point in the shifting away from this view, and the managerialism of Frederick Winslow Taylor, came with the Australian psychologist Elton Mayo and his colleagues, who originated my favorite management study of all time – the "Hawthorne Experiments". Beginning in Chicago's Western Electric telephone factory in 1927, the experiments, ostensibly meant to measure dry performance of workers under different physical conditions, morphed into the biggest evidence and analysis of how if you treat humans like humans, listening to them, observing them as a team, you get completely different results.

The entire human relations movement, and what has become known as "the Hawthorne effect", began by stumbling across the importance of work culture. Not for nothing did the great management legend Peter Drucker, an Austrian who moved to America, say that "culture eats strategy for breakfast".*

There's just one problem. Despite the fact that everyone talks about it, creating and maintaining culture has remained elusive, and insufficient, certainly when it comes to trying to woo people back to the office. Remember the ice cream carts and the free massages which were first on offer post pandemic? And the unlimited time off? Well, that's all gone now.

But so too has the idea that good office culture is drinking yourself silly after work, or being groped at the office Christmas party, or

---

* Drucker's quote is also included in the Beyonce Column in Chapter 6.

even staying late and working beyond the hours you are paid for. Similarly, the DEI movement shows that culture has come to mean something very measurable, if messy: the perception of exclusion and the quest for inclusion.

All of which is deeply difficult to get right in an environment changing as dramatically as the current one. Workplace culture now has to balance between creating community, cohesion and creativity and stemming its opposite, a clash of cultures, of values, and a breakout of cultural hostilities within single organizations and wider discussion.

> *It's over a hundred years since we have begun to think seriously at work about the impact of what we feel about belonging, and how individuals and groups interact, and increasingly this is defined by a single word with multiple interpretations: Culture.*

Intensely Human

Cultural drama of the highest order played out in American universities following 7 October 2023.* The presidents of Harvard University and UPenn were forced to resign after failing to persuade the public that they were controlling unbridled student activism on campus. Pro-Palestinian sentiment was being openly expressed as anti-Semitism.

In the ensuing row a prominent Harvard alumnus and donor, Bill Ackman, single-mindedly "took on" his alma mater and its culture. But his "victory" enraged and engaged others and his wife became the target of media attention. At the heart of it is a workplace concern: the charge of academic plagiarism. This was what caused the resignation of Harvard President Claudine Gay, kicking off a firestorm of argument and counter-argument about human error, AI-detectable plagiarism, and what is intentional and what is what you might call "unconscious bias".

When Ackman's wife, a prominent former MIT professor called Neri Oxman, got brought into the brouhaha and was accused of plagiarism by *Business Insider*, Ackman wrote a very long post on X in which he invited founders of AI companies wishing for investment to produce plagiarism-detecting software, admitted his wife's error, but said, with no irony, that she was "intensely human".

This is a mess. And it's ongoing. The university campus rows have stirred up a hornet's nest of cultural stings around values, beliefs and behaviors, which go back a century just at a time when they need to go forward.

---

* Day of the Hamas attack on Israel.

WORKING ASSUMPTIONS

Workplace culture has to reinvent itself for new times. How do you get workers to love their work and their workplace? How do you manage to insulate external politics from internal workplaces becoming overwhelming? This is the heart of the dilemma and it's by no means solved yet.

Work culture has become a holy grail of managers and leaders trying to create fresh collaboration and cohesion among a more distributed workforce, which will rely much more on remote working and automated tools. My gloomy working assumption is that nothing much will change until leaders and managers accept that "culture" is often used as a brand message rather than a lived reality for the workforce. But there is a reason to be optimistic. The twin effects of the profound isolation resulting from Covid, combined with the aggressive growth of generative AI, will strengthen efforts to nail down the human experience at work, and this will hinge on providing ways to be social, to network, and to build community, both in person and virtually. Workplace culture, which has already become rebranded as workplace experience, or WX, is still quite a lot of corporate waffle. Actions speak louder than words. My working assumption is that the organizations which try to fix their failures first will be the ones which can say "we have a great culture".

> *A proxy war is raging in the battle between hyper-stressed managers trying to meet the clear employee demand for freedom and the equally clear C-suite demand for presenteeism and monitored work.*

CULTURE CLUBS AND CLASHES

Work Is The Color Gray (And Pink)

Part of the way through finding a new set of values, beliefs and behaviors, a new workplace culture, is to see clearly what popular culture is showing us so that we might respond to it.

The original "lunch" photograph is of course black and white, but the color of work is depicted in films in all kinds of hue. There is a famous scene, for instance, in *The Devil Wears Prada*, a film set in the not-unlike-*Vogue*-world of a fashion magazine, which at one point stars the color "cerulean blue". Meryl Streep at her sweeping best berates a young assistant, played by Anne Hathaway with devil-may-care insouciance, about the significance to jobs in the fashion industry based on this color.

Work's color, literally and culturally, is box office (this film grossed $300 million on a budget of $35 million).*

> *ChatGPT3.5's Response to:*
>
> *'List ten notable films of the twenty-first century set in workplaces'*
>
> *Answer:*
>
> **1. The Social Network** *(2010) – Directed by David Fincher, this film explores the founding of Facebook and the dynamics within a tech startup workplace.*
>
> **2. Up in the Air** *(2009) – Directed by Jason Reitman, this film follows a corporate downsizer who spends most of his time traveling and delivering layoffs.*

---

* boxofficemojo.com, statistics on *The Devil Wears Prada*.

> **3. Office Space** (1999) – Although released in the late 90s, this workplace comedy has remained popular in the 21st century, satirizing office life and corporate culture.
>
> **4. The Devil Wears Prada** (2006) – Directed by David Frankel, this film provides a glimpse into the high-fashion magazine industry and the challenges faced by a young assistant.
>
> **5. In Good Company** (2004) – Directed by Paul Weitz, this movie explores the dynamics of a corporate takeover and the relationships among employees.
>
> **6. The Intern** (2015) – Directed by Nancy Meyers, this film tells the story of a retired executive who becomes an intern at an online fashion retailer.
>
> **7. Horrible Bosses** (2011) – A dark comedy that focuses on the trials and tribulations of employees dealing with terrible bosses.
>
> **8. The Belko Experiment** (2016) – A thriller directed by Greg McLean, this movie takes place in an office building where employees are forced to participate in a deadly social experiment.
>
> **9. The Internship** (2013) – Directed by Shawn Levy, this comedy features two middle-aged salesmen who intern at Google, highlighting the culture clash between generations.
>
> **10. Thank You for Smoking** (2005) – Directed by Jason Reitman, this satirical comedy centers around a tobacco industry lobbyist and the challenges he faces in his workplace.

I was pleased to see *The Devil Wears Prada* in this list as that scene about cerulean blue is etched in my mind. The movie of the moment which also gave a nod to fashion was *Barbie* in the

CULTURE CLUBS AND CLASHES

summer of 2023, but as I wrote in a column, the color pink clashed with the color gray...

Oscar Wilde's assumption that life imitates art might need a rethink. Right now, it looks like the other way around. Especially when it comes to work, popular culture is reflecting back what life is like.

You might expect me to take this view, as the author of a column called Working Assumptions. *But take some of the more recent hit movies or bestselling books and you'll find that how we work is the subject or subtext of the story.*

Let's start with Barbie, *the summer's blockbuster movie. By popular consensus the dominant color is "dopamine dressing" pink, but I actually see gray. For me, the most memorable scene is when Barbie hurtles through a grim, gunmetal set of office cubicles trying to evade dastardly corporate executives who want to put her, quite literally, back in her box. The production designer Sarah Greenwood told* House Beautiful *the color scheme in the film for the corporate headquarters of Mattel Inc., Barbie's makers in the real world, was deliberately chosen to contrast with the hot pink of Barbie Land.*

The main message of Barbie *may be a feisty feminist one (including the fact that Ken World turns out to want to turn back the clock on President Barbie or indeed any working Barbies not in the service of Kens), but it also reveals quite a strong one about corporate life, too. That it's colorless and oppressive.*

You don't need to page Dr Freud to understand the message here, any more than you do the eerily similar office chase scenes in Everything Everywhere All at Once, *the incumbent best movie at the 2023 Academy Awards. Both of these highly successful films are set in multiverses in which the cold, hard, venal reality of work, tax, and corporations are portrayed bleakly with the office villains.*

The summer bestseller, Yellowface *by Rebecca F. Kuang, resonates in no small part due to a recognizable takedown of the publishing industry. "This will, for sure, be the book of the season" the lead character is told by her publisher, who is unaware that she is passing off her dead best friend's work as her own. The success of this satire is how relatable the story is.* Yellowface *describes a culture where the already-successful always have unfair advantage over the less confident and lesser known. I'm sure you, dear reader, have not taken credit for a colleague's creativity, but I imagine you might know someone who has.*

Away from the office, contemporary fiction also serves up compelling drama about a very different work experience. In Barbara Kingsolver's Pulitzer-prize-winning novel Demon Copperhead, *it's Walmart and the cold realities of shelf stacking in supermarkets – monotonous, low-paid work – which feature in the lives of characters in a coal mining community which has fallen victim to economic hard times and the opioid crisis.*

It isn't just literary fiction which tells this story of unfair work, or not enough work, or shift work. Billy Joel performed "Allentown", a song about the decline of the manufacturing sector during the last century and the feeling that working life was a series of broken promises, at his sellout gigs at Madison Square Garden and London's Hyde Park forty years after he first wrote the song.

In this respect art does imitate life. Work's themes are either eternal or cyclical.

Hard times and hustle culture crop up a lot in a slew of non-fiction books explaining work culture and history. In On Work: Money,

CULTURE CLUBS AND CLASHES

Meaning, Identity, *Derek Thompson writes that* "Today the norm is to think about employment and unemployment as a black-and-white binary, rather than two points at opposite ends of a wide spectrum of working arrangements."

This point is echoed in The Workplace You Need Now: Shaping Spaces for the Future of Work *by Sanjay Rishi, Benjamin Breslau and Peter Miscovich, executives with real estate property company JLL. The book predicts a future where work becomes "liquid", noting that "employers and managers now need to view their workforces in terms of both employees and nonemployees, which presents a challenge to creating a cohesive and integrated workplace ecosystem."*

The last word goes to a recent futuristic Danish novel, The Employees: A Workplace Novel of the 22nd Century, *a sci-fi book set on a spaceship "some time in the future" in which "someone touched me on the shoulder and I saw that it was a humanoid co-worker."*

Perhaps Oscar Wilde was prescient for our times. Pretty soon life will imitate art, and the distinction between the humans and humanoids will echo some of sci-fi's outer realms. At least we were entertained by art along the way.

[August 24, 2023]

◇

The brilliance of *Barbie* the movie was how many messages about culture it contained – not least because it's a post #MeToo-era film. In 2014, when British writer Laura Bates' bestseller *Everyday Sexism* was published, Sony acquired the rights to develop the live action Barbie movie, five years after Universal Studios first announced it. The culture changed further in 2017 when *The New*

York Times ran its historic allegations of sexual abuse (in a work context) against Harvey Weinstein, citing on the record quotes from actresses Rose McGowan and Ashley Judd.

Workplace sexism and sexual violence is now a working assumption rather than what prevailed for decades, a kind of jolly plain-sight denial of its true nature. *Mad Men*'s seven-season success was as much about its depiction of rampant sexism as advertising, but its run ended in 2015, just when the cultural tide turned.

> *The main message of* Barbie *may be a feisty feminist one (including the fact that Ken World turns out to want to turn back the clock on President Barbie or indeed any working Barbies not in the service of Kens), but it also reveals quite a strong one about corporate life, too. That it's colorless and oppressive.*

Toxic Workplace's Starring Role

Depiction versus reality. This is the tension at the heart of what workplace culture is about. This is why we turn again and again to what feels like a realistic depiction of culture at work, in fiction, in drama, in art. It's preferable to the intense pretence so much of work makes people feel. Not all of it, and not all people, and not all of the time. But as a norm, the workplace has become associated with dysfunction and disengagement.

This is why so much of corporate workplace strategy hinges on words like engagement, experience, and alongside that recruitment and its all-important counterpart, "retention". We know what happens when people do not have shared values and beliefs and do not care about their people, or their people do not feel cared about: they leave, underperform or rebel.

The toxic workplace is alive and well. It's systemic. In the spring of 2024 a festering sore of workplace corruption caused by a bad IT system erupted in the UK as a direct result of a piece of culture – a TV show called *Mr Bates vs The Post Office*.* Within days of airing such was the outrage that Parliament convened to discuss it, and faster action was taken in two weeks than in the fourteen years since the problem first began to surface.

Culture about corporate culture: how ironic that this is the only way in which people can face what's happening.

From grappling over bad management, the exact terms of returning to the office; from external politics to identity politics, culture has

---

* *Mr Bates vs The Post Office* was aired in the UK on ITV from January 1 to 4, 2024.

all too often come to mean not creating great places to work but crisis management to cover up terrible error long after it's known or even exacerbating tensions instead of calming them down.

In the case of corrupt practices to cover up a bad IT system at the UK Post Office, 700 people were wrongly convicted by the Crown Prosecution Service between 2010 and 2021* which repeatedly appeared to enlist its IT supplier Fujitsu to corroborate the claim that the tech worked and the workers were corrupt. At the time of writing, few corporate heads had actually rolled – although the former chief executive had to return her CBE "Honor" (how very British).

A different kind of sour culture is cancel culture. Well before Covid, thanks in large part to social media and possibly as an unintended consequence of the movement to focus on DEI (diversity, equity and inclusion), corporate culture started to become increasingly mired in everyday controversy. During the pandemic a whole slew of corporate executives canceled themselves in some shape or form by trying to "flex shame" – a brilliant term coined by the British HR academic Gemma Dale. Sir Alan Sugar, a man who has made millions from the very tech which has enabled working from home to thrive, accused British workers of being "lazy gits", for instance.† Charming.

A further irony is that the very people lampooning appalling management and behavior began to inexplicably display it themselves. They say pop will eat itself – well, culture appears to cancel itself too: in 2023 Scott Adams, whose refreshingly irreverent Dilbert cartoons

---

* The British Post Office scandal is a series of miscarriages of justice between 1999 and 2015.
† X post by Sir Alan Sugar, May 5, 2022.

CULTURE CLUBS AND CLASHES

on corporate culture ran globally from 1989, made inexcusable racist remarks in an online rant.* Even without the obvious need to go, Dilbert's demise is testament to a febrile, fractious mood in which people lose their cool and say and do stupid things.

Culture isn't working at work as well as the story that it is.

So rather than papering over the cracks, the best thing to do is try to resolve problems. I wrote a piece about what this could entail:

As Big Tech lays off thousands, workplace conflict is back in a big way. Here's how to keep the peace.

Humans aren't harmonious beings. Judging by the number of ongoing wars and ever-increasing hate online, we live in a world geared more for conflict than conflict resolution. The workplace is no exception. If anything, it can be the rule.

Now that business life is moving beyond the fog caused by Covid and into a new territory where actionable ideas are the order of the day, it's time to negotiate a new peace between warring factions. At the same time, the US tech giants are under extreme pressure, with brutal layoffs at Twitter Inc. by email and reported cuts at Meta Platforms Inc. In fact, US Surgeon General Vivek Murthy released guidelines in October that directly address toxic workplaces.

The focus was very much on mental health and wellbeing, and on avoiding egregious activity like bullying. My working assumption:

---

* Dilbert is an American comic strip written and illustrated by Scott Adams, first published on April 16, 1989.

bosses and workers need something more strategic and systemic to address the underlying issues that cause pressing tensions in the first place. Turns out, there's a roadmap to harmony that can be found in places ranging from the classic tenets of political diplomacy to the traditional business school curriculum to the La Brea Tar Pits, but it has to be learned – and applied in real time.

Certainly if leaders can get better at reading the room, that's a good place to start. The power balance changed during the pandemic. Management can no longer blithely impose its will and priorities on the workforce, or at least it will pay a far steeper price for resorting to the corporate dominance strategies common in the pre-pandemic era. Notice the 2.3 million members of the subreddit r/antiwork group (tagline "Unemployment for all, not just the rich!"). Goldman Sachs Group Inc. warned a year ago that a shift in work preferences and lifestyles posed a "long-run risk" around labor force participation.

There's a well-documented disconnect between managers who place a premium on presenteeism and those who don't. The former suffer from a "productivity paranoia" that translates to just 12 percent of leaders having full confidence that their team is productive versus 87 percent of employees who claim they are, according to the latest Microsoft Work Trend Index. Elon Musk qualifies for this category, rolling back Twitter's work-from-anywhere policy after calling employees back at Tesla Inc. earlier this year.

Finding common ground requires sensitive negotiations in each workplace, away from the gaze of social media. For example, a decade ago a 100+ day lockout by the National Hockey League and its union, the National Players' Federation, over hockey-related revenue ended with the shuttle diplomacy of a federal mediator.

Workers aren't feeling understood, or listened to. Many feel they are in a so-called "psychic prison". It's one of eight organizational metaphors social theorist Gareth Morgan identified thirty-six years ago, which means essentially groupthink – a faulty mindset too fixed for its own good. Morgan's lessons have almost certainly cropped up in the reading of everyone in the MBA class of leaders who dominate much of corporate life.

Given that an MBA is said to increase salaries by more than 40 percent on average, those who enjoy this hard-won perk shouldn't put their learning on the shelf. If more leaders reapply case studies, they might find ready-made answers not just from Morgan, but also Dutch sociologist Geert Hofstede's "power distance" data. These teachings arise from his job in the personnel research department at International Business Machines Corp. and demonstrate how excessive hierarchy and distance from decision-making incubate trouble in teams.

New advice and case studies are available, too. One comes in Amanda Ripley's book High Conflict, which retells the story of how predatory animals followed each other into a sticky end because "conflict, once it escalates past a certain point, operates just like La Brea Tar Pits… more and more of us get pulled into the muck." It's a cautionary tale for the workplace that could be entitled "When You Are in a Hole, Stop Digging".

Ironically, in order to have what Ripley calls "good conflict", we have to get into a different kind of muck altogether: psychological chaos. This is definitely messier than the feel-good messages around wellbeing, but more realistic. In Gabriella Braun's book about using psychoanalysis to create workplace dialogue, All That We Are, she's clear that to really resolve conflict people need to "consolidate the *return from their disturbed state of mind." In other words, you have to get down and dirty with it. A sophisticated approach to conflict resolution isn't the avoidance of it, or the sugar-coating of "differences", but a recognition that humans do unravel, and then they can reassemble themselves. Workplaces are no different. Or they shouldn't be.*

Evolutionary anthropologists argue about whether we always fought or fall into two camps: the optimist doves and the pessimist hawks who will always find our casus belli *– cause of war. But we can use negotiation and bargaining to ease through conflict, not with a battering ram of take-it-or-leave-it policies but with nuance, patience and a willingness to shuttle between warring factions in order to seek – and make – the peace.*

[November 7, 2022]

◯

The cultural peace is without doubt being stressed by the politics of remote and hybrid work. Dave Cairns, a provocateur real estate consultant who calls himself a "digital homad" and whose posts on LinkedIn make for compulsive reading, articulates well the worker–worker tensions of a new way of working in which the always-on, always-in culture is being disbanded:

> *When I had a child, all of a sudden I couldn't show up to the 8.30 Tuesday meeting that my team was having because it meant that I would have to bring my daughter to the daycare at 7:15 in the morning and subject her to a day of being there from 7 until 5:30, which is not fair to a fifteen-month-old child, right? And so, all of a sudden I come in later. I'd had a partner who was in his fifties, who had kids that were older.*

CULTURE CLUBS AND CLASHES

And then the rest of the staff on our team had no kids. And so all of a sudden the leper, they're like looking at me, like I'm not contributing. You know what I mean? Because it's this bias of proximity, right?

> *The working assumption for years was that men didn't want to even do childcare, and that women's childcare issues didn't count. But we know otherwise. The working culture has to meaningfully catch up and reflect this. And the person to set the bar, to set the scene, has to be the leader.*

Follow The Leader

Proximity bias is of course a perception, and one driven by cultural sensibility. If your boss wants you in, does that mean you need to be in, or they need you to be in? How do you redraw the boundaries so that compromise can happen – and, even more importantly, so can experimentation and iteration? This has to involve mindset shifts, which also take note of the available technology.

The working assumption for years was that men didn't want to even do childcare, and that women's childcare issues didn't count. But we know otherwise. The working culture has to meaningfully catch up and reflect this. And the person to set the bar, to set the scene, has to be the leader. As one of the characters in *Things Change*, the 1988 David Mamet gangster movie, asks of a fellow mafioso: "Are you the guy... or the guy behind the guy?"

Well, let's assume you're the guy (gender neutral meaning here). I wondered what would be gained if another cultural occasion in one setting – the commencement speech – could work transposed to another, the corporate one:

◇

The annual academic ritual provides a useful model for welcoming new recruits.

As spring turns to summer, college students turn to graduation, the ritual celebration that signals the end of formal university education and the beginning of a professional career. A key aspect of this ceremony dating back to the Middle Ages is the commencement address.

CULTURE CLUBS AND CLASHES

The speeches themselves are often examples of memorable oratory. I'm thinking in particular of Winston Churchill's address to Harrow School in 1941 ("We have only to persevere to conquer.") or Martin Luther King's Springfield College address in 1964 ("No nation can live alone. No individual can live alone. We are all caught in an inescapable network of mutuality.").

My working assumption is that emulating the commencement address in person and in the office as newbies arrive could be rather a good model for leaders who want to recruit and retain talent. According to data from consulting firm Mercer, annual turnover rates are rising to nearly 25 percent in the US across businesses. So something needs to change there.

I view the commencement speech – whether valedictory in educational terms or welcoming in corporate terms – as a key cultural moment. As Kevin Ellis, PWC's UK and Middle East chairman, told me, "The only long-term advantage of any business is its culture." The new recruits are increasingly not all graduates by the way – PWC dropped its stipulation that they would only employ graduates in certain roles in 2022 in a bid to boost diversity – but the principle applies irrespective of who is "commencing" the work.

Work itself features often in great commencement speeches. King invoked it several times as he exhorted his audience to push for social change. Perhaps most famous in this genre was Steve Jobs (himself a college dropout), who in 2005 told his audience at Stanford University that "the only way to do great work is to love what you do. If you haven't found it yet, keep looking. Don't settle." And in Michelle Obama's 2016 commencement speech as first lady, she cited how her father's "blue collar job helped to pay the small portion of my college tuition that wasn't covered by loans or grants or my work-study or my summer jobs."

The value of an inspiring, well-delivered commencement speech – and lucky Harvard University, which has bagged the actor Tom Hanks as its principal speaker this year – is to set out values themselves. This is both a challenge and tremendous opportunity for corporate leaders. The challenge is partly one of oratory itself. Let's face it, not everyone can be media trained to perfection or has natural public speaking abilities. So don't be afraid to invite someone who is able to be the best messenger, and let that person make commencement memorable at companies, too.

CULTURE CLUBS AND CLASHES

This challenge in itself can create an opportunity, especially as leaders continue to be vexed by the best way to bring people more into their office buildings. It's not limited to speeches, either. Why not see the initiation of new recruits into your workplace as an initiation ceremony every bit as vital and memorable as a college commencement itself?

Remember the commencement ceremony is just that: a ceremony. It can become a way to introduce alumni, to unveil the team, to launch a whole series of initiatives which also build trust, camaraderie and networks – the all-important cultural glue of any organization.

I have already argued in this column about the value of making Thanksgiving a workplace ritual which takes place in rather than outside of working hours and spaces in order to emphasize that not only is work itself an institution as important to many as college or family, but that it takes up as much commitment and time.

The human resources and people management industry is full of ideas for addressing the "recognition revolution" wrought by hybrid working – a way to keep the peace with restless teams as the balance of power swings somewhat in favor of employees in tight labor markets. This both maximizes recruitment and retention potential but has another benefit. In doing what McKinsey calls "continuous listening", a new set of signals is being sent to employees: that they matter.

Don't worry about convention. It's better to design your own, integrating the corporate culture and location of the business as universities often do.

The American Council on Education conferred "wide latitude" on the exact time and manner of celebrations and this is seen especially

WORKING ASSUMPTIONS

in a fairly latitudinous dress code: the pinning of sunflowers to lapels is traditional at the law school of University of Texas at Austin, or lei flower garlands in Hawaii for instance. In India, convocation ceremonies now favor attire made out of Indian handloom in response to direct wishes from Prime Minister Narendra Modi, while in Italy some wear imperial laurel wreaths as a symbol of triumph.

Let leaders use commencement ceremonies to introduce new workers as triumphant standard bearers for the next generation of corporate life. Let them enjoy a commencement ceremony, too: not to mark the end of an era, but the beginning of one.

[May 24, 2023]

◯

Well, the triumphant standard bearer would be nice. Culture eats strategy for breakfast, but it has to be strategic. And it has to come back to our old friend tasks and jobs, to productivity and our other old friends, inputs 'n' outputs. And the best way to measure this, and certainly to implement it, is to understand how best to collaborate.

Collaboration is in the eye of the beholder*

00 00 01 02 CC
Apollo 11, Houston. You're good at 1 minute.

00 00 01 06 CDR
Roger.

00 00 01 54 CC
Stand by for mode 1 Charlie.

00 00 01 57 CC
MARK.

00 00 01 58 CC
Mode 1 Charlie.

00 00 01 59 CDR

One Charlie.

00 00 02 03 CC
Apollo 11, this is Houston. You are GO for staging.

00 00 02 17 CDR
Inboard cut-off.

---

* nasa.gov transcription of the Technical Air-to-Ground Voice Transmission (GOSS NET 1) from the Apollo 11 mission.

00 00 02 19 CC
We confirm inboard cut-off.

00 00 02 44 CDR
Staging.

00 00 02 46 CDR
And ignition.

00 00 02 55 CC
11, Houston. Thrust is GO, all engines. You're looking good.

00 00 02 59 CDR
Roger. You're loud and clear, Houston.

08 02 57 19 CC
11, Houston. You can go ahead and turn it on.

08 02 57 24 LMP
Okay. I'll have to go to command reset to do that.

08 02 57 34 CC
11, Houston. That's negative. All you have to do is turn it on. That'll be fine.

08 02 57 44 LMP
I guess I don't know how to turn it on, then. I got PCM, ANTILOG RECORD, FORWARD; high bit rate, and barber pole.

08 02 58 03 CC
11, Houston. We'll send the ON command from down here, see if it works.

CULTURE CLUBS AND CLASHES

> *08 02 58 07 LMP*
> *Okay.*
>
> *08 02 58 56 LMP*
> *Got our friend the Moon whipping by the field of view right now.*
>
> *08 02 59 01 CC*
> *Roger. Copy.*
>
> *Transcript, Technical Air-to-Ground Voice Transmission (GOSS NET 1) from the NASA Apollo 11 Mission, 16 July 1969.*

I was four when a man walked on the moon, and I don't know if we watched it or not. But when I read the transcripts of the teamwork to put him there, I get goosebumps. Four hundred thousand workers of one kind or another supported Neil Armstrong, the American eagle who landed, consolidating America's place in the world as the technological powerhouse it remains today, and, incidentally, 650 million people watched, the biggest news TV event in American history.

If you want to see workplace culture represented *well* at work on the screen, it's there in teams which have a purpose, a method, and who trust each other: *All the President's Men, Apollo 13, Moneyball,* and one of my favorites from 2015, *Spotlight,* based on the *Boston Globe*'s investigative team, which won Best Picture and Best Original Screenplay at the Oscars that year.

The story of how organizations have tried to create culture with a capital C can be best seen with another C-word: collaboration.

WORKING ASSUMPTIONS

This was a column I wrote in December 2022, just as the desire to get people back to the office was arguably weaponizing the charge that you could only collaborate well in-person.

◇

What the management theory "forming, storming, norming, performing and adjourning" can teach us.

The universal working assumption is that productivity depends on collaboration, but there's no agreement on what's the best way to achieve it. While the market for digital tools, platforms, teleconferencing and software to facilitate collaboration is worth nearly $20 billion, technology alone isn't the answer. In the end, it's about the humans, not the machines.

For one, the understanding of teamwork predates the widespread use of office technology. Bruce Tuckman and Mary Jensen wrote a model of group development back in 1977. Their five-stage "forming, storming, norming, performing and adjourning" process still stands as key to designing the iterative process of collaboration. For instance, the "norming" phase is when a group gets into the teeth of a project and learns to trust each other and assign roles, while "performing" relies on interdependence. In a testament to the endurance of their principles, Slack, one of the highest performing collaboration software providers, cited them in a 2019 blog post.

The mid-seventies were a rich seam for management theory and coincided with the start of what I describe in my book The Nowhere Office *as the Mezzanine Years (the time between the supremacy of offices and a tech-enabled future which could operate outside them).*

CULTURE CLUBS AND CLASHES

COLLABORATION IS IN THE EYE OF THE BEHOLDER

It's important to frame the plethora of technological platforms and applications which have flooded increasingly into the workplace as only ever as good as the human minds using them. Nothing can replace this – the technology is a utility to augment the creativity and dynamics of what happens when people work together.

That said, the development of technology to support people working is impressive and reflects that the workplace isn't a fixed place all the time anymore for increasing numbers of white collar workers. Not only are we seeing the rapid evolution of dominant players, such as Zoom Video Communications Inc., moving beyond teleconferencing, but new models of co-working apps like Polywork and hybrid working platform Kadence underscore the reality that collaboration isn't always done from an office. In September, for example, remote jobs were 14 percent of all posts on LinkedIn, but got 52 percent of US applications.

The more new technology supports new patterns of work and keeps it simple and user-friendly the more it's likely to succeed. Let's not forget that perhaps the best example of an early workplace collaboration tool is Google Docs, designed sixteen years ago by Jen Mazzon. She wrote at the time: "Everyone told us it was crazy to try and give people a way to access their documents from anywhere – not to mention share documents instantly, or collaborate online within their browsers."

Everyone knows the pain point of a badly designed interface or something overly complex: the phrase of the year may well be "Toggling Tax", from a Harvard Business Review *paper showing the sheer scale of interactions required these days to switch between different applications. Which is why the clunky complexity of the metaverse makes me wonder whether it will ever live up to the hype as being the next big thing in collaboration-enabling technology.*

It's thirty years since the phrase "metaverse" was used in Neal Stephenson's 1992 sci-fi story Snow Crash. *He correctly predicted the possibility of a real-time synchronous 3D world in which digital facsimiles of humans – also known as avatars – will unite and enhance co-working and community. The metaverse currently looks like it's in a distinctly beta phase when it comes to being used for collaboration, notwithstanding that the global market is predicted to grow by 50 percent by 2029. This is partly because at the moment it just doesn't seem cool. Let's not forget the story that the European Commission was left with egg on its face trying to attract Gen Z to engage with them by throwing a metaverse party which few attended.*

The metaverse isn't working yet because it's putting technological design before function. Analysts at Tech Target noted that industry watchers have questioned if the metaverse will ultimately be much different from the digital experiences we have today or if the masses will be willing to spend hours in a headset navigating digital space. Recent research by the University of Primorska's Faculty of Mathematics, Natural Sciences and Information Technologies shows significant productivity losses and mental health issues from trying to work in virtual reality for prolonged periods of time.

COLLABORATION IS IN THE EYE OF THE BEHOLDER

All of which brings us back to the human in the machine age. As long as collaboration technology is underpinned by collaboration management in the next phase of work, the teams that come together can get their work done – whether in person, in cyberspace or in between.

[December 15, 2022]

> It's important to frame the plethora of technological platforms and applications which have flooded increasingly into the workplace as only ever as good as the human minds using them. Nothing can replace this – the technology is a utility to augment the creativity and dynamics of what happens when people work together.

Wild Boars and Humans

A brilliant example of human-led collaboration is the famous Tham Luang cave rescue in Thailand where twelve young boys and their football coach from the Wild Boars were rescued after flood water trapped them. A global pop-up team of over 10,000 divers, technicians and local mountaineers converged on the area, deploying technology as advanced as drones and as basic as handheld radios. Coincidentally, Elon Musk, the most famous technology entrepreneur in the world, offered to send a mini submarine, and was rebuffed.

The movie, *Thirteen Lives*, directed by Ron Howard in 2022, brilliantly captures the team effort, and the instant culture of concentration and cohesion which formed on those impossibly rainy slopes for eighteen long days.

> *"It's a physical activity. But a thinking activity with logistics and planning"**
>
> **Rick Stanton, cave diver who co-ordinated the "Wild Boars" Thai Cave Rescue in 2018**

---

* Don Riddell, "Thai Cave Diver Rick Stanton reflects on the mission to save 13 lives that transformed his own", CNN, January 30, 2022.

Family Gathering

In the end you need a workplace culture which enshrines *belonging*, even if thanks to new distributed ways of working – freelancing, being a solopreneur, or in the gig economy – you work in different places, and not all of the time. The Thai cave rescue, rather like the Normandy Landings, took place in a workplace which did not exist before or after its work was done.

It's an important point for those arguing that workplace culture is place-based, because if that place is grains of sand or rock, surely the salient culture arises from the people and the technology on that speck of land?

And what about not belonging? Exclusion and denial? A friend of mine in London worked for a year in an organization and was invited to the Christmas party, only to be crushed and humiliated when she was the only one not given a present. "We don't do that for sub-contractors," someone explained breezily. My friend resigned a week later. It didn't say much for the organizational culture, did it?

The model of belonging most common to all of us is the family, and for all sorts of reasons this is problematic to emulate in the workplace. Families are not all cuddly happy places, for a start; the model of a family is not uniform; and not all workplaces should be encouraging over familiarity if boundaries protect rights and responsibilities.

And yet, when you look at depictions of good workplace culture, or when you look at what works well, it is often based on the family model. The idea of breaking bread with someone is not new, and office refurbishments are spending more on enlarging kitchen and shared community spaces to eat and drink in than they are the old cubicle model.

For this reason I wrote a column about the transferable model of Thanksgiving to the corporate or organizational table:

People feel pretty gloomy about jobs and the workplace right now. The working assumption is that something is irretrievably broken, that workers don't care about work and that work doesn't care about them.

For anyone wondering how to turn gloom into optimism, there is a surprising opportunity to relaunch the kinship and community of the workplace by borrowing something from home: Thanksgiving.

Thanksgiving has been a national holiday in the US since 1863, and except for when it was briefly named "Franksgiving" after Franklin Delano Roosevelt changed the date in 1939 to try to boost sales after the Great Depression – it's about not *working. In the US and many countries around the world it's an annual holiday: very few workplaces – even fully remote ones – are open for business on Thanksgiving.*

That said, plenty of people celebrate Thanksgiving with at least a handful of colleagues, because friendships formed at work that can be as strong as family and in some cases a proxy for it. There's a scene in Amazon Prime's show Bosch, *based on the Michael Connelly detective novels, in which the hero detective Harry Bosch and colleagues gather around turkey and trimmings. They wisecrack and argue, and everyday tensions are put to the side while they serve, eat and drink. I'm guessing your own family Thanksgiving* may be a little like that, too. It isn't just that work for some is like family (for plenty it isn't) but that it conveys a similar interdependency and intimacy which we can all recognize.

The plate-sharing of Thanksgiving is a great equalizer. This is something to build on when trying to recreate fractured workplace communities. Lack of connection is often at the heart of why work appears to be so unpopular. Data published by research firm Workplace Intelligence and logistics company Airspeed showed that 96 percent of executives said that "if their employees felt more connected to each other it would boost their motivation and productivity."

It's why so much cutting-edge workplace and office redesign puts socialization at the heart of bringing people back to offices. In their book Unworking: The Reinvention of the Modern Office Jeremy Myerson and Philip Ross say that "food and drink needs to take center stage as the means by which to encourage attendance and interaction." Thanksgiving's origins for centuries have been highly tied to work and giving thanks for the food produced and harvested – by workers. In modern times, Japan formally created its Kinrō Kansha no Hi after the Second World War to celebrate production and workers' rights. Creating and enabling community spirit is key to restoring confidence in the workplace.

Data from a study that Workplace Intelligence conducted with think tank Workforce Institute shows the scale of the problem when workers feel disconnected from meaning or belonging. Some 45 percent of employees across ten countries don't want to work anymore, 77 percent want to spend less time working and "more time doing things that matter to them" and 46 percent wouldn't recommend their company or profession to any young people they care about.

And yet, this isn't the whole picture. Yes, people are disaffected, but not necessarily by work itself, just badly managed work, or badly paid work or inflexible work. In fact, the same dataset shows that 84 percent of those surveyed would still work, even if they won the lottery, and just under one third of them would work the same hours. How do we explain this apparent contradiction, and does it let managers off the hook if the majority of people want to work anyway?

The political philosopher Hannah Arendt never believed there was a contradiction about people wanting to both live and work. In The Human Condition, *published in 1958, she called for a sense of "vita activa", namely focusing on labor, work and action, rather than a life of mere contemplation, or "vita contemplativa". She noted that "the human condition of labor is life itself."*

This may be unfashionable and unwelcome news to those arguing today for anything from universal basic income to a limit on working days to no work at all. But now is a good time to be thankful for the rewards of work: it gives us more than pay, it gives us meaning.

But no, it doesn't let those off the hook who foster disconnection at work. Togetherness takes effort and time – just like preparing the Thanksgiving meal. But showing your team that you're grateful for them and that you understand they are actually grateful for the work, too – well, that brings you all nicely together.

[November 15, 2022]

Network Effects

A family is just one kind of network. During the pandemic I started to use WhatsApp groups as a network and they remain a flourishing part of my personal network today. They are a mobile, intimate, trusted part of my "family" of connections. It doesn't matter if you don't want to call your colleagues your family. What matters is whether you feel you belong. Because if you don't, your soul is crushed.

I will end this chapter with a piece of mine which to some degree went viral when it was published, being widely circulated and syndicated in, among others, the *LA Times*.

◯

Beyoncé's "Break My Soul" is full of cultural data. And it's telling us how young people feel about their jobs

Does culture eat strategy for breakfast?

The phrase has reverberated around boardrooms for decades, even though it's a misquote of the late great management guru Peter Drucker, who in fact said "culture, no matter how defined, is singularly persistent."

Indeed, it is.

This is a problem, because the culture of dissatisfaction around work is all too evident.

One manifestation is the dip in wellbeing. Data from Deloitte shows that about one-third of employees and executives struggle with fatigue and mental health issues. Citing Gallup's latest workplace data, the World Economic Forum noted that "workplace wellbeing and satisfaction have plateaued after almost a decade of improvements."

But this can't all be blamed on the pandemic. In May of 2019, before Covid-19 was sweeping throughout the world, the World Health Organization declared burnout "an occupational phenomenon". In fact, concern about work and wellbeing goes back centuries and was always linked to culture: it was Aristotle, after all, who worried about what it would take to create a sense of flourishing or eudaemonia.

Now that CEOs around the globe are trying to maintain or reinvent both corporate culture and future strategy in the wake of a pandemic that rewrote the rules of work, it's popular culture that leaders should consider to win the hearts and minds of their workers – specifically pop music.

Take this year's zeitgeist tune "Break My Soul" by Beyoncé Giselle Knowles-Carter, known to her fans simply as "Queen Bey". It's a dance-based rallying cry for workers rejecting old constraints in new times from an album entitled Renaissance. *And it's rich in cultural data.*

The song is an anthem not so much for the Great Resignation as the Great Resentment. The chorus energetically exhorts listeners to release "ya anger", "ya mind", "ya job", "the time" – in that order. A word that crops up defiantly throughout is "motivation". The implication being that it's a bit thin on the ground.

"Break My Soul" isn't the voice of an innocent generation from yesteryear during which work culture was infantilized and power lay strictly above the heads of the rank and file. A good example there is the innocently jolly "Heigh-Ho" from Walt Disney Co.'s Snow White *in 1937.*

Nor is it quite the pay and conditions anger of Generation X, those born between the 1960s and 1980s, who grew up with 1970s hit songs like the distinctly unsubtle "Take This Job and Shove It" by Johnny Paycheck or indeed Dolly Parton's feminist rallying cry in the song and film 9 to 5 from 1980, now reprised for the new times in a successful touring musical.

Beyoncé is speaking instead to the millennial generation and their younger Gen Z co-workers who are the future of the workplace, and whose emotional literacy expresses their resentment and disappointment that the world of work, even if well paid, still doesn't deliver for them.

They feel betrayed by broken promises of prosperity, security, status and wellbeing. Beyoncé told Harper's Bazaar *magazine last year that "I worked to heal generational trauma and turned my broken heart into art that would help move culture forward and hopefully live far beyond me."*

Exactly 100 years before Queen Bey's 2022 anthem to existential generational malaise was streamed to millions, T.S. Eliot's modernist poem The Waste Land *was published to thousands, with notable similarities. Both are in their very different ways landmark commentaries which simultaneously address working life – Eliot writes movingly of the "violet hour, the evening hour that strives Homeward" – and yet move well beyond it to a bigger picture: our inner selves. Written in the aftermath of the First World War,* The Waste Land *is the cultural equivalent of a pop song, with its long lyric to broken-ness.*

Today's global workforce feels similarly broken, fragmented and discombobulated as if by war. Covid-19 universally left its losses and scars, which have opened up longing for a new fresh start.

CULTURE CLUBS AND CLASHES

Leaders need to do two fundamental things to get on the right track.

The first is to acknowledge the sense of loss and pain.

Every workplace has to rebuild and redesign itself. There is no business as usual. Aim for a corporate culture which prioritizes comfort, security and certainty in an uncertain world. That does not mean providing a rigid set of rules but a flexible approach where possible to respond to the complexity of their lives.

Be like Beyoncé: release your mind to think afresh.

There is no playbook ready to help you that isn't out of date. So co-create new rules, new norms and ditch the top-down approach.

In order to do that you have to do something else: listen. Don't tell, ask. Spend as much on employee evaluation as you do on getting under the skin of what customers think. Go beyond online evaluation forms and begin face-to-face and teleconferenced feedback sessions. They will be worth every dollar spent.

Culture doesn't compete with strategy – it complements it. But it has to be authentic. Let's stop trying to make the workplace naively upbeat (Disney) and instead match the knowing beat (Beyoncé).

[October 14, 2022]

Out of culture comes a healthy, functional workforce. This too has been disrupted by changing values and norms – and by Covid itself. The post-pandemic age can see some amazing opportunities. I'm more optimistic about changing health and wellbeing at work than I am about work culture. So: on to that.

> *We've come very far, very fast in the idea of illness and work (and indeed what healthy management is). "Working through" illness is a working assumption we have jettisoned. It's just not on now. But Covid brought with it fear of illness and for some, fear of something else: other people.*

5

HEALTH AND SAFETY NETS

"I'm a positive person, Jerry. I only talk positive, I only think positive. But me having to generate all the positive energy right now is making me feel so negative…"

Leslie Knope in *Parks and Recreation**

The toxic workplace displayed through comedy is very familiar to us. But here's a scene from the movies which captures a different and new workplace health perspective more than half a century after it was made: Billy Wilder's Oscar-winning 1960 masterpiece *The Apartment.* Our hero Jack Lemmon, a hapless but ultimately heroic accountant in a giant corporation, sits miserably at his desk in a gigantic warehouse, surrounded by his manual adding machine, bits of paper, a telephone – and a pile of tissues. He is coughing and sneezing his way through a terrible cold in a way which would run shivers of anxiety down co-workers' spines today. He is called by his boss and protests weakly that he can't keep working and needs to go home. His boss says no – he needs his apartment for his afternoon tryst!

---

* *Parks and Recreation*, "Pawnee Parade", written by Stefan Gibson.

We've come very far, very fast in the idea of illness and work (and indeed what healthy management is). "Working through" illness is a working assumption we have jettisoned. It's just not on now. But Covid brought with it fear of illness and for some, fear of something else: other people. It's a terrible irony that the shift from miasma theory to germ theory, one of the biggest advances in medicine, was somewhat overturned by Covid. The "bad air" idea, dating back to Hippocrates in the fourth century, came back in 2020: the air you breathe could kill you. This could partly account for the vaccine skepticism which swept through parts of society: why trust new, modern science, focused on vaccines and antibiotics, if we were thrown back to the deep past where humans had little control over their lives?

As I write, in the early spring of 2024, another "highly infectious" variant of Covid is circulating: JN.1, and as I write, my old friend Derek Draper, a workplace psychologist who was one of the first to succumb to Covid in the UK in March 2020 finally died of Covid-related complications and long Covid. His illness and death transfixed Britain and left all who knew him utterly heartbroken. Covid will never leave the collective memory of anyone alive today.

Only wars or revolutions have had the same impact on so many people at the same time. We are all left feeling deeply fragile. Recovery is slow and ongoing. It's another irony of course: our trust in health has taken a huge knock, precisely at the point when AI advances in predicting, preventing, diagnosing and treating health conditions are at unprecedented levels. I had the rather eerie thrill of watching Reed Jobs, who runs the "medtech" venture capital firm Yosemite, give a presentation at a tech conference in New York where he and others on the platform basically said cancer will be curable by the middle of this century. If the son of Steve Jobs says this will happen due to technological advance, I am inclined to think he's on to something.*

But we're not there yet. Nor are we there with workers who work at optimum capacity, even if they are technically well. We're still grappling with this problem despite the eye-watering technological advances. And yet one advance matters in the way we see health and indeed safety at work – and that's psychology. Here's Octavius Black, founder of MindGym, which puts organizational transformation through the lens of workplace psychology:

> We started in my kitchen on New Year's Day, 2001. We would have started in the garage if I'd been an American, but we couldn't afford a garage in London. So, we ended up being in the kitchen. We felt that the eighties were seen as a decade of the body, you know, gyms and fitness, and the nineties as a decade of the soul, the spirit. And therefore, what were the 2000s? We thought it would be decade of the mind, because it made sense in a sequence: mind, body, soul.
>
> At the beginning behavioral science, as it's now come to be called, didn't really exist. This is pre-Malcolm Gladwell, pre-the presence really of Ted Talks and his significant nature. All the popular behavioral science hadn't been heard of at that stage. And we were the first to come out and say, actually, if you understood human behavior from a scientific perspective, a bit like medicine at the beginning of the twentieth century, psychology in the twenty-first century redefines how you approach, in particular, the world of work. So, it was really a

---

* Founder's Forum conference.

kind of zeitgeist hunch. It was zeitgeist in the sense that no one was talking about psychology at the time.

Billions are spent by businesses on trying to improve corporate health wellbeing. Fifty billion last year, due to become a hundred billion in three years' time. It makes no difference at all. Yeah. You know, by and large there's a massive self-selection bias.

So, I did go to my own gym, now I'm going to the company gym. Or I did used to eat fresh fruit, now I'm eating some company fresh fruit. I think we can agree a tiny bit, can't we, there is quite a lot of wellbeing babble. There's a lot of wellbeing babble, and what we're doing is cutting through it. So, we're saying basically the 50 billion is by and large wasted in terms of improving wellbeing. Maybe it's a lovely employee benefit, maybe nice virtue signaling, maybe all sorts of good things about it, but it's not changing body mass index, cortisol levels, sleep patterns, or anything else you like. And there are lots of studies I can share to do that. But the much more interesting question is: what should we be doing as companies instead?

And the answer to that is there are five drivers of wellbeing, psychological needs, that when they are met, wellbeing increases significantly. And they are certainty, competence, autonomy, belonging, and purpose.

Social Health

"The presence of physical, mental and social wellbeing, not merely the absence of disease or infirmity"

World Health Organization definition of health, 1948

Well, Octavius Black is on to something. Covid and generative AI have fast-forwarded our understanding of both physical and mental health. It is a reasonably certain working assumption that preventative interventions led by customized monitoring will become more mainstream in the workplace, as it is becoming throughout society. Underlying health metrics will be a factor in how workers and their managers get insight into performance.

This is not entirely positive, even if full of potential. Because the surveillance culture which has mushroomed since both Covid and the advent of generative AI means that privacy is increasingly a luxury. This undermines the idea of "psychological safety" which at present remains a widespread management concept.* The stress of being monitored, controlled even, will have to balance against the benefits of personalized schedules and workplace treatment. But if corners are cut, employers will know more about you than is helpful. We know so much about disease and illness that fear of it will become greater, not less, and this will mean that far more sophisticated clean air and other preventative policies will start to become mainstream. Above all, the tension between "good" social interaction and the risks of malignant bullying and hidden bad actors in the metaverse and online will rise.

---

* Psychological Safety defined by Professor Amy Edmondson.

WORKING ASSUMPTIONS

So, we're in the curious position of looking forward with really unprecedented optimism through a lens of unprecedented gloom.

I began writing about what I call social health in 2017, after a bout of severe ill health. I wanted to understand the connection between not only psychological and physiological vulnerability but also how external factors contributed, specifically the always-on internet era. In my case I felt there was a connection. I wrote a book, *Fully Connected: Surviving and Thriving in an Age of Overload*. The subtitle was changed for the paperback to "Social Health in an Age of Overload" because I had attempted to update what "social wellbeing" could mean today.

I am still constantly fiddling with the best definition, but ultimately it means the most productive and successful way that people can connect to each other and to technology in the age first of the internet and now AI. This question has become more pressing. So many are experiencing anxiety, long Covid, job insecurity, AI trust issues and fear of actual replacement by tech – what could even be "full sentience" by the middle of this century.*

It's for this reason that I've written fairly often about uncertainty. This book opens with a column on turbulence, but here's a snippet from another I wrote in which embracing uncertainty played a starring role:

Leadership is often thought of as a solid state, with decisiveness running like the stripe through a stick of candy. But the challenges

---

* BBC, "Can Artificial Intelligence Ever Be Sentient?", March 7, 2023.

HEALTH AND SAFETY NETS

at the beginning of the Covid-19 pandemic were overwhelming and unpredictable, meaning that leaders needed to be flexible.

As lockdown loomed in the UK in early March 2020 Kevin Ellis, UK chair and senior partner of PWC, realized that for the firm's 25,000 employees the uncertainty was undermining confidence.

He told me: "We were all watching daily updates from the prime minister. We thought: if you can't solve the medical catastrophe we're going through, you can't solve the isolation of lockdown, what can we do? You can tell our people that their jobs are safe. So, we then looked at our cash flow, we looked at our business, we looked at our facilities. And we worked out that even if the worst-case scenario carried on for six months (and we thought six months was the longest it could go on), we could carry on not only paying the 25,000 people that were already here, but actually honoring the additional 3,000 job offers that were already effectively made to people."

Jude Jennison, a British-based strategy coach and author of Leading Through Uncertainty, writes that "uncertainty requires a new set of skills and a framework within which to flex and operate." The PWC framework was to make staff retention a priority through staff reassurance. This strategy seemed to work both morally and financially: Revenue for UK and Middle East operations rose 12 percent for the year ended June 30, 2022. Uncertainty isn't going away any time soon, as any student of the VUCA theory (volatility, uncertainty, complexity and ambiguity) knows, but it's good to see a tangible example of how to embrace it.

[March 10, 2023]

It seems as if we need to reach a balance now between the turbulence, uncertainty and unpredictability of the era – not knowing if your job is safe; not knowing how ill you need to be to avoid work or a workplace; and not knowing what the new rules of engagement at work are overall – in other words what a sense of a healthy, functional workplace actually is. Set against increasingly positive ways to identify very precisely the mind–body ways we can improve our wellbeing. This is what you might call the "beyond beanbag phase", and it's welcome.

> *Covid and generative AI have fast-forwarded our understanding of both physical and mental health. It is a reasonably certain working assumption that preventative interventions led by customized monitoring will become more mainstream in the workplace, as it is becoming throughout society.*

Burnout Is Back

Perhaps unsurprisingly burnout, a catch-all phrase first used half a century ago, remains oddly widespread and applicable. From quiet quitting to mental health breakdowns, all of which has risen dramatically since 2020,* we can agree on this: burnout is back. Here's my column from August 2023:

It's the fiftieth anniversary of "burnout" entering the corporate lexicon when Herbert Freudenberger, a New York psychologist, first identified it. I wish I could tell you that we've banished it, but instead burnout is back with a vengeance. Recent data from Deloitte and the research firm Workplace Intelligence cites about half of workers saying they are either exhausted or stressed and 60 percent of employees say they would consider changing jobs to find better wellbeing provisions.

The working assumption that current corporate wellness programs are sufficient for the times is being severely tested. Here's why.

First and foremost, never underestimate the power of the toxic workplace. It's no accident that the most streamed show in the US during Covid-19 in 2020 was The Office, *which satirized the daily grind.*

I've written here before about the need to address what can be done to combat stress in the workplace itself. Susie Orbach, psychoanalyst and social critic, told me: "Work is where we live

---

* "What is 'quiet quitting' and how is burnout affecting the UK?", Open Access Government, October 21, 2022.

and where we hope to have our need for connection, contribution, stimulation and engagement occur. When work has little personal recognition or stimulation it produces ennui and dissatisfaction."

The World Health Organization added burnout as an "occupational phenomenon" in its 2019 classification of diseases: not as a medical condition per se, but as "a syndrome conceptualized as resulting from chronic workplace stress that has not been successfully managed."

In other words, bad work or badly managed work makes you unwell, which in turn impacts productivity.

The author and workplace culture expert Bruce Daisley believes that the idea of "resilience" – which the American Psychological Association describes as a "process and outcome of successfully adapting to difficult or challenging life experiences, especially through mental, emotional, and behavioral flexibility" – places unfair emphasis on an individual's stiff upper lip in dysfunctional workplaces. Resilience, as he told me "is associated with the toxic reframing of excessive demands."

If the first reason for burnout being back big time is the old problem of bad management and toxic workplaces, the second is a more recent phenomenon, namely the havoc wrought by long Covid. That's outside of the control of both employee and employer and has been devastating to mental and physical health at home and at work. According to Brookings Institute, 16 million working-age Americans have long Covid.

Around the world, the Organization for Economic Cooperation and Development reports that a third of workers experience strain at work. In the UK, 30 million working days were lost from 2021 to 2022 with nearly 1 million of these due to work-related stress, depression and anxiety. The World Health Organization reported a 25 percent increase in stress and anxiety worldwide since Covid.

This brings into sharp focus how out of step modern workplace wellbeing has become with the post-Covid-19 experience. Despite the huge scale and scope of the corporate wellness market, which is set to double from more than $50 billion to $100 billion by 2032, many of us associate it with soft stuff, from an emphasis on mindfulness to the idea that this is about selling offices as nice places to work rather than helping people do their best work.

It's a far cry from the original, deeper psychological emphasis of the worker assistance programs of the 1940s onwards. Popular consciousness doesn't equate wellbeing at work with Centers for Disease Control and Prevention of the ACE score or "adverse childhood experiences", but they should.

There are always bright spots, good initiatives and positive action being taken around wellbeing.

Syreeta Brown, chief people officer for Virgin Money, the UK bank, told me: "It's not that there is more stress per se since Covid, but the nature has changed. All jobs are 'always on' now, and there is an expectation that your diary can be filled up by others if they can find a gap. Stepping away from your laptop can feel mutinous."

Brown cites their program, "A Life More Virgin", which she says is "location-agnostic, totally flexible on office/home working, and encourages people to work the hours that suit them for the role and meets our customer and operational needs."

WORKING ASSUMPTIONS

Virgin Money, like many companies, also give employees "wellbeing days" in addition to their existing holidays, but I'm struck above all by the commitment to reframing what workers need rather than the old, rigid model of what a manager might want them to need.

It's time to locate work and working within a bigger framework. Let's remember that the original WHO definition of health includes "social wellbeing".

This means one thing above all: it's time to take care of each other and ourselves in new ways for new times.

[August 7, 2023]

○

It's worth also emphasizing how unwell American workers were before 2020 due to the Opioid crisis. According to *The American Journal of Public Health*, a marked escalation in liberalized prescribing led to more use, and chillingly, 57 percent of all opioid deaths related to attempts to relieve pain from work-related accidents.*

An entire generation have not experienced the world in a healthy or functional way and it's taking time to recover. Even babies born in 2020 are fundamentally affected by the absence of early experiences we should all take for granted: eye contact, mimicking, taking in the world around us. Every parent of a child, teenager or young adult knows all too well the complex toll the stop–start years of lockdowns, illness, recovery and long Covid took and continues to take.

---

* "Work Environment Factors and Prevention of Opioid-Related Deaths", Shaw, Roelofs, Punnett, 2020.

And yet a new form of communication, not without its merits, became mainstream: teleconferencing, i.e. Zoom and Teams. This had unexpected benefits for shy people, some neurodivergent people, or simply people whose schedules and lives were in fact improved by remote access (especially after the schools reopened: to be a working parent during the pandemic was an emotional and psychological health hazard in itself). The lesson is the one we know of health itself: it's personal, not one size fits all.

Someone who has intrinsically understood the impact of mental and emotional health on workplace performance is the entrepreneur Arianna Huffington. I became an editor-at-large for her wellbeing platform Thrive Global before I joined Bloomberg, and as part of a series of Bloomberg Originals videos looking at ways to "Work Smarter" in the autumn of 2023 I went back to see her in her offices on Broadway in Manhattan. There she expanded on Octavius Black's five measures of wellbeing at work, and upped it to six:

◇

When Arianna Huffington collapsed from burnout and exhaustion in 2007, she hit her head on her desk and broke her cheekbone. That's when she began to realize that burnout wasn't just a problem she was having, but, she says, a global epidemic. "It was based on this collective delusion that in order to succeed, in order to perform at our best, we have to be always on," she said. "And the science makes it very clear that the human operating system is very different than machines."

The phenomenon is coming even more to light since the pandemic with the Great Resignation, quiet quitting and trials of a four-day work week – some of which found that people used the extra time to sleep. More than 40 percent of people with desk jobs felt burned out at work, according to a survey released earlier this year from the Future Forum, a research consortium backed by Salesforce Inc.'s Slack Technologies. And in a report last year, the US Surgeon General said it's up to bosses to create more supportive environments, rather than expecting employees to take on the burden of establishing boundaries – which can often backfire, especially for workers from underrepresented backgrounds.

The co-founder of the Huffington Post has since founded Thrive Global, a company that sells services and tools that help employers and staff avoid burnout and boost productivity. Work Shift contributing columnist Julia Hobsbawm talked with Huffington about Thrive's philosophy for avoiding burnout, how Covid has changed the conversation and the integration of artificial intelligence into the company. (Questions and responses have been edited and condensed).

JH: When you started to say that burnout and wellbeing was important, did people push back?

AH: There was definitely pushback because for centuries we believed that being always on was the way to be amazing at work. You snooze, you lose. I'll sleep when I'm dead. And yet it was just impossible to avoid the reality that people were suffering and we were in the middle of a cultural transformation.

JH: And we now have an epidemic of burnout post-Covid, but the World Health Organization declared burnout an epidemic before the pandemic.

AH: Yes, in 2019. So, it's interesting how long it takes for cultural transformation. And we're still in the middle of it. There are many, many more companies, many more people who acknowledge the *science-based reality that it takes daily behaviors that together affect our health and our productivity.*

JH: You call them micro steps?

AH: *Daily behaviors are broken down into micro steps and the six daily behaviors are sleep, food, movement, stress management, focus and connection. And they are interconnected. The truth is that if I'm sleep deprived, it's going to have an impact on what I'm eating, on how much I'm moving, how I manage my stress. And we wanted to bring everything together, but also break it down into tiny incremental daily steps as opposed to big New Year's resolutions that we break after two weeks.*

JH: Thrive is dealing principally with human behavior, but it's using technology and AI to achieve it. Tell me a bit about that.

AH: *AI is going to revolutionize how we can affect human behavior. Behavior change is notoriously hard. We are much more successful when the micro steps can be really personalized. AI helps us personalize the micro steps. We link to whatever wearable they're using and we ask a lot of questions, which is great with ChatGPT. They're given very specific and personalized micro steps that work for them and very personalized content, ranging from videos, articles, sleep meditations and long form curricula on mental health, onboarding, etc. All of that has to be served up at the right moment, in the right way.*

JH: You've made the point that burnout is a public health emergency, but we are still facing a public health crisis from Covid and its resurgence. It's stopping people yet again from coming back to offices. How is that adding to the stress for leaders, the managers, the workers?

AH: *We are never going to go back to the pre-Covid world. There is always going to be more flexibility. We are recognizing that being together in an office has a lot of advantages, especially for younger employees. We see in the data about women returning to work, that women, when they are given more flexibility to manage their family lives, their children and their work, they are more likely to stay in the workplace.*

JH: When it comes to working smarter is it one single thing or six micro steps?

AH: *These six behaviors all lead to productivity, but they also lead to greater health. We see chronic diseases going up every year – diabetes, cardiovascular disease, hypertension – and that we can't address them just with drugs or surgery. So we need to address behavior as truly a miracle drug.*

> How to measure people who aren't toiling away in front of you requires a leap of faith and imagination, the ability to trust on a task base, not time-based measurement of productivity.

The AI "Eyes" Have It

I'm one of millions of people who have precarious, uncertain health. In 2021, in the middle of the Covid pandemic, I developed a severe auto-immune condition which affected my eyesight, and as I mentioned in the introduction, I now spend around half a day a month at Moorfields Eye Hospital in London. I receive a miracle drug (good news) directly into my eye (not so good). In between I have to balance a cocktail of medication with lifestyle adjustments. Stress has to be kept low – not always great with deadlines and the adrenalin required to make speeches and travel – and sleep matters *a lot*. But loving what I do, having great colleagues and a workplace I can choose to be in on my terms helps significantly, as does having a great tech set-up at home and virtually. Having a trusted technology guru on WhatsApp speed dial who sends me a Microsoft Teams link pretty instantly to solve problems makes a difference. Because if there is one thing which raises my stress levels through the roof it's technology which directs you to solve its problems *without human intervention*.

Let's not underestimate the very unglamorous and very present stress of technology not working, or of having to interact with an automated system. Our daily lives involve constant interaction with technology, which until AI came along was pretty Luddite: slow, hanging-on-the-telephone kinds, greeted by humans in a call center working to a rigid script. Outsourcing can create an additional language barrier. You're often talking to someone in a different time zone, using voice intonation it's difficult to decipher, and a script which is somehow more enraging for being delivered by a human than if it was automated. I've ended up venting at them, I'm ashamed to admit. Systems which snare humans in delivering poor service bring out the worst in other humans.

Sadly, I'm not the only one. They call it "call center worker attrition", where call center workers quit, and it's around 50 percent. Call center waiting times on average tripled during the pandemic, which didn't help, and remote-based call center workers undoubtedly faced the ire of people who felt they were taking time off in a working day with less apparent flexibility than those taking their call. Tempers rose. Turnover in call centers is super high.

It's not surprising then that the focus of early successes with generative AI in the workplace is in call centers. A key feature is to detect *stress* in a human voice, and "know" when to escalate to a human of sufficient seniority to diffuse a situation. Quite a gamechanger.*

Also, another plus: for the same reason that technology can screw up our working day, it can liberate it. Not only will the customer save time pressing buttons and listening to terrible muzak, or getting gobbledygook chatbot messages on text, but something else beneficial for our workplace health too: time and tedium is undoubtedly being eased.

However, the electronic eyes remain a real and present danger to mental health. Show me someone who likes the idea of being spied on as they work. A friend of mine has had to rig up a way of taking a toilet break and a tea break without detection – and she's a "senior" manager working in retail. Ironically, her stress levels are high because she has no office to go back to, or rather a

---

* Bromuri, Henkel, Iren and Urovi, "Using AI to predict service agent stress from emotion patterns in service interaction", Open University Publications, September 10, 2021.

HEALTH AND SAFETY NETS

pared-down one, out of town, at which a desk is only available to her once a week. She's lonely and isolated, and frustrated by being rewarded with spyware.

There is a risk with new workplace wellbeing techniques assisted by AI that they can become part of the problem and not the solution. One of the big failures of HR in recent years has been the de-humanizing of services, in which an emphasis on algorithm-derived screening at scale has excused many from even bothering to acknowledge an application: something which I have been told many times by workers, especially young ones, is intensely demoralizing.

The manager responsible for workplace wellbeing needs to stay human, act human, be the human in the loop, no matter how many what used to be called *gizmos* in my day are being used. The risk with AI and workplace health is too much outsourcing to electronic eyes which can monitor stress levels, and track eyes to detect loss of focus.

Some of this might also seem Orwellian. The American Psychological Association reports that over half of people say that surveillance software adds significantly to their workplace stress.* It's clear the rather than engaging with "employee monitoring software" it's better – far healthier – to engage in discussing with employees what success looks like, what levels of presenteeism and productivity are required, and actually inviting them to co-create a good *modus vivendi*.

That, in essence, is social health too: developing systems between people and tech, people and other people, in terms of getting the job at hand done well.

> *Some of the healthy benefit of AI coming post Covid is that the jobs themselves are often improved.*

---

* Michele Lerner, "Electronically monitoring your employees? It"s impacting their mental health", American Psychological Association, September 7, 2023. *See also* World Health Organization, "Occupational health: Stress at the workplace", October 19, 2020.

The Jagged Frontier

The Wharton College academic Ethan Mollick has written wonderfully about AI's "jagged frontier" in which not all benefits are equal, and often create opposite side effects. But he is also clearly right that some of the upside, some of the healthy benefit if you will of AI coming post Covid, is that the jobs themselves are often improved. In his blog of predictions at the start of January 2024 he reiterated his research, cited in my column on page 238, that AI can boost quality results by up to 40 percent on complex tasks; that it "acts as a leveler, helping low performers more than high performers"; and that "the frontier is what AIs can do is constantly expanding".*

Note, by the way, the plural: AIs. It's not a single definitive "thing" at work but a shapeshifting mix of software, applied via apps, hardware and wearables, in real life, teleconferencing and in cyberspace, the cloud and the metaverse. This in itself is, of course, complex and stressful: we constantly oscillate between the benefits and drawbacks of technological progress. The individual worker can not only feel the pressures of the toxic workplace, or of isolation through remote work, or of fear of physical illness or its effects, but something else: the loneliness of tech. Do you feel you are the only one who doesn't understand it? That's more common than you may think, especially among older workers.

---

* Ethan Mollick, "Signs and Portents", One Useful Thing Substack, January 6, 2024.

Rebooting The Corporate Mindset

The jagged frontier is the zig-zag state of AI and technology at work, and how it becomes less of a puzzle and more of a piece which fits together. That often requires strategy, leadership, and a new mindset.

Arianna Huffington and Octavius Black have got the right approach. We have to feel motivated to work, and supported in ways which are scientifically proven to improve performance because they improve our mental and physical health. But not all workplaces are on board. And the problem often lies within the board itself. At the moment many workplaces are riven with conflict. Parts of the C-suite, the executive brain and decision-making body of organizations, want good health from workers for moral and practical reasons: in the UK the days lost to ill health are now topping 35 million working days a year – a huge post-Covid surge partly but not exclusively attributed to long Covid – and in the US the number of work absences through sickness has also doubled.*

But for others it's got a scintilla of skepticism. Like the leaders who whisper forcefully to me, behind the fan of their fingers, that they want their workers in all the time, or that long Covid is partly an attribute of the workshy. The board function at the forefront of dealing with this is a group I have called "the bullied child of the C-suite"† – HR, or human resources.

---

* TED: The Economics Daily, 78 million workers had an illness-related work absence in January 2022, February 9, 2022.
† *The Nowhere Office* podcast.

Health And Safety

I want to be fair to HR. I really do. So I wrote this optimistic take on how it is responding to unprecedented pressure and new challenges.

The corporate function with the word "human" in its name will matter most in a world of generative AI.

Let's be honest. The human resources department has never been the cool kid in the workplace. Behind their back many people used to call this function "human remains". In fact, the working assumption for years has been that HR is more often on the side of the top brass and too bossy itself. A Harvard Business Review article once put it like this: "We don't like being told how to behave – and no other group in organizational life, not even finance, bosses us around as systematically as HR does."

Distrust of HR reached a zenith pre-pandemic when an admission in a regulatory filing from Uber Technologies Inc. ahead of its public offering noted within the summary of risk factors: "Our workplace culture and forward-leaning approach created operational, compliance, and cultural challenges." This was a reference to sexism which the HR department sat on and ignored until engineer Susan Fowler blew the whistle. The situation led, ultimately, to the resignation of founder Travis Kalanick.

But HR is changing. Far from being an enabler of whatever the C-suite wants, it's now moving big time into strategy, data and talent acquisition using generative AI. The HR thought leader Josh Bersin, head of human capital advisory firm The Josh Bersin Company, told me: "Despite HR's history as a compliance and administrative function, today's professionals play a business-critical role in reskilling, leadership development and job transformation. As the job market remains highly competitive (and getting tougher), they are responsible for employee retention, engagement and productivity. It's a vital role and a huge step up in responsibility for the profession."

This chimes with data from LinkedIn's Future of Recruiting 2023 report which shows that 87 percent of recruiting professionals globally say talent acquisition has become more strategic in the last year, while in France, Germany and the UK, the second fastest growing C-suite role was that of chief people officer. Brett Baumoel, vice president of global talent acquisition – engineering at Microsoft Inc. is quoted in the report saying, "You used to be able to say 'these hires helped our company'. Now you can say 'I changed the makeup of our company, I changed where we work.'"

HR has always been a bellwether for the challenges faced by an industry and its executives. It was Henry Ford in the 1920s who made use of Frederick Winslow Taylor's so-called scientific principles of management to improve worker productivity. Although his work was ostensibly focused on assembly line efficiencies in the 1920s, it's not coincidental that by 1926 the Ford factory introduced the five-day week which acknowledged the "human" aspect of workers and their need for rest and leisure. The emergence of contemporary human relations management is the direct descendent of the awareness that scaled corporate activity needs humans who must feel like more than cogs in the machine where they work.

The receding waters of Covid-19 have left a tidemark of issues which challenge everything to do with the productivity, placement, recruitment and retention of people. The person with the word "human" or "people" in their job title is going to be very visible and indispensable if they can deliver for all sides.

Right now HR is the department which picks up the pieces for the fluid nature of return-to-office policies. Leaders have oscillated considerably around this causing consternation with Google the latest to be caught up in the chaos. And it's the department which handles an increasingly complex issue called "talent mobility" in HR speak.

Until 2020, the aspect of HR which handled movement of people was relatively niche and focused on relocation and virtual assignments driven by globalization. Today it warrants reports of its own, such as the EY 2023 Mobility Reimagined Survey which argues that workforce mobility programs are of "powerful strategic and operational importance in the global race for talent."

For many who love to hate HR, the annoying box-ticking character of Toby Flenderson on the popular television satire The Office provided endless entertainment and reinforces our bias against HR.

But we all need to look at our bias, and we need to look beyond the stereotype. Organizations need brokers who can parlay between different teams and they need strategists who can see what's happening in one group (employees or talent) and another (managers).

It turns out that the much maligned and often self-sabotaging HR manager might just become the hero of this very complicated moment in corporate history after all.

[June 26, 2023]

The broader truth is I'm not entirely sure that the function of HR isn't pretty outdated, or overloaded, or both. In other words, that the management tasked with making the workplace healthy don't feel a little plagued by dysfunction themselves.

Both culture (chapter four) and health (chapter five) rely less on top-down policies, or self-conscious statements about caring for employees, and more actions rather than words. The academic Carl Benedikt Frey reminded me that one of the first chatbots, a prototype AI, was called Eliza, after George Bernard Shaw's famous Eliza Doolittle in *Pygmalion*, a story about what would happen if you could train and retrain a human in a mechanistic way.

My favorite film as a child was *My Fair Lady*, the musical romance in which Eliza, played by Audrey Hepburn, is taught, not without torment, by Professor Higgins, played wonderfully grumpily by Rex Harrison. In one scene she rounds on a suitor with a song in which she says she is sick to death of words and wants instead for him to show me! Show me now!

> *The problem now is that irrespective of whether we can or can't work hybrid, remote, part time, flexitime, the technology we have access to is often always on, winking its lights at us throughout the day and night. This may be convenient, but it's also impossible to do what machines themselves actually have to do: to reboot.*

Boundary Management

The workplace has to be a place where actions speak louder than words. How you are invited to work, how you are treated, managed, all count as much as how your own personal performance is affected by factors you bring in with you. Humans and machines and humans and other humans: a complex bit of machinery which can work well or badly, depending on the fine-tuning.

But being healthy at work is also about something else: boundaries. The problem now is that irrespective of whether we can or can't work hybrid, remote, part time, flexitime, the technology we have access to is often always on, winking its lights at us throughout the day and night. This may be convenient, but it's also impossible to do what machines themselves actually have to do: to reboot.

I finish this chapter with a column I wrote about practicing (or trying to) what I preach, namely the ability to insulate oneself from work and not be always on, especially in that sacred time called "vacation" or "holiday".

Switching off fully on vacation keeps boundaries between paid and unpaid leave and better reflects the new life-work balance.

The summer holiday season is upon us and airlines are clapping their hands with glee: The US Transportation Security Association expects that the number of passengers will surpass pre-pandemic levels this summer. Over the recent Memorial Day weekend, nearly 10 million people passed through one of America's 400-odd airports. But the working assumption that everyone is going on vacation is wrong.

That's because many travelers will be on a so-called workation, part of a growing trend that takes the idea of hybrid working a bit too literally. Billed as part of "work from anywhere" slots, which are increasingly cropping up, they prove that an unhelpful blur is developing between paid and unpaid leave.

This is happening for three reasons.

First, culturally, Americans think holidays are for wimps. Gerri, a key character in Succession, *the highly successful HBO drama about an American business dynasty, described a European business rival this way: "They're soft. Hammocked in their social security net. Sick on vacation mania and free health care. We've been raised by wolves." Not surprisingly less than half of employees use their vacation days and the US is way behind most advanced countries on offering minimum annual leave.*

America isn't so much sick of vacations as phobic about them, a problem stretching back to the early industrial era. As an article published forty years ago in the Industrial Relations Law Journal *on the politics of vacations put it tartly: "Parties tend to write ambiguous vacation eligibility provisions." Wolves don't need holidays, the argument goes.*

Second, fairly genuine attempts are being made to assuage the itchy feet of people who can't stand to work only from the office. In response, Japan's StarFlyer airlines introduced the "Star Pass" to attract domestic commuters flying in and out of Tokyo for both work and leisure. Although not completely new – back in 2017 a fellow Bloomberg journalist asked the reader if they were "Jealous of well-to-do friends who do their 'working from home' at a beach house in the Hamptons?" – the idea has gained momentum since Covid-19.

As I wrote in this column in September: "The pandemic tipped a low rumbling about flexible working into a roar." This roar shows no sign of abating, signaling as it does a desire for life-work balance in that order.

But the third reason is less well-intentioned than the second, and more in line with the first. The trend to workations can be a backdoor way to keep people working, even when they need to switch off.

A proxy war is raging in the battle between hyper-stressed managers trying to meet the clear employee demand for freedom and the equally clear C-suite demand for presenteeism and monitored work. Perhaps this explains why one in five US companies doesn't have transparent policies on hybrid working. Yet it's not just the "soft" Europeans introducing flexible working around the world. Kenya is among the latest to look into to doing so and the "right to disconnect" is at the heart of debate.

So much for the old demarcation of life and work made famous by the chocolate bar Mars television advertising back in 1960 with its slogan "A Mars a day helps you work, rest and play."

As regular readers of this column will know, I'm a keen advocate of increased flexibility in the workplace – both of flexible mindsets and practices around time and location for getting work done. And I'm all for tightening some unfair (and unhealthy) workarounds: in the UK, for instance, people are rather scandalized by new research from a nicotine pouch company Haypp showing that the average smoker ends up with a twenty-minute paid break a day, amounting to thirty-nine hours a year – about a whole week's extra vacation.

WORKING ASSUMPTIONS

What I'm not in favor of is slippage between actual time to reset, rest and recharge and working flexibly. Yes, technology assists the always-on camp: sales of PCs and desktop computers slumped by more than 25 percent at the end of last year while the global laptop market is expected to rise by 4 percent (more than 5 percent in Asia) to $234 billion by 2030. And yes, there is a convenience in having agency to work a bit here and there and not be compelled to burn up vacation days.

But you used to leave your desk and your desktop, once upon a time. And it's time to reinstate that boundary with your laptop. Once in a while at least.

[June 11, 2023]

◯

> "They're really annoying, especially in the workplace.
> They're like: 'Nah, I'm not feeling it today, I'm gonna come in at 10:30 a.m.' Or in emails, I'l! tell them: this is all grammatically incorrect, did you not check your spelling? And they're like: 'Why would I do that, isn't that kind of limiting?'"
>
> Jodie Foster on Gen Z, 2024*

---

* Kevin Rawlinson and Emma Brockes, "Jodie Foster says Generation Z can be 'really annoying' to work with", the *Guardian*, January 6, 2024.

6

THE AMAZING AGE

amazing
/əˈmeɪzɪŋ/
adjective
causing great surprise or wonder; astonishing.

The times, sang someone called Bob Dylan, they are a-changing. And indeed in the time between the advent of Covid-19 and ChatGPT an entirely new generational era has begun – the "Amazing Age" of AI. Debate rages about whether "full sentience" will be reached or not, i.e. whether AI can ever feel like a human, but already in trials 60 percent of people could not tell a human from a chatbot, and it is becoming harder and harder to separate not just human from machine but humans from *their* machines.*

Are you, for instance, ever not within arm's reach of your smartphone? Does your car now start with an app? Are your books, groceries, documents, communications all done via the interface of *something* rather than *someone*?

---

* Brad Stone, "AI Leader Proposes a New Kind of Turning Test for Chatbots", June 20, 2023.

WORKING ASSUMPTIONS

Those of us born before the 1980s grew up working alongside technology, which was "over there", not "always on". I was born in 1964, and therefore am a young boomer.* It wasn't just the manual typewriter I grew up with but the corded phone, the four-channel black-and-white television, the manual airline ticket and the filing cabinet. Millennials, Gen Z and Alphas – those born after 1981, and who I call the *AMaZing Generation* – have experienced technology's advances directly, and used them from the get-go. Headphones and smartphones and iPods and AirPods; screens and touch screens, with agency in technology and yet very little control outside in the world. Since the 1980s the AMaZing generations in the developing world have been born into a background of rising insecurity, outsourcing, competition for rising economies, and now, generative AI. Schooled in social media and immersive media, they are less and less socially mobile, and so for them the idea of the "career ladder" is, well, pretty old-fashioned.

Covid connected families back to each other in strange ways. The generations saw each other a lot more, close-up. It's not that surprising that post-Covid the youngest working cohort, Gen Z (Alphas don't reach working age until 2026), want to work radically differently from the Boomers and Gen X, the two dominant "elders" in the workforce right now. We were always in and always on, because, well, the rewards were there. But we burnt out, we neglected ourselves, and our young kids noticed.

Like all kids, they don't want to be like their parents. And that includes the grown-ups in the workforce. But here's the problem.

---

* Pew Research Centre, The Baby Boomer Generation – born 1946–1964, Generation X – born 1965–1980, Millennials – born 1981–1996, Generation Z – born 1997–2012, Generation Alpha – born 2013–2025. January 17, 2019.

THE AMAZING AGE

> *Since the 1980s the AMaZing generations in the developing world have been born into a background of rising insecurity, outsourcing, competition for rising economies, and now, generative AI. Schooled in social media and immersive media, they are less and less socially mobile, and so for them the idea of the "career ladder" is, well, pretty old-fashioned.*

We need each other. We can't go in for generation wars now, when generational AI can potentially sweep away the distinction between what it means to be a human at work or a bot or a robot.

So yes, we communicate differently – show me someone born before 1980 who doesn't prefer leaving a voicemail or using an actual phone call, or who genuinely prefers an emoji over a text. And show me someone of my generation who did not naughtily laugh *out loud* at actor/director Jodie Foster's remarks about Gen Z – but that isn't the point. Here's the point: at this point in history, us humans need to stick together.

Here's a bit of a song for you. Written and sung by the best man at our wedding, Simon Toulson-Clarke, and a hit in the 1980s, the start of the AMaZing generation. As it happens, there's a recording up there of me on backing vocals, but that's not why I'm reproducing it with Simon's kind permission.* I always thought it

---

* BCG Music, 1986, reproduced with personal permission of Simon Toulson-Clarke.

225

was the best anthem for a political party, pitched at all the generations at once. Do stream it, its chorus is very rousing:

> *From the very very young to the very very old*
> *everybody now say aye.*
> *From the center of the earth*
> *to the corners of the globe*
> *Everyone of you say aye.*
> *Nobody better let me down*
> *We will see on the other side, lean on me*
>
> *Ah-li-ayo!.**

> " Here's the point: at this point in history, us humans need to stick together.

---

* "Lean on Me" – Red Box, 1986.

Grown-Ups In The Room

Here's what I wrote about the preoccupations at the World Economic Forum in January 2023. The column somewhat dials down my generational complaining about snow-schlepping, which I dislike, or super early starts, which I also dislike now I'm older. But it was a window on the world of the issues preoccupying "leaders", and it showed that among all of the key concerns, the young, and in particular Gen Z, had their attention:

◊

I'll be honest and say that my working assumption about attending the World Economic Forum at Davos was that it was going to be all about the parties and networking and less about learning anything I didn't already know. Conferences are often better socially than they are intellectually. I was wrong. This was both. Conversations over dinners, at private parties, bumping into people on the promenade and the famous Davos shuttle bus plus the main sessions all increased my understanding of key developments on the future of work.

The event – which combined being a talking shop with initiatives anchored around the word "impact" – ran from 7 a.m. to midnight for five days against the vista of the highest town in Europe. It's fair to say that you don't go to Davos for convenience: it's all shuttling and trudging and snowy schlepping. Arguably it underscores the point about return to office made by business leaders like Jamie Dimon of JPMorgan Chase & Co., namely that the cultural benefit is worth the commute. But it also demonstrates what I and plenty of others say about immersive in-person gatherings: they should be considered *primarily for the social benefit. As Greg Tomb, then president of Zoom Video Communications Inc., told me: "Seventy percent of our people don't even live near an office anymore." We were speaking in the Zoom pop-up space along the Davos Promenade, another metaphor for the transience of office space for many now.**

Davos in 2023 was in more ways than one a microcosm of exactly the debates going on everywhere else about how work is working out. Only a small set of the hundreds of sessions that are held publicly and privately addressed the topic of work directly and yet the issue pervaded everything from economics to culture. The takeaway? Work continues to be at an inflexion point.

As Gilbert Houngbo, director general of the International Labour Organization, pointed out: "We will never go back in terms of how we organize industrial relations and work–life balance," and US Labor Secretary Marty Walsh went further: "The workplace is not going back to what it was pre-pandemic."

Hybrid, reskilling, AI, talent, diversity and inclusion are all changing so fast that in addition to bluntly titled sessions like AI and White Collar Jobs, a running joke was that "this session will be chaired by ChatGPT next year." Demographically, the preoccupation with flexibility wasn't just for "millennials in Brooklyn" as Ben Smith, the co-founder of Semafor, who chaired the session entitled "Quiet Quitting and the Meaning of Work", put it, but everyone. Karien van Gennip, minister of social affairs and employment of the Netherlands described much of the discussion about flexible work as "very much for the upper class. Because if you look at many of the jobs they're still in-person service jobs. Also, if you go to a four-day

---

* Zoom orders workers back to the office, August 7, 2023.

work week, you have to be quite serious about what it means for pay per hour."

Davos is also a good place to launch initiatives and make some noise. The Human Rights Campaign presented a white paper on LGBTQ+ inclusion at work, while Valuable 500, an advocate for disabled people, launched a white paper calling for standardized measures and targets for disability inclusion.

Generational workplace issues were also on display. A ten-country study of Gen Z was unveiled over breakfast by management consultancy Oliver Wyman and Gen Z media group The News Movement. It emphasizes that of the cohort which will make up 27 percent of the workforce by 2025, 85 percent prefer hybrid or remote work, and cites buzzwords like "acting their wage" to describe how values now align with work and workplace choices. Some 80 percent also said they are more likely to be less engaged at work if their employers aren't engaged in social issues.

All of which shows that leaders have to wake up. "It's on leaders and companies to change," Anjali Sud, former chief executive officer of video platform Vimeo,* said at a Davos event. "How are we going to communicate and engage with distributed teams, and how are we going to align people and connect with them in a digital world? Actually it is a bit of a house on fire. Because I don't think most leaders feel equipped to do that."

Touché. The fact is that we are about to enter yet another phase of turbulence, which will test all but the most open-minded and skilled of leaders. Some will rely on economic headwinds to gain the upper

---

* Angeli Sud moved to content and streaming platform Tubi in 2023.

WORKING ASSUMPTIONS

hand over employees, but the smart money will be on those who use this moment to reset and have their own internal talking shops more. It's all about impact, isn't it?

[January 26, 2023]

> " What's fascinating about this generation is that they've grown up in households where there's a lack of deference. And a real emphasis on: what do you think? Let me hear your views; and a real, much more democratized culture within families. And then they entered education, where they faced a much more childcentric learning experience.

The Gen Z Difference

This especially impacts Gen Z, the generation coming actively into the job market since approximately 2017, just three short years since the sudden hard stop of Covid. For many, they were still in college, or unable to get to college, so the concern among the corporate class has focused on this generation: they don't want to lose their pipeline. The Millennials are not just older, they have the responsibilities which employers want them to have: families and mortgages. But what has become clear is just how poorly understood this generation has been.*

> *"Gen Z have had a smartphone in their pocket since they were in their early teens. Which means it's generated a different attitude towards money. And particularly making money. So if you go on eBay or if you go on Depop, you can switch fluidly between buying, being a buyer and being a seller. Whether you're talking about TikTok shop or whether you're talking about Depop, this is a generation that has been able to generate money"*
>
> Dr Eliza Filby, Generations Expert

I have lost count of the times leaders and managers, older Millennials, have come up and looked into my face searchingly to ask what I can now call the Jodie Foster Question: how can I get Gen Z to stop thinking about themselves? Equally, I lost count of the times I encountered Gen Z postgraduates or non-graduates who were clearly working in a wholly different way to my generation:

---

* See also Pew Research Center, "Generation dominates online searches for information on the post-Millennial generation", January 16, 2019.

they worked as if they were gig workers by choice: they worked as baristas or in hospitality, they worked on short-term contracts, they lacked the sense of a lifelong career. And they didn't seem at all anxious about it.

In order to make sense of this, I sought out the generations historian Dr Eliza Filby and asked for a primer on this group who have become the generational focus of workplace attention:

EF: *There was an assumption up until the Covid pandemic that young people were eventually going to become older and get mortgages and have kids and discover that their lives will pan out just as their parents' were and have.*

What's become clear is that with Gen Zs, but also Millennials as well, we're looking at a very different attitude towards work. And that's for a number of reasons. Number one, of course, and we cannot underestimate this, is that Gen Z have had a smartphone in their pocket since they were thirteen. Which means it's generated a different attitude towards money. And particularly making money. So if you go on eBay or if you go on Depop, you can switch fluidly between being a buyer and being a seller. Whether you're talking about TikTok shop or whether you're talking about Depop, this is a generation that has been able to generate money from having the world's marketplace in their pocket since they were thirteen. A recent report from the Harvard Business Review found that 70 percent of Gen Z teens were making their own pocket money.

And they weren't doing traditional things, because the Saturday job has been in steady decline since the 1990s, like working in a bar, like doing a newspaper round. These teenagers were making money online. And that has continued into their twenties. So, we have to firstly appreciate that this is a generation that will really not believe in the one salary model of revenue. Multiple streams of revenue is the norm for this generation. And that is fundamentally disruptive to work.

THE ATTENTION DIVIDEND

The second thing is, of course, they are highly individualistic, and that sense of individualism hasn't just come from having a smartphone in their pocket since they were thirteen, but also coming from smaller families where actually parents paid them, ironically, a lot more attention, perhaps even if they had less time, than previous generations of parents.

So what's fascinating about this generation is that they've grown up in households where there's a lack of deference. And a real emphasis on what do you think? Let me hear your views and a real, a much more democratized culture within families. And then they entered education, where they faced a much more child-centric learning experience.

And then, something else: they had social media, which was all about what are you having for dinner? Tell us what you're doing. Tell us what you're thinking. There's no deference on social media. These kids have had a voice on social media. And then they enter workplaces built on hierarchy around age. They're built in very formative structures, fully formed, rigid structures. And it doesn't necessarily fit the way they've even been parented, let alone the cultural norms of social media.

WORK FLUIDITY

That disjunct, and that individualism has also, I think, planted a really important seed in their heads, which is: I don't necessarily want a fixed identity. I want a fluid identity. That could be in terms of your sexuality, it could be in terms of your gender, it could be in terms of your career.

So this idea of I'm going to study this thing at university to become this thing for life, we know that sort of died with the Gen Xers and the Millennials, right? Certainly the job for life died with the Boomers, but the career for life you've seen upended with Millennials anyway. So with Gen Z, they're not thinking, what do I want to do for life? But, what do I want to be now? Maybe for the next five years, eight years. And it's no surprise to me, therefore, that this is a generation that's been estimated will have over seventeen different employers over the course of their working life and five different careers. And, you know, I'm forty-two and I've had three distinct careers.

That fluidity is becoming the norm and it will be most pronounced because these trends take time in that Gen Z generation. So in all sorts of ways this generation even started work, forget the pandemic for a moment, with a very different sort of gestation, right? And then you entered the pandemic years, where for a lot of this generation, it was their last experience of education.

And let's not forget that a number of universities – up to 50 percent of courses in the UK – still teach in some kind of hybrid format. And let's not forget that that comes at a £9,000 a year cost. So for many of them, they've finished their education in a hybrid environment and entered workplaces in, if they entered the work-

place in COVID or just after, in a heavily Zoomified culture. And for many of them, they weren't working from home, they were working from bed. Their experience of work was disengaging, demotivating.

THE UNREWARDING REWARDS OF WORK

Critically, and I think this is really important in the workplace, everyone assumes that when you're talking about work, people want role models: who do I want to be in twenty years' time at this company?

Actually, most of us think much shorter term than that. Most of us are thinking, who do I want to be in five years' time? Can I see anyone here who I want to be in five years' time? And the really critical thing for Gen Z-ers is they look at the elder Millennials, still part of the generations who worked pretty nonstop, and they're thinking: actually, the rewards of work aren't what they used to be.

And so that questioning that happened around Covid was a combination of things, including: this isn't a great entry point into the workplace. My networks have been shrunk. My communication skills have been restricted. I'm not managed very well. I'm staring at a green dot twelve hours a day. And in this economic environment, work doesn't pay either.

Eliza is currently writing a book about the way in which for Millennials and Gen Z: *it's not what you earn that's important anymore, because wages fundamentally have stalled significantly since the 2000s. It's not what you learn anymore, because the value of a degree has declined as more and more of us have got them, and also the price of that degree has gone up. It's essentially, do you have the safety net of Mum and Dad, or do you not? And for those that do, they're reaping the benefits of the inheritance economy, where Mum and Dad are lubricating the wheels of adulthood for them and enabling them to define their opportunities and smooth that pathway into adulthood.*

What bigger corporations are really struggling to understand is how to attract and retain Gen Z. The money and stability have gone out of those industries, and therefore the gig economy is an inevitable way in which we are transactional and less stable, dynamic with each other as buyers and sellers of skills. But what's interesting is that even in the fixed professions, those professions that were so sexy and aspirational in the nineties, it's becoming the same.

STRESS LEVELING

I'm a very geriatric millennial. I was born in 1981. In 2001, the idea of getting on a graduate recruitment scheme was such an aspirational thing. That aspiration, not for all, but for a proportion of Gen Z, has gone, and one of the reasons why it's gone is quite often they've seen their parents in those professions, and again, they've seen both parents working in a digitalized work environment where potentially they saw their parents stressed and uninspired.

I've just done a focus group with a load of Gen Z girls talking about what it was like to grow up with professional working mothers, and the overriding consensus from those Gen Z girls was, I never saw my mom and when I did she was really stressed. And I don't want to work as hard as her.

So as much as they're looking to millennials, they're also looking to their parents. I was talking to one woman the other day and she was saying that her girl, who's fifteen, told her that they're doing a jobs event and careers event at her school. And her mum, who was a senior partner at a firm, one of the big four, said, "Oh, I'll come in and talk about my career." And she was like, "No, Mum, I don't want you to come in. No one wants your job. No one wants to be you."

What's interesting is I then interviewed the Gen X mothers in their fifties in senior positions and a lot of them said, my daughter's right. I spent far too much of my career stressed. I spent far too much of my career working, and you know, I am beginning post Covid to think, where's this all going? What's the point?

THE NEW TRADITIONALISTS

However, what I'm also seeing is a very high proportion of traditionalist Gen Z-ers that no one really talks about. You know, not all Gen Z-ers are Greta Thunbergs, not all Gen Z-ers are quiet quitting. There is a growing constituency of Gen Z-ers who really do aspire to traditional sectors and want that stability and will be motivated by money. And quite often they don't have the responsibilities of looking after children (we know the birthrate is dropping around the developed world) at such an age, but many of them need to fund their parents – not the other way round.

THE UNIVERSITY OF (LIFE) SKILLS

*JH: **What about the new skills, the new AI?***

EF: Well, good question. The new skills and AI are instant, short form, pivot based, skills based. And this is contributing to an unravelling of the old university-based, college-based system which saw an emphasis on sending as many people to college as *possible. The US have always sent a lot of kids to college, but globally, the big story of the last thirty years was let's get as many people to university as possible. And the cost of becoming part of a graduate workforce in a knowledge economy has gone through the roof. What we are seeing now is the gradual, and this always happens gradually,* although COVID I think has put a massive accelerant under it and AI will further, the gradual erosion of that belief in higher education as setting you up for the workforce of the future. It's a massive drop in confidence. Even if you study computer science at university now, that doesn't necessarily set you up for life as a computer scientist or a data analyst or whatever, because in so many ways, universities are not necessarily at the forefront of that information or are not necessarily guiding you or equipping you with the skills you need.*

So if you look at the PWCs in this world, if you look at the big organizations, they are having the most successful recruitment strategies with school leavers rather than graduates. Who are more loyal, more grateful, and more willing to learn. The disillusionment of Gen Z with education, I would say generally, but particularly tertiary education, is because it costs so much money. There are now interest rates on top of that. And obviously for the screen-based, attention-short TikTok generations, let's be honest: it's boring. It's slow. It's not fast enough. And it's turbulent. So what you're seeing there is the rise of apprenticeship degrees, the rise of condensed courses, two years, the rise of staying at home during your graduate years, during your undergraduate years.

---

* Ethan Mollick, "Signs and Portents" post, One Useful Thing Substack: Some hints about what the next year of AI looks like, quoting Amara's Law: "We tend to overestimate the effect of a technology in the short run and underestimate the effect in the long run."

So even the university experience. That's combined with parents who are not as rich, who themselves went through that sausage factory of sink-or-swim education culture and going, yeah, actually, I'm not sure you need that. And I think I stress this a lot. The nuance has to be important, has to be teased out here.

But it's striking that degree apprenticeships, for example, are harder to get into than Oxbridge. What's important is that essentially we have that great turn that is happening, that great question mark that is hovering over higher education.

But I'm not undoing the point and purpose of universities. I still think there's a critical place for universities. But I do think this idea of pushing everyone into university and expecting there to be a reward on that investment is now debunked. And that leads me to the final big point here: The life cycle is really critically important in that. We know that the Lynda Gratton argument, which is quite right, that the twentieth century was really about the three-stage life. It was about your education, and that being a fixed end point, maybe at eighteen, or maybe at twenty-one, if you were lucky, but you didn't have to pay for it. And then you had your working life, which was sustained and arguably in one career, but you were building for the last stage, which was retirement.

But although it goes back to the 1860s, really retirement is a late twentieth-century phenomenon. As people aged and acquired wealth, retirement came into its own. Well, that is completely being disrupted now for all sorts of reasons. Number one, of course, is there's no way we can leave kids finishing their education at twenty-one. It doesn't make sense in the age of AI, right? It doesn't make sense that we saddle them with all that debt age twenty-one as well. So education cannot stop. It has to continue. Second of all, the way we're procreating is fundamentally changing, right? Women increasingly want to be child free.

So the way in which the family dynamic is changing is that we cannot assume that a woman in her thirties is about to have children. Nor can we assume, of course, that a woman in her fifties isn't looking after teenagers. So we need to think about, what does procreation look like in the twenty-first century, where women are having fewer children, they're having them closer together, and they're having them much later in life, if at all.

And as women have stepped up in the professional sphere, men inevitably, in dual income households, for it to even work, have to step up in the domestic sphere. And so, therefore, it's not just the domestic sphere being looking after children, it's, as you've already alluded to, within your own circumstance looking after the elderly because in an ageing society we're going to have to look after our elderly because the state won't.

So our caring responsibilities are different to what they were in the twentieth century. And then our acquisition of assets is coming much later because we're entering adulthood later. Adulthood: when we get married, when we have kids, financial independence from our parents, when we leave home. So we've got this delayed adolescence, but also this protracted old age. And this idea that we retire at a fixed point has long been questioned, but particularly for Gen Xers and Millennials coming after them. They won't retire in the same way. I don't think they'll have a fixed point. They'll downsize their career like they're downsizing their homes. They won't want to, you know, it won't be golf courses, grandkids, and cruises to places that Millennials probably went to in their thirties. The whole aspiration of retirement and what it looks like is going to be so fundamentally different.

Quite often what I find is when I go into a boardroom and I talk about the changing dynamics of twentieth-century family life. The board don't understand it because they're still living in the 1950s, very often with stay-at-home wives.

◯

"I was quite frightened once or twice because Eliza was doing it so well. You see, lots of the real people can't do it at all: they're such fools that they think style comes by nature to people in their position; and so they never learn."

George Bernard Shaw, *Pygmalion*

The Eliza in question here isn't Eliza Filby but Eliza Doolitle, George Bernard Shaw's classic character in a story of class and of course of love, which is intergenerational: nowadays Professor Henry Higgins would be deeply frowned upon for falling in love with "flower girl" Eliza Doolitle as he taught her to speak properly, but whatever else this play is about it is about different generations learning from each other.

A totally different take on this is the film *The Intern*, made in 2015 and starring Robert de Niro as an ageing widower who takes up a job working for Anne Hathaway, a stressed, brilliant dotcom founder. The film is charming and probably played at the back of my mind as I mulled on this question. I had written in my book *The Nowhere Office* that generational identities are shifting in terms of what we do at work, and revisited this idea for Bloomberg early in 2023 – a year which saw two Gen Z figures change corporate history: Sam Bankman-Fried was convicted of epic fraud and jailed, and Sam Altman, co-founder of ChatGPT, was fired and re-hired, having made the world perhaps a little too dependent too fast on the next generation of AI.

⬡

Just as the constraints of the physical office and dress codes loosen, so do the ways workers define themselves.

Are you a Learner, a Leaver or an In-Betweener?

Three years after Covid-19 ushered in the most tumultuous period in the history of modern work, it isn't just the place of work undergoing a fresh identity crisis, but the person doing the work. The working assumption is that the way people define themselves at work doesn't need changing. I think it does, and here's why.

Before the pandemic, the identity of the office itself was relatively stable: there was no controversy over going to the office, flexible hours or working from home because none of it was mainstream. It is true that possibilities for working differently began to emerge most notably over the last fifteen or so years when the internet, the iPhone, and co-working spaces like WeWork made mobility and working flexibility visible and desirable. Nevertheless, in 2019 the commute was largely unavoidable, city business centers unassailable and any individualization of working hours for white collar employees was a perk rather than a right.

The lockdowns flipped this stability on its head, and ever since the office itself has borne the brunt of the identity crisis engulfing the world of work. Fixed locations have come to be seen by many as an unwelcome constraint, almost like an outdated uniform. Why "wear" a commute if you can "clothe" yourself in work from a laptop anywhere?

Fashion is also a useful prism through which to observe the changes in working identity because it shows how the rigidity of what people wear at work has loosened as values shift. Note the loss of casual Fridays, which used to be an office mainstay but disappeared when every day became casual, and the growth of the "athleisure" market (hoodies and track pants to you and me) during the height of the pandemic.

These trends around the place of work and its dress code demonstrate a lessening of constraints on workers. As leaders mix the right cocktail of policies around people and place to bring teams back together again in a rhythm approaching predictability – not easy in a hybrid world – they should look at the way people have come to live and work now and increasingly have different needs depending on their career stage and age.

Those in the early stages of entering the workforce are the "Learners". They need mentoring and immersion into the culture of office life more than the cohort who are mid-career. "Leavers", on the other hand, are typically older and not looking to build and stay in their careers in the same way as Learners. While Learners want freedom to have the best of office life and to not work in ways which cramp their style – a key reason for the appeal of hybrid and remote working – Leavers actually need flexibility to dedicate time to responsibilities other than their jobs.

They benefit from communicating with and mentoring the Learners and the social interaction that comes with in-person work – some of their time. As their demographic often includes those *with heavy caring responsibilities – both for children and parents – their headspace is different as are in some cases their income needs. They can either afford to opt out or are more prepared after the pandemic experience to work and live differently and downsize. In Britain, an argument is raging right now about the best way to attract back well over half a million over-fifties who have left the job market since the pandemic.*

Then there are those who are among the growing number of "solopreneurs" who are freelance or part time, and for whom dropping in and out of a fixed place on a fixed schedule matters less. More than a third of the US workforce was freelancing six months into the Covid-19 pandemic. The solopreneur is the white collar equivalent of the gig economy blue collar worker and a group I also call the "In-Betweeners". They operate in patterns based on asynchronous work, requiring attendance some of the time and not necessarily at the same time as their co-workers.

The good news is that the trend for declaring your status in relation to how you work is growing. As I was writing this article I received my first automatic reply from someone with the following message: "I support flexible working and I'm sending this email now because it suits the hours I'm working today. Please don't feel obliged to reply straight away if it is outside the hours you're working."

That email line, which I hadn't encountered before, feels like progress. Just as office buildings and dress codes are morphing, workers are assuming new identities as the next phase of post-Covid-19 work begins.

[January 13, 2023]

Enter The Queenager

New work identities for new times. I secretly cheered when Jodie Foster, a heroine of mine, gave her interview about being not completely deferential to the idea of working with Gen Z, and I realized that her being outspoken is a typical trait of a gendered generation called "the queenager", women whose careers began to take off in earnest precisely when the AMaZings were little babes in arms and who knows what they have learned about life and are acting on it (and speaking it).

I wrote about this generation of women for Bloomberg and it was one of the most widely read and syndicated of my pieces (credit firmly where it's due to British writer and entrepreneur Eleanor Mills, who coined the term "queenager").

◇

In ongoing discussion over the progress women have made – and still need to make – in the workplace, one key group is often overlooked. Meet the queenagers, women in midlife who began their careers in the 1980s, the decade when the "glass ceiling" was first identified and when breaking through it became a possible if incredibly difficult-to-achieve goal for ambitious, corporate women.

Now, many of those senior female executives are leaving the workforce. In rejecting unsatisfactory jobs they also debunk the working assumption that one size fits all for every phase of a working woman's life.

To understand the challenges ahead for women today it's crucial to consider what queenagers have accomplished and how the playing field has shifted since they first made inroads into a male-dominated business world. Queenagers range in age from about sixty-five all the way down to forty-five. These women typically have relatively high incomes and a high degree of freedom in the choices they're now making, either because they have moved beyond their child-rearing years or because they chose not to have children in the first place.

Noon, a website dedicated to serving this group, coined the term queenagers and describes the group as being in "the age of opportunity". Unlike their younger colleagues having babies and bringing up families, with every spare penny eaten up by childcare, queenagers enjoy a high degree of autonomy and spending. But above all they prize freedom.

"The important thing to understand about this cohort of women is that they are pioneers, the first generation of women to work all the way through," says Eleanor Mills, Noon's founder.

The question now is, will a new generation of rising corporate women do as well? And what can the successful queenager do to show solidarity with younger women and guide them on the path to their own successes?

For women it often gets back to a critical phase: how to successfully navigate the years of juggling careers with having kids – and the often huge financial costs required to do so in a society where men, on average, still significantly out earn women. The International Labour Organization shows that women still earn on average about 80 percent of what men do.

The rising numbers of women in the workforce has been stagnating since the turn of the century, even allowing for the latest return to pre-pandemic participation levels. And at the heart of this stagnation is pay.

Let's zero in on mothers and caregivers. It seems remarkable that it's only this year that The Pregnancy Workers' Fairness Act has become federal law in the US, updating rights ranging from breaks or remote work for employees that are expecting. In the UK, the aptly named Pregnant Then Screwed campaign took the government to the Court of Appeal in 2021 for discrimination against the way income for pregnant women was taxed – and won.

Childcare costs eat up livable income. In the UK they are the highest in the Organization for Economic Cooperation and Development, even while there is a clear correlation between the positive impact of early years provision and labor force participation. Iceland always tops the list.

Both the logistics and the cost of childcare hinder working women and their families. Claudia Goldin, a professor of economics at Harvard University and author of Career and Family: Women's Century-long Journey to Equity, *writes of a study she conducted of careers of male and female MBA graduates at the University of Chicago Booth University between 1990 and 2006. As she explains in her book, "we know from an in-depth analysis of these MBA histories that the growing gap in earnings doesn't appear randomly. Rather, it emerges with the arrival of children. Children and the ensuing caregiving responsibilities are the main contribution to lesser job experience."*

For women, Noon found that flexibility is sixteen times more important to women aged forty-five to sixty than status – and way above the value they place on reaching the corner office or receiving a swanky title as rewards of seniority. For many, particularly those who had worked in corporations for a couple of decades and had the financial resources to go it alone, starting their own company or consultancy was seen as a way to get the flexibility and autonomy they craved, according to Mills.

So how can a queenager lend a hand to younger workers who are right now in the thick of potentially raising families and fighting to compete and rise up in the workplace? It may be nothing more than reassuring them that they, too, can get there. Or it may be throwing energy into the more gritty and hard-fought campaigns, such as Pregnant Then Screwed, and joining corporate boards and organizations to promote policy changes.

There are also green shoots of optimism. And one of them is that at the end of the day men and women in 2023 are not all that far apart in what they want from a career and work experience. When it comes to how people feel at work, a recent survey of 4,500 workers across five countries on Belonging in the Workplace conducted by research firm Opinium and commissioned by ISS, the facilities management business, found that men and women are neck and neck at around 70 percent feeling a sense of belonging, with the caveat that more than half of both men and women said they can't always express themselves freely.

Women and men are equal in one way, then: they both want to talk about how they feel about work. Let's all of us – queenagers and beyond – make sure that discussion includes continuing to change the workplace so that it's fair and equitable for everyone.

[July 20, 2023]

Women's experience of work has changed, and Covid lifted the lid on two generations struggling with old norms. The queenager could remove the shackles of expectation, seize life by the shoulders and shake it out on her terms, while working women finally had the opportunity to take advantage of a little more by way of flexibility to better reflect the endless juggle and struggle of childcare-plus-career.

WORKING ASSUMPTIONS

Time Warp

But the queenager is not entirely a generation continuing to work happily. Sixty-eight percent of workers in the UK marked as becoming inactive post Covid were fifty- to sixty-four-year-olds.* In the US less than 20 percent of those above sixty-five continued in the workforce post Covid.† Part of the reason is the same one hitting the young: economics. The cost of living crisis has been so huge, work has stopped paying enough. It isn't only the childcare trap but the care trap: an ageing workforce needs more care, which is a mess. Only the lucky or the wealthy get to age gracefully, safely and well – or affordably.

But it's more than this. Technology, the great enabler, requires a cognitive function which slips as you get older anyway. I cannot be the only parent of a Gen Z who rolls their eyes as I struggle with the sheer quantity of things to do to stay connected: plug-ins, downloads, authentifications, user IDs. The average person now has seventy to eighty digital passwords to either store safely or remember: in practice, that's not gonna happen, is it? The annual cost of cybercrime is rising across the world – $10 billion per annum and rising in the US according to the FBI. What's the guessing that a large proportion of the victims are over fifty?‡

My mother was eighty-eight when Covid hit the world. She lived alone in an apartment near to all the family, and she spent most

---

* Felicia Rankl, "Why have older workers left the labour market?" The Office for National Statistics (ONS), March 14, 2023.
† Brian Scheid, "Oldest employed Americans have left the workforce, never to return", S&P Global Market Intelligence, June 13th, 2023.
‡ Luke Barr, "Americans lost $10.3billion to internet scams in 2022, FBI says", ABC News, March 13th, 2023.

of her time either walking to the local "University of the Third Age" to learn, I kid you not, Italian literature, but also to be on her computer, writing a memoir, communicating with her vast circle of friends, and, with a bit of help, watching interesting things on YouTube or reading the *Guardian* on her iPad.

But it was a fragile truce with technology. Because by 2020 her mind was becoming mired by early stage Alzheimer's. Trying to help her use Zoom during the pandemic was complex. We visited her apartment but, as per the rules and anxieties of the time, did not enter for months. By the time the pandemic was over her mental health had deteriorated significantly. By the time she entered a home in the summer of 2022 she could no longer work her mobile phone, a radio, or the channels on the TV.

It isn't just that dementia is rising exponentially across the world: it affects around 55 million people today, but is set to afflict triple that number by 2050.[*] It's that technology isn't designed for the old, let alone the old at work. For all the talk of reskilling and retraining, there isn't yet a mainstream discussion about providing this at different speeds for different cognitive abilities. Being old is a form of neurodiversity. The workplace should do more than be inclusive, equitable and welcoming: it should actively help the elderly to learn and use technology. Maybe AI is coming to the rescue here. It should.

Up until she left her independent life for managed care, Mum clung to the one piece of technology which never gets old, a physical desk diary. Writing in this was tremendously important to her, even when the days and dates swam in her mind. I don't think

---

[*] Alzheimer's Disease International, Dementia Statistics.

that's sad, I think that's sane. Do you still use pen and paper, ever? I sincerely hope so. I still have a desk diary, a notebook and a pen, even as I use of course a digital diary.

For this reason I commissioned the workplace historian Dr Andrew St George to remind the listeners of *The Nowhere Office* about the history of the desk diary:

> The desktop diary. This is the place on our desk where past and present meet. Tangible proof that we live life forwards and understand it backwards. Of course, now this place is digital and portable, tied into our mobile phones with their complex array of contacts, invitations and scheduling.
>
> But it was not always this way. The desktop diary, invented and produced by John Letts in London in 1812, brought together for the first time the journal, where you recorded what you had done, and the calendar, where you planned what you would do, or which marked out high days and holidays. This was the world's first known commercial diary, and focused on future events rather than past recollections.
>
> A simple and powerful idea that changed how we think about time. Of course, we all know of great works that record the past or chart the present as it occurred. Marco Polo, Samuel Pepys, Anne Frank, all renowned diarists. Or notebooks that caught artistic ideas. Da Vinci or Beethoven. And equally, we can think of calendars from the great civilizations and religions.
>
> The oldest solar calendar is the Jewish. in use for nearly 3,000 years. There are less portable versions, too, like the arrangements of stone circles in Aberdeenshire, Scotland, the world's oldest lunar calendar, 10,000 years old. It could predict days and hours, but not what would happen in them. That was the job of John Letts.

> *Remember he bound past and present in one book. You could tell what you did last week and what you would be doing next, and of course the diary never lies. How much time did you spend in meetings? Where were you last Monday? Who did you meet? Who are you having coffee with tomorrow? And measure time and effort, record what you did and what you plan, and you are in your own modern time and motion study.*
>
> *You are managing time. Fast forward, turn the pages into the future because you can, and discover all those meetings, commitments, undertakings and appointments that lie in wait. And go further still. To the project, the Gantt chart, and the Agile Sprint. The desktop diary lets you learn from the past.*

Do we learn from the past? Well, I'm not sure we do. But equally, I'm not sure we are taking full advantage of the present either. Because the resistance to change in terms of how we work (beyond desk diaries or digital ones) still hinges hugely on where and when we work, on our patterns of working, reflecting our life stages and our life choices. Professor Steven J. Davis of Stanford University refers to the pandemic as "this big forcing event"* and it's time to learn from it and put in place different ways to live, and to work.

If I could wave a magic wand, the one thing we would do to better understand the present of work and make workable working assumptions about the future is to address the past. To learn from it. The future is coming at us so quickly, but we need to pause and

---

* *The Nowhere Office*; Stephen J. Davis co-authored "The Evolution of Working from Home" with Jose Maria Barrero and Nicolas Bloom, Stanford Institute for Economic Policy Research, July 2023.

understand two things. Firstly, how generations are changing, and secondly, how we can create a truly amazing age, in which it isn't about one generation being in the driving seat, but several at once.

> *What will the workplace look like a year from now? The snowglobe of work has been undeniably shaken to its core since the arrival of Covid-19. And the swirling mist is far from settled. But one thing is clear: the working assumption that office life can "go back" to what it was before 2020 is just wrong.*

Where Do We Park Our Spaceships?

The futurism of technology, the perpetual state of humans: these are the challenges we face now and always did face. In work and in life. They are increasingly blended. Although I have consulted the internet and AI for this book, every word has been researched and written by me, and fact-checked by humans. And although I'm sure I could have asked ChatGPT to creatively produce words for me, I chose to ask a highly skilled human, the poet Mr Gee, to read the columns and this book and to write a poem about work.

As it turned out, unprompted, he wrote about the generations. And here it is.

Where do we park our spaceships? A Poem by Mr Gee

At school, I told everyone that I dreamt of flying a spaceship,

One that could navigate between the falling shards of a failing glass ceiling,

One that would fuel my motivation to never burn out,

But my career advisor cautioned me on the importance of staying grounded,

On being anchored to an idea,

He proposed that my journey into work should involve:

"A meaningful path where a person might seek value"

He assured me that once I had grasped this elusive treasure, I would recognize it immediately,

WORKING ASSUMPTIONS

> *This all seems like another lifetime ago, He was from a different world, a different era, a different commute, He only knew one beginning and one ending, So what advice could he really give to an unclear career Thus my rocket-heads remained unused, I left them to seek rust in nostalgic playgrounds*
>
> *But yesterday is simply today plus some change Post-Covid strategy has reimagined its own culture, Its own social cohesion of distance, One which requires a flexible hustle with a dream attached, This hybrid path now juggles many heads Each one twisting sideways every day to avoid decapitation, Our breakfast muesli is now ingrained with such turbulence*
>
> *Some say that AI now knows all of the answers, Its convictions are remotely based on the strength of my Wi-Fi signal, And my ability to avoid microaggressions, Perhaps my true value has been submerged within its code As I try to decipher whether or not the advice it gives sounds authentic to me, Who does this algorithm want me to be?*
>
> *Good morning,*
>
> *For today's meeting I have many questions:*
>
> *1) How many times has the water cooler leaked?*
>
> *2) Can any office show its color under ultra-violet light?*
>
> *3) When the wolves are on holiday, how anxious is their howl?*
>
> *And finally:*
>
> *4) If our saviour is a potato, where do we park our spaceships?*

Back To The Future

I will end on a column I wrote at the end of 2022, predicting the following year at work. It's interesting to see how much stayed in place. But whether you read this in 2024, or 2025, or further out, how much will feel wrong, and how much will feel like it just... evolved?

A new model of where and how to work is emerging and it hinges on learning from past mistakes.

What will the workplace look like a year from now? The snowglobe of work has been undeniably shaken to its core since the arrival of Covid-19. And the swirling mist is far from settled. But one thing is clear: the working assumption that office life can "go back" to what it was before 2020 is just wrong.

Three out of every four workers say that working hybrid is now non-negotiable for them. The coming year will see a return of a kind for the office, but one which is organized in a very different way. Here are three predictions for a healthier, happier and more productive workplace.

An End to Flex-Shaming

Early in 2022, the British HR expert Gemma Dale coined the phrase "flex-shaming" in a LinkedIn post. It captures well the bad faith some leaders showed to workers who aren't physically in front of them. Among the most famous is David Solomon of Goldman Sachs, who in 2021 called working from home "an aberration we're going to correct as quickly as possible." In October, Solomon told

CNBC that about 75 percent of its people were in the office on any given day of the week pre-pandemic and now it's about 65 percent. Even if bosses think they can impose their will, legislative changes around the world are favoring flexibility. Over a billion people from Greece to Thailand are already being affected by changes in the law to facilitate remote or hybrid work. What matters is creating a culture of trust and transparency between bosses and employees to reach solutions, not as dry policy but by mutual agreement. There's no place for flex-shaming in 2023.

Softening Hybrid's Hard Edges

This is not to say that hybrid work is a picnic. Recent global data from property consultancy JLL show that compartmentalizing between office and home is a major problem. Some 25 percent of hybrid workforces feel socially isolated and 59 percent expect wherever they work to pay attention to their health and wellbeing. Anxiety around social cohesion and productivity in hybrid offices is gaining traction: Marc Benioff, the founder and chief executive officer of technology firm Salesforce Inc., who also sits on the board of the World Economic Forum, recently told a company-wide Slack forum that new hires weren't being productive enough, and asked "are we not building tribal knowledge with new employees without an office culture?"

Joanna Swash, group CEO of the call answering and live chat company Moneypenny, who has built a pub in her Wrexham headquarters in Wales to make her office as attractive as possible, nevertheless told me on my Nowhere Office podcast that "I'm a big believer in the office, but I'm also a big believer in wherever somebody's working, it's got to be the right environment for them."

In other words, iterating workplace by workplace is the only way forward. Speaking recently at the Global Drucker Forum in Vienna Frauke von Polier of German manufacturing group Viessmann, voted European CHRO of the Year 2022, said that piloting changes for as little as three months or as long as a year should become the new normal until things settle down.

The Workplace as Social Space

In a recent LinkedIn post von Polier said: "How do you ensure that your culture is reinforced? Well, you start from the top and serve food to the people… and of course, dessert must be for free!" Since joining Bloomberg Work Shift as a commentator, I make a point of coming into the London office frequently to check in with colleagues. The elevator always comes to the same floor first. It's called "The Pantry" and is designed as a social hub for meeting, snacks, hot drinks and exchanging face-to-face contact before people continue on to workstations or meeting rooms. The Instagram @bloombergpantry is labeled "where our purpose & our people meet".

Although data shows that 84 percent of the reduction in office space is associated with hybrid working, the repurposing of both offices to be more social, plus an investment in the experience of work, is growing. The US Office Occupier Sentiment Survey from property firm CBRE shows that 36 percent of leaders are curating workplace experiences and events as part of their strategy to create community and increase presence in offices. I expect this percentage to grow. People need a reason to come to a place which goes beyond mobile technology they can access from anywhere. That reason is simple: other people.

WORKING ASSUMPTIONS

While the base of work's snowglobe has shifted from place to person, we all do need to work and meet somewhere. Here's hoping 2023 is the return of the office in its new, improved form.

[December 28, 2022]

> Turbulence is here to stay, and stability is long gone. That's my overall working assumption. The five-year plan? Forget it. Five months is more practical. The combination of Covid and ChatGPT has shortened the time horizon against which we work. Trying to lengthen it again, invoking stop–start delays and pushback, as has broadly happened with return to office policies, is obviously a management mistake. Iterating, learning, listening, responding: this is the opportunity.

CONCLUSION: THE UNITED STATE OF WORK

This book has been about working assumptions, but I'd like to end with some wishful thinking. This is because I'm an optimist in a pessimistic world. I do see upside, albeit against a blizzard of challenges. The snowglobe of change around the world of work I first wrote about in *The Nowhere Office* has become a snowstorm.

Turbulence is here to stay, and stability is long gone. That's my overall working assumption. The five-year plan? Forget it. Five months is more practical. The combination of Covid and ChatGPT has shortened the time horizon against which we work. Trying to lengthen it again, invoking stop–start delays and pushback, as has broadly happened with return to office policies, is obviously a management mistake. Iterating, learning, listening, responding: this is the opportunity.

We're all in a new state of work – I call it The United State of Work. The global workforce is more united than at any point in its history. United by anxiety, united by technology's proximity, united by unease between managers as wrong-footed by the speed of change as workers wrong-footed by a working life not living up to expectation.

WORKING ASSUMPTIONS

Common challenges render differences narrower than at any time in the last century. Jobs which were dominated by class, by educational difference, are all facing the same challenges and a blurring of roles within those jobs. We can see this now with fresh eyes. We may not all have 20:20 vision but we all have clarity post 2020 about how things were, how they are and how they can be.

Every workplace has the same components: elements of construction, marketing, administration, management. Planning, operating, providing, communicating, learning, delivering. People remain at the heart of any operation. The phrase of the moment is *keeping the human in the loop*. Well, it was ever thus. Focusing less on the difference and more on the similarity will help.

Why? Any organization which pulls in the same direction is more successful than the one which doesn't. We are all united by what we face right now. Not an enemy exactly, but without doubt a very powerful universal competitor who everyone is cheerfully calling "a co-pilot". This doesn't quite do justice to what's happening.

From now on, and it's happening already, every human in every workplace in the world will to some degree have to work alongside a very fast, very shiny new kind of worker who doesn't need as much sleep, doesn't need as much hand-holding, doesn't have feelings which need managing – and is here to stay. The chat bot, the robot, the programmed software to interpret their keystrokes or their past behavior or to monitor how their eyes move on a screen and then *provide a response*: these are our co-workers, our co-pilots. Everything, everywhere, all at once. We humans have to stick together more and not less as the new knowing technology threatens to remake us, control us, or at the least increasingly define us.

CONCLUSION: THE UNITED STATE OF WORK

It is the human spirit, character, essence, which will continue to differentiate us, and hold the biggest possibility to make of life and work what we always have had the capacity to do: amazing things. The potential for this now is only increasing. Notwithstanding the risks of cyberattack, surveillance nightmares, job disruptions, plus of course the risk that bad management continues to resist a necessary evolution, the balance for optimism is greater than pessimism.

This lesson is explored in another blockbuster movie, *Poor Things*, which also swept the awards boards in 2024. In this, a remake of the Frankensteinian 1992 novel by Scottish writer Alasdair Gray, the heroine, played by Emma Stone, discovers humanity as a baby does: at exceptional speed. The character, who has been given a baby's brain as an implant, provides a metaphor for much of what we are learning today: to see the world with fresh eyes; to accept the fundamentals of love and decency and community which bind us, but to accept as well the advances of science and technology, without which we cannot prosper. The closing scene, set in an idyllic garden, with both work and rest on beautiful display, is clearly intentional. How we live and how we work: it's not that different in the end.

The lesson of *Poor Things* is also one that all workers learn who survive in hostile environments: to arm themselves with knowledge and support systems. Having the right skills, networks, mentors, trade unions and well-chosen workplaces are all vital. What is a "well-chosen workplace"? Anywhere which doesn't trumpet their culture as if it's a branded slogan, backed up by rigid policies, but instead embodies a culture which responds to the times and keeps it real. A place which operates in person, remotely, hybrid, using the best technology and with the best human psychology, which shows those who work in it, and its consumers, that it is fair and relevant and open to change.

The optimist in me does see a management culture which is changing. I do have great faith in people who are attracted to working in "People", the newly rebranded HR function. I do see HR communities as being a bit like carers in health and social care. Generally speaking they want to help. Generally speaking they get the thin edge of the wedge in terms of support. They are often forced to work within the part of "the system" which is most outdated, or most disrupted – often both. But they care. They know that their job matters. Stick with the People people, I say.

What of those who call themselves, a little too proudly in my book, "leaders"? Well, they need to learn. They need to convey uncertainty as much as conviction. This is not a certain time, and respect to the leader who admits this openly. They could start with dusting off some of the most interesting case studies of the last century (start with the Hawthorne effect) because the present and the future always have elements of the past we need to know and remember the past in order to move forwards.

In doing so fresh new case studies from across the world can be created. What are the lessons being learned and how do we access them outside of the ivory tower of academia? We badly need a global dashboard of data – I struggle to find one – which shows what works well in different countries against certain obvious metrics: employment, skills, gender equality, stress and sickness, and productivity being chief among them.

There is much we can learn from the Scandinavian or Canadian childcare model, or the South Korean R&D model, just as there is much to watch from the connection between flexible working laws and productivity: the UK will be an interesting test case in this.

What of America? Will the American work ethic of always-on and always-in ever regain its momentum? At first sight, it's going to be a climb. When the cost of ill health, from rampant opioid addiction to the quarter of the workforce who say they will only work again if remote work is an option and the quarter of the workforce who say government aid packages during Covid actively disincentivized them to look for work afterwards* is laid bare.

I think that Americans love work, they just don't like working for no benefit: insecure jobs that don't pay enough to pay the rent. They are becoming more disillusioned faster with their "dream" than in other countries because for so long it held out such promise and reward, and because the American Dream was so tied up with work. The scales are falling from American eyes and they are hurting. As Johnny Paycheck sang all those years ago, if it isn't right, take this job and shove it.† Beyoncé echoed it all those years later in "Break My Soul".‡ The tools of social media and the post-Covid landscape give workers, especially the "AMaZing" generation, much, much more power now. They can be listened to not only through their pop songs but in their own actions.

The soul of the American worker matters – it's not just the economy (stupid). If it has taken a pandemic and a threat to the world order of work to get this message through, then all I can say is this: better late than never.

---

* US Chamber of Commerce paper, "Understanding America's Labor Shortage", 2024.
† "Take This Job and Shove It" – Johnny Paycheck, 1977.
‡ "Break My Soul" – Beyoncé, 2022.

Plus, you can already see green shoots of change in America. New initiatives to promote new skills, a painful but necessary reckoning that the Ivy League universities have to some degree lost their way and that a degree-only management class trained on the MBA is not the only way to develop world-leading brands or services. A $250 million dollar American initiative, supported by Bloomberg Philanthropies, to prepare high school students to graduate directly into healthcare jobs* is a good example of fresh approaches. Again: let's have that dashboard to see all such initiatives, all over the world, collected not in conferences for the few, but for all of us to learn from and emulate or improve on.

America matters, not only because it is the largest economy in the world right now, and not only because it's one of the largest employers in the world outside of its own shores; not only because it created the very fabric so much of the world relies on – from mass transport to mass production to mass communications and now the latest mass AI – but because of its art, its culture and its stories. The way we see ourselves and our lives, if we look, has always been a story told predominantly by America. So America's survival as a great nation of work is important not just to America – but to all of us. We see ourselves in America, and we always have done.

> *The soul of the American worker matters. If it has taken a pandemic and a threat to the world order of work to get this message through, then all I can say is this: better late than never.*

---

* In January 2024, Bloomberg Philanthropies announced an investment of $250 million to create "Healthcare High Schools".

CONCLUSION: THE UNITED STATE OF WORK

Workin' Day and Night

I'm optimistic that the current dramas around working patterns and working time will calm and settle. At the moment it's extreme and volatile: some bosses want everybody back in, some economies want everyone working more and not less. The four-day week campaign is, for me, a symbol of a time which says: Who we are now are blended selves with work and home lives which need to work. Let the tech help not hinder us, whatever that working model is. Wishful thinking, but also a working assumption: ever since Henry Ford connected his workers with their consumer selves – they worked to earn to consume his products during their leisure time – and ever since the smartphone and the internet embedded the tech we use for work within the tech we use to live – a new system of living and working was inevitable.

It took 2020 for this to happen. Times change. And they change suddenly. When Michael Jackson, one time global "king of pop", sang of too much work in "Workin' Day and Night" in 1979, it was five years after he debuted the most famous dance move in the world: his robot dance. He articulated two of the biggest shifts at work in short order: the fact that humans and machines are becoming more and more aligned, and the tendency to work more and more is sapping our strength and our souls. Whatever else his legacy left the world (including terrible sexual abuse allegations and the reality that the most famous man for a time in the world was apparently addicted to opioids) he did what culture does best: sings a truth of the moment about the way things are or the way things will be in a way which touches the soul. Again, an American story the whole world recognizes.

Charlie Chaplin, Michael Jackson: American twentieth-century icons used movies and music to move to the beat of work as the central story, exploring how we live and how we work, as souls and as humans working with machines. This timeless truth comforts me. Because nothing is that new, after all. It's just a new era now. A new era and new opportunities.

> *Everyone today, regardless of collar or qualification, faces having to make their own luck in jobs which require a series of stackable skills overlaid upon each other – can you drive? Can you cook? What languages can you speak? Can you code? Can you type? Are you – and you will need this on your resume – "proficient at prompting" when it comes to ChatGPT?*

CONCLUSION: THE UNITED STATE OF WORK

New Luck for New Times

London's hot theatrical night out is an immersive trip to *Guys & Dolls* at the Bridge Theatre where the hot ticket is to stand with the actors in the stalls. This timeless musical was made famous in the 1955 American movie in which the gamble of life, love, work, ultimately pays off. "Luck Be a Lady" is one of the most famous songs. Everyone wants Lady Luck. Why does it resonate so much today? Well, it's joyous. It's about the reality that we all duck and dive in life, that we all love, we all pine, and we all hope to get lucky.

Everyone today, regardless of collar or qualification, faces having to make their own luck in jobs which require a series of stackable skills overlaid upon each other – can you drive? Can you cook? What languages can you speak? Can you code? Can you type? Are you – and you will need this on your resume – "proficient at prompting" when it comes to ChatGPT? There is a new equality to this moment like never before. The AI workplace will be far more of a leveler, or will level up: the early indications all point to lower skilled workers benefitting more.*

Tomorrow's worker will have to learn to use an ever-changing new generation of technology; to stay "authentic" in an age of replacement or "augmentation"; to keep a job which could be outsourced to a robot or a different time zone remote worker; and to learn how to live well, live better, work less but earn enough to live. This worker may wear overalls or a suit and they may work from a fixed place *temporarily* or a fixed place *never*. We're in a new placeless, timeless world. Today the National Theatre, where

---

* *See* Microsoft Trends Survey, 2023.

WORKING ASSUMPTIONS

I first saw *Guys & Dolls* in a production in 1982 (that famous year, the year of the queenager's career beginning and the AMaZing generation being born) has taken its workplace – the theater – out to the cinema. It's become virtual. Today you can watch its productions anywhere in the world. Culture has taken a leaf out of work's book. Virtual meeting? Sure. Join us. Join in. It's a sign of the times.

The worker of tomorrow won't have a single place of work, or if they do, it won't be for long. The workplace of the future is full of solopreneurs, people who move their skills in a stackable set across industries, countries, sectors. And why not? This is what AI is letting us do: be fully imaginative in how we access information, and, crucially, how we share it.

> *If our cognitive computation can be augmented by AI, replaced by it, what we have left is the essence of how humans work together. Time is really of the essence here: we have to learn to do this before the elder generations pass through the system of work and out.*

Co+Laborare = Collaborate

Above all the United State of Work is one in which we are going to have to work together intergenerationally and pass on knowledge of how to do the one thing humans can do better than machines: collaborate, innovate, imagine, argue, and find ways through.

If our cognitive computation can be augmented by AI, replaced by it, what we have left is the essence of how humans *work together*. Time is really of the essence here: we have to learn to do this before the elder generations pass through the system of work and out. A quarter of the world's workforce is already made up of the AMaZing generation, dominated by Millennials and Gen Z and soon to be joined by Alphas: far younger than me, younger than anyone born before 1982.*

To collaborate is to *col-laborare* – the Latin for working together, which became "collaborate" in the nineteenth century. Today and tomorrow, in the future of work how we do this doesn't matter but that we do it does. The means of production has always changed. Will it matter if the surgeon remotely instructs the robot in a different time zone if they get the result we all want? We have always worked in different modes. Standing at a production line. Sitting at a desk. Sitting in traffic on a highway or crowded commuter trail. We've sent messages by telex, by fax, by snail mail, by email, by Slack, by Dropbox. By WhatsApp. On Twitter. We have communicated and collaborated to do what we do in person, or at a distance.

---

* McKinsey, EY, and many other sources cite the percentage of GenZ working as above 25 percent, so this is a conservative estimate when you count in Millennials, as well.

Whatever we do to get a job done, an important job done, requires technology which changes. But the essence of a successful endeavour doesn't. It's the human. The human spirit, the human ingenuity, and the human will.

There is a beautiful illustration of this in the 2024 movie *One Life* about the late Sir Nicholas Winton (played by Sir Anthony Hopkins), who rescued over 600 Jewish children on Kindertransport from Prague to the UK during at the beginning of the Holocaust in the Second World War.

He ignores the telex from his stockbroker boss to "return to office" and instead works tirelessly using pen, paper, photography, and footwork to queue and queue-jump a hugely bureaucratic system to pursue his goal: rescuing children at risk of certain death.

So yes, the bowler hat days are gone. The always-at-your-desks days are gone. The commute days are gone. Get over it. So what? What matters is how we humans work, and how we work with each other and our machines.

> *Whatever we do to get a job done, an important job done, requires technology which changes. But the essence of a successful endeavour doesn't. It's the human. The human spirit, the human ingenuity, and the human will.*

CONCLUSION: THE UNITED STATE OF WORK

Walking In The Air

The snowglobe of work has become a snowstorm. We're shaking and shifting, disrupting and arguing, waiting for the blur to settle. The most famous snowman flies, in the book and movie *The Snowman* by British writer Raymond Briggs. The animated film, made in 1982 – the generationally significant year – is all about possibility, about belief, as well as being about a small boy and an imaginary snowman. I urge you to download the movie or the song, or both, immediately. I bet you will be moved.

Movement: in our lives and in work. From one place to another, be that a room or a metaverse "place". Be that to our car or to the commuter train. From one city to another. The small boy looks down from high above the place he lives to "the people far below". Well, that's us. We're what they call a "distributed workforce" now. The way we work and the place of work is redistributed itself – and that's actually a good thing. Long overdue.

Turbulence is a weather system we're stuck with in climate change and in society. I began this book with a column about being in a plane, high above the people down below, in a turbulent place. But I knew I'd land safely. These are the odds. I think the same is true for work overall. It's not about to crash out of the sky and jobs aren't about to be swallowed up by clouds. Work will remain part of the fabric of society. No, this isn't a working assumption or even wishful thinking. This is a prediction. Take my word for it. The detail, however? That's still up in the air.

FURTHER READING

Given the tsunami of information which is "incoming" (as Americans say), please regard these recommendations as mere dips in a very large, roiling ocean. I've focused on relevant books, podcasts I have encountered since 2022 which have informed my thinking in some shape or form for this book (You can also find an extensive reading list in my book *The Nowhere Office* on thenowhereoffice.com). In my LinkedIn posts and on Substack, and my personal mailing list I also make recommendations on articles, Substacks, Reddits, TikToks, Instagrams of relevance to the world of work on a regular basis: see more at juliahobsbawm.com

Acemoglu, Daron, and Johnson, Simon, *Power and Progress: Our Thousand-Year Struggle over Technology & Progress*, Public Affairs Hachette, 2023

Berwick, Isabel, *The Future Proof Career: Strategies for Thriving at Every Stage*, Harper Collins, 2024

Cass, Orin, *The Once and Future Worker: A Vision for the Renewal of Work in America*, Encounter Books, 2018

Daisley, Bruce, *Fortitude: The Myth of Resilience, and the Secrets of Inner Strength,* Penguin Books 2023

Edmondson, Amy, *Right Kind of Wrong: Why Learning to Fail Can Teach Us To Thrive*, Cornerstone Press, 2023

Goldberg, Emma, *Life on the Line: Young Doctors Come of Age in a Pandemic*, Harper Collins, 2021

Gratton, Lynda, *Redesigning Work: How To Transform Your Organisation and Make Hybrid Work for Everyone*, Penguin Books, 2022

Ibarra, Herminia, *Working Identity: Unconventional Strategies for Reinventing Your Career*, Harvard Business Review Press, 2023

Ibarra, Herminia, *Act Like a Leader, Think Like a Leader*, Harvard Business Review Press, 2023

Kellerman, Barbara, *Leadership from Bad to Worse: What Happens When Bad Festers*, Oxford University Press, 2024

Kissinger, Henry, Schmidt, Eric, Huttenlocher, Daniel, *The Age of AI*, John Murray, 2022

Hirst, Alex and Penny, Lizzie, *Workstyle: A revolution for wellbeing*, Nicholas Brealey Publishing, 2022

Khurana, Rakesh, *From Higher Aims to Hired Hands: The Social Transformation of American Business Schools and the Unfulfilled Promise of Management as a Profession*, Princeton University Press, 2007

Lake, Andy, *Beyond Hybrid Working: A Smarter & Transformational Approach to Flexible Working*, Routledge, 2024

Langlois, Richard N, *The Corporation and the American Century: The History of American Business Enterprise*, Princeton University Press, 2023

Leonhardt, David, *Ours Was the Shining Future: The Story of the American Dream*, Hachette, 2023

Levitan, Sar A and Johnston, William B, *Work Is Here to Stay, Alas*, Olympus Publishing, 1973

Lipman, Joanne, *Next! The Power of Reinvention of Life and Work*, Harper Collins, 2023

Li, Fei-Fei, *The Worlds I See: Curiosity, Exploration, and Discovery at the Dawn of AI*, Flatiron Books, 2023

Merz, Charles, *And Then Came Ford*, Doubleday 1929

Suleyman, Mustafa, with Bhaskar, Michael, *The Coming Wave: AI, Power and the 21st Century's Greatest Dilemma*, Penguin Books, 2023

Sutton, Robert I & Rao, Huggy, *The Friction Project: How Smart Leaders Make The Right Things Easier and the Wrong Things Harder*, St Martin's Press, 2024

Toffler, Alvin, *The Third Wave*, William Morrow, 1980

Thompson, Derek, *On Work: Money, Meaning, Identity*, Atlantic Editions, 2023

Ton, Zeynep, *The Case for Good Jobs: How Great Companies Bring Dignity, Pay and Meaning to Everyone's Work*, Harvard Business Review Press, 2023

Viney, John *The Culture Wars: How American and Japanese Businesses have outperformed Europe's and why the future will be different*, Capstone Publishing, 1997

Watts, Steven, *The People's Tycoon: Henry Ford and the American Century*, Alfred. A. Knopf, 2005

White, E.B, *Here is New York*, Harper & Bros, 1949

PODCASTS

Acquired: Every Company Has A Story with Ben Gilbert and David Rosenthal

Belabored: A podcast about labor organizing, hosted by Sarah Jaffe and Michael Chen

Better Life Lab with Brigid Schulte

Azeem Azhar's Exponential View

The Nowhere Office: The Past, Present and Future of Work with Julia Hobsbawm and Stefan Stern

Eat, Sleep, Work Repeat with Bruce Daisley

Elon, Inc.

Flex Perspectives with Rob Sadow

It's All Relative with Dr Eliza Filby

Keen On with Andrew Keen

Let Go and Lead with Maril Macdonald

FURTHER READING

The Future of Work Podcast – International Labor Organization

Talent Angle – Gartner Podcast

The Way We Work – Fast Company

Work Appropriate – Anne Helen Peterson

Work In Progress from WorkingNation

WorkLife with Adam Grant

You Don't Know Me with Chloe Combi

The Valley Labor Report with Jacob Morrison and Adam Keller

We Make It Work – the CRE Podcast from Cushman & Wakefield

Working It with Isabel Berwick

> *Who we are now are blended selves with work and home lives which need to work. Let the tech help not hinder us, whatever that working model is.*

ACKNOWLEDGMENTS

A book is a production line of work, automated by humans and machines. The most visible person, the author, is never the whole story. I have a long and heartfelt list of people to thank for this book. While mistakes and omissions are entirely my own responsibility, there is a long line of interviewees, colleagues, supporters, critical friends and of course family who have made this particular book possible on the tightest turnaround I've ever had.

There are many people who helped bring this book to you who I can't name, because I don't know their names. They work in the book-related supply chain and production business, in typesetting or warehouses, or they are the people who indulged me on my travels: air stewards, baristas, taxi drivers, bartenders, hotel teams and broadcast crews who I gently pump for information by asking one question which they always, always seem happy to answer: How's your work going? Where do you think work is going?

Firstly, the team at Whitefox, especially Julia Koppitz and John Bond. Together with Kiana Palombo, Miranda Ward and Jill Sawyer, they show a new way to publish collaboratively with an author – and I like it. Whitefox worked seamlessly with Fiona McMorrough, Kealey Rigden and Katrina Power at FMcM who are also wildly good at what they do. In the US I've been so lucky to work with Marissa Eigenbrood and Sophia Moriarty at Smith Publicity, and in New York to have the peerless support of Tracy Lovatt and Maria Gianoutsos in hosting a salon for me.

To Sophie Radice, my friend and wise editorial eye extraordinaire: thank you for being there for this book as you were the last. Likewise to my brilliant friend Sophie Levey for her late-stage fact-checking.

To the ad hoc writer's room who at short notice read and helped me keep my pecker up: Andrew Davidson, Elizabeth Diaferia, Cathy Meade, Peter Miscovich, Saskia Sissons, Stefan Stern as well as those who helped me sense-check when asked, including Henry Coutinho-Mason, Andy Hobsbawm, Emma Jacobs, Giles Gibbons and Rob Sadow.

To Lynda Gratton for writing the preface to this book. She is both a friend and a mentor to me.

My gratitude goes to Bloomberg. In the spring of 2022 Adam Blenford covered my book *The Nowhere Office* shortly before its publication. A few months later John Micklethwait introduced me to Brian Bremner, who brought me in to write on and off for Work Shift, a new section dedicated to the emerging trends in work and workplace custom and practice. Brian gave me creative license to really write what I want to about the history, politics and culture of work – a freedom which I relished. I really enjoyed the time I spent working on Work Shift and am grateful to Nicole Bullock, Matt Boyle, Jo Constantz and Natasha Solo-Lyons, in particular.

Much of this book draws together threads from interviews or conversations. Some are informal, some regular, some one-off. Some featured directly in columns or broadcasts for Bloomberg or

ACKNOWLEDGMENTS

my podcast *The Nowhere Office*, which I have co-hosted since the summer of 2021 with my 'podcast buddy' Stefan Stern and which is now in its sixth series. But some have just lodged in my mind, sparking ideas or leading me to direct sources of information I would not have otherwise had. I thank in particular: Tom Adeyoola, Azeem Azhar, Roy Bahat, Matt Ballantine, Stephen Barber, Octavius Black, Margaret Bluman, Nicholas Bloom, Gabriella Braun, Adam Browne, Dave Cairns, Richard Carvalho, Louise Chester, Chloe Combi, Caroline Corby, Michael Creamer, Matthew d'Ancona, Steven J. Davis, Steve Frost, Charles Handy, William Eccleshare, Davie Eisenberg, His Excellency Ahmad Belhoul Al Falasi, Eliza Filby, Carl Benedikt Frey, Giles Gibbons, Emma Goldberg, Arpit Gupta, Mary Jane Greenhalgh, Arianna Huffington, Herminia Ibarra, Barbara Kellerman, Binna Kandola, Nick Lichtenberg, Gemma Lines, Sophie Levey, Richard Lee, Skender "Sketch" Mehmed, Eleanor Mills, Dambisa Moyo, Aled Maclean-Jones, Peter Miscovich, Karla L. Miller, Adrian Monck, Sanjay Nazerali, Ben Page, Laline Paull, Ed Pilkington, Indrani Sen, Michael Skipwith, Elizabeth Sheinkman, Anya and Joseph Stiglitz, Rory Sutherland, Drew Smith, Richard Straub, Joanna Swash, Juliet Schor, Bridid Schulte, Alice Sherwood, Alice Thwaite, Brigitte Trafford, Gleb Tsibursky, Nikhil Virmani, Rachael Ward. And to everyone on the "Corona Conversations" WhatsApp group: you know who you are and I thank you.

To the backroom gang who have produced and edited *The Nowhere Office* over six series including Calum McCrae and Kevin Hirshorn and Hayden Brown, my longtime design collaborator. To Nicola Streeten, the graphic artist and illustrator who so readily agreed to share the illustration spotlight with ChatGPT's DALL-E. Collaborating with generative AI may be fast – twenty seconds to ask for an illustration on average – but it was infinitely more rewarding to work with Nic and see what her hand and eye produced over days (our office was WhatsApp and Zoom). Grateful thanks also go to poet Mr Gee and historian Dr Andrew St George, whose words never fail to elegantly and lyrically capture as intended, and to Simon Toulson-Clarke for permission to reproduce his lyrics to "Lean on Me" (ah-li-ayo).

Gratitude to Leo von Bülow-Quirk and Eithne Jones and their teams who handle my speaking and corporate teaching work and who work hard to keep me busy. There's a team at Moorfields I'm eternally grateful for and admire each and every time I see them at work: the clinical and administrative staff who take bloods, dish out meds, organize the appointments, and generally work like a silent, well-oiled machine. To Harry Petrushkin, Richard Lee and their colleagues down in the bustling basement of Clinic 15 at Moorfields, and upstairs in the colour-coded retinal therapy unit. Thanks doesn't begin to cover it. Plus the wonderful Gloria Else, and Michael Skipwith. I think they call it integrated medicine. I call it keeping the show on the road.

And finally, the family without whom I cannot live, let alone work. Alaric, my husband and lodestar; my big brother Andy who is always first on the tech zeitgeist; to the Fischbein cousins in London, Vienna and New York: that's the next book project. Lastly, to our five Millennial and Gen Z kids who are just, well, amazing: Rachael, Max, Roman, Anoushka and Wolfie. And to our Generation Alpha grandson Jace: there's a lot riding on you, kids.

INDEX

accidents caused by technology 79–80
Ackman, Bill 155
acronyms for models of working 129–31
Act Like a Leader, Think Like a Leader (Ibarra) 59
Adams-Prassl, Jeremias 54
Adams, Scott 164–5
adulthood, delayed 240
ageing 250–2
AGI (Artificial General Intelligence) 86
AI (artificial intelligence)
  behaviour changes 207
  bias concerns 75, 77
  call centers 210
  co-pilots 76, 134, 262
  current assumptions of impact 4, 6
  cyclical emergence 122–3
  DALL-E xxiv, 48
  facial recognition 77
  fakeness 152
  future predictions 269–70
  generative AI and authenticity 51–2
  generative compared to predictive 51
  hybrid working 134–5
  impact on creativity 3, 4, 152
  market growth projection 53
  plagiarism 155
  predicted use in workplace 2, 56–7, 119, 213
  prompts 72, 269
  replacement anxiety 52, 53–5
  safety 76–7, 79–80
  sentience 198, 223
  skill set requirements 70–2, 230, 251
  terminology 72
  see also ChatGPT
Al Falasi, Ahmad Belhoul 101
all-collar workers 58
All That We Are (Braun) 167–8
'Allentown' (Joel) 62, 160
Alphabet Inc. 23
Altman, Sam 85–6, 87, 242
always-on culture xxi, 25, 168, 198, 222, 223–4, 265
AMaZing generation 224, 265, 270, 271
Amazon.com Inc. 25–6, 82, 83, 129
American Dream 265
anchor days 145
The Apartment (film) 147, 193
Apollo 11 175–7
Apple Inc. 23, 85
apprenticeships 102, 238
Arendt, Hannah 187
Aristotle 189
Armstrong, Neil 177
artificial intelligence (AI) *see* AI
Ashore 147
assembly lines 53, 93, 216

'At Lunchtime, A Story of Love' (McGough) 11
athleisure 243
Australia 98, 112, 113
authenticity 51, 55, 73
Authors Guild 54
autonomous vehicles 128
autonomy 94–5
avatars 73–4, 180

Bahat, Roy 70, 75
Baltimore ship disaster 80
banking, AI and operating profits 72
Bankman-Fried, Sam 87, 89–90, 242
Barbie (film) 158–9, 161–2
Barrero, Jose Maria 133
Barrett, Oli 130
Bates, Laura 161
Battenhall 142
Baumoel, Brett 216
behavioral science 195–6
belonging, sense of 152–3, 184, 186–8, 248
Benioff, Marc 258
Benvie, Drew 142
Bersin, Josh 215–16
Bethlehem Steel 46
Beyoncé 1, 188, 189–90, 265
Bhaskar, Michael 51
bias
    AI (artificial intelligence) 75, 77
    generational 122
    HR stereotype 217
    proximity bias 169–70
    unconscious bias 155
    women in the workplace 32–3
Black, Octavius 76, 195, 205, 214
Blair, Euan 74
Blake, William 137
Bloom, Nicholas 23–4, 41–2, 45, 56–7, 133–5
Bloomberg
    Bloomberg Beta 71
    Bloomberg Originals 41, 205
    Bloomberg Philanthropies 266
    workforce forecasts 56

'Working Assumptions' column xvii–xviii
blue collar workers, flexible patters 131
board responsibilities 87, 89, 91
Boomers 7, 224
Bosch (TV series) 185
boundary management 219–22
Braun, Gabriella 167–8
'Break My Soul' (Beyoncé) 1, 188, 189–90, 265
Bregman, Rutger 97
Breslau, Benjamin 161
Briggs, Raymond 273
British Library 77–8
Brown, Syreeta 203
Buffet, Warren 90
'Builders of the City Enjoy Luncheon' 151, 153
burnout 189, 201–4, 205–8

Cairns, Dave 168
calendars 253
call centers 210
cancel culture 164
cancer 194–5
Career and Family (Goldin) 247
career changes 59
career identity 58
career stages 100, 208, 243–4
caring responsibilities 168–9, 240, 244, 247, 250
cars
    autonomous vehicles 128
    commuting 105–6
    Ford Model T 69, 105
    self-driving 77
Carter, Stephen 148
cash registers 66–7
The Cat in the Hat (Seuss) 30–1
change
    behaviours 207
    embracing 122
Chaplin, Charlie 1, 268
Chapman, Tracy 105
charisma 90, 91

INDEX

chatbots 72–3, 218, 223
ChatGPT
  anxiety about 50–1, 53–4
  assumptions of impact 4
  copyright infringement 70
  list of office films 157–8
  mistakes disclaimer 76
  prompts 72, 269
  speed of change 2, 48–9, 70–1, 268
  see also DALL-E
Chief Critical Officer 87, 92
childbirth rates 240
childcare costs 247
China 45, 102
Churchill, Winston 171
Cialdini, Robert 90
city design
  fifteen-minute cities 112–13
  redefining central business
    district 110, 113
  suburbia 26–7, 110–12
  zoning 123–5
civilization, goal of 4
Clegg, Nick 73
climate change 9, 106, 109, 120, 137, 273
co-pilots, AI 76, 134, 262
co-working spaces 27
coffee 139–43
collaboration 28, 178–82, 183, 184, 271–2
The Coming Wave (Suleyman & Bhaskar) 51
commencement speeches 170–4
commuting
  cars 106, 108–9
  climate change 109
  discounts 112
  effect of Covid-19 pandemic 110
  future predictions 127–8, 136
  worker dislike 26–7, 108, 125, 242–3
computing power, Moore's Law 53
conferences 145–8, 227–8
Connelly, Michael 105, 185
conspiracy theories 113

consumerism 10, 267
copyright infringement, ChatGPT 70
correction fluid 69
cost of living crisis 7, 250
Courpasson, David 27
Coursera 38–9
Coutinho-Mason, Henry 16
Covid-19 pandemic
  changing assumptions about
    working through illness 193–4
  impact on children 204
  impact on work 4, 19–20, 22–3,
    42, 62–3, 92, 110, 191, 242
  long Covid 6, 81, 194, 202, 214
  mortality 6
  as tipping point 31
  vaccine skepticism 194
  value shift 6–7
Covid pandemic xv
creativity
  impact of AI 3, 4, 152
  replacement anxiety 152
cryptocurrency 89–90
culture
  cancel culture 164
  popular, about work xxi, xxiii, 1,
    12, 18, 157–61, 163, 189–90, 217,
    220, 267–9
  sense of belonging 152–3, 184,
    186–8
  see also wellbeing; work culture
culture wars
  identity politics 17
  Middle East conflict 6, 155
  working from home 31
Cushman & Wakefield Plc 27
cyber security 77–8, 137, 250
cyberspace 27, 50

Daisley, Bruce 202
Dale, Gemma 164, 257
DALL-E xxiv, 20, 21, 43, 49, 67, 95,
  141, 150, 283
Davis, Steven J. 133, 253
Davos 102, 146, 227
deepfakes 52, 55

dementia 251
Demon Copperhead (Kingsolver) 160
desktop diaries 252–3
The Devil Wears Prada (film) 157–8
diaries 252–3
digital nomads 147
digitization 8, 80
  see also AI
Dilbert 164–5
Dimon, Jamie 227
disease, office design 137
diversity 164, 172
doom loop 132
Dostoevsky, Fyodor 13
Draper, Derek 194
dress codes 243
Drucker, Peter 51, 86, 154, 188
Dylan, Bob 223

The Economist 43–4
education
  Generation Z 233–4, 237–40
  MBAs 101–3, 167, 266
  reskilling 102–3
  teaching online 38–9
  see also universities
Eisenberg, Dave 102
eleven, symbolism of team 152
Eliot, T. S. 190
Ellis, Kevin 172, 199
emerging economies 99
The Employees: A Workplace Novel of the 22nd Century (Ravn) 161
employment
  gaps since Covid-19 81
  workforce forecasts 56, 57
Energy Plaza, Houston, Texas 27
energy transition 14–15
Enron 89
equity 120, 164
ethics, board responsibilities 91
European Commission 180–1
European Union, employment law reform 25
events business *see* conferences
Everyday Sexism (Bates) 161

Everything Everywhere All at Once (film) 5, 159–60
eye conditions 3, 209

facial recognition 77
families 184, 233, 240–1
fashion 243
'Fast Car' (Chapman) 105
Ferris, Joshua 138
fifteen-minute cities 112–13
Filby, Eliza 231, 232–41
films about work, ChatGPT list 157–8
five-day week 10, 93–6, 216
Flexetariat 23–4, 29, 58
flexible working
  acronyms for models 129–31
  blue collar workers 131
  caring responsibilities 168–9, 240, 244, 247
  globalization 35–6
  increasing demand 23–4, 29, 40, 63, 242–3
  inequality 228–9
  legislation 25, 258
  management attitudes 24–5, 35–7
  models not yet settled 97–8, 100
  productivity 42–4
  start of careers 100, 208
  women 33–4, 208
flying, fear of 7
follower power 87, 90
FOMO 90
Ford, Henry 10, 53, 93–4, 96, 216
Ford Model T 69, 105
Forster, Robert 60–1
Foster, Jodie 225, 226, 245
four-day week xxiii, 24, 96–8, 100, 228–9, 267
Fowler, Susan 215
Frankenstein (Shelley) 53
Frederick the Great 91–2
freelance work 23, 59–61, 244
Freudenberger, Herbert 201
Frey, Carl Benedikt 18, 45, 218
FTX 87, 89, 91

INDEX

Fujitsu 24, 36, 164
Fully Connected (Hobsbawm) 198
furlough 19
Future of Jobs 2023 Report (WEF) 8–9, 14

Gay, Claudine 155
Gaza 6
Geddes, Patrick 114
Gee, Mr 255–6
General Electric Co. 131
Generation Alpha 119–20, 224
Generation Glass 19
Generation X
  always-on 224
  attitudes to work post-Covid 7, 237
  pay and conditions protests 190
Generation Z
  attitudes to work 6–7, 190, 224, 229, 231–2, 235–7, 245
  communication 225–6
  health and wellbeing focus 119–20
  individualism and identity 233–5
George, Bill 51–2
Germany xxiii, 94
gig economy 58, 232, 236, 244
glass ceiling 245
Glengarry Glen Ross (film) 147
Global North 63, 99
Global South 99
globalization 35–6, 108, 128, 217
Gog, Soon Joo 8
Golconda (Magritte) 21, 27
Goldberg, Emma 17, 109
Goldin, Claudia 32, 247
Goldman Sachs Group Inc. 31, 130–1, 166, 257–8
Goldstone, Nancy 92
Google 137, 217
Google Docs 180
Google Gemini 76
graduates, work choices and lifestyle 19
Graham, Bette Nesmith 69, 79
Granovetter, Mark 59, 62

Gratton, Lynda 11, 97, 239
Grau, Erin 33
gray 159
Gray, Alasdair 263
Great Refurb 136–8
Great Resignation 1, 20–2, 81, 82
green jobs 14–15, 81
Greenwood, Sarah 159
groupthink 167
Gupta, Arpit 132
Guys & Dolls (musical) 269, 270

Habsburg Empire 91–2
Haigh, Gideon 114
Hamlet (Shakespeare) 131
Handy, Charles 36
Hanks, Tom 172
Harman International Industries Inc 24
Harvard University 101–3, 155, 172
Hawthorne Effect 153–4, 264
health
  definition 197, 204
  opioid crisis 204
  personal, not one size 205
  social 198, 212
  see also illness; wellbeing
health and safety 79–80, 137, 215–18
health insurance 99–100
healthcare jobs 266
'Heigh Ho' 189
Hidalgo, Anne 112
hierarchies 167, 233
High Conflict (Ripley) 167
Hippocrates 194
A History of the World in 6 Glasses (Standage) 141–2
Hoffman, Christy 98
Hofstede, Geert 167
holidays 219–22
Hollywood artist strike 54, 83
Holmes, Elizabeth 89–90
home working *see* WFH
Homeland (TV series) 1
Horton Hatches the Egg (Seuss) 30, 35
hot desks 27, 142

Houngbo, gilbert 228
Howard, Ron 183
Huffington, Arianna 205–8, 214
The Human Condition (Arendt) 187
human gymnastics lab, MIT 28
human resources (HR)
    future predictions 264
    globalization 35–6
    health and safety 214–18
    see also recruitment; retention
hybrid have/have nots 2, 41
hybrid working
    effect on office space 2
    effect on team culture 2
    impact of AI 134–5
    increasing demand 17, 23, 29, 39, 41–2
    management attitudes 24, 38, 42, 221, 229, 257–8
    models not yet settled 97, 117, 119, 126, 144
    most common model 133–4
    productivity 42–4
    workers' preference xxii, 31, 257
    see also WFH

'I Hear America Singing' (Whitman) xix
Ibarra, Herminia 59
IBM 56
Iceland 247
identity
    authenticity 51–2
    culture wars 17
    Generation Z 234
    work as identity 58
illness
    working days lost 214
    'working through,' changed attitudes 193–4
In-Betweeners 244
inclusion 120, 164, 184, 229
India 99, 174
individualism 233
Industrial Revolution, Fifth 9
inequality 99

inflation 19
inflexion points 14
Informa 146, 148
Infosys 99
inheritance economy 235–6
innovation
    AI contribution 84
    productivity 45
insecurity 56
The Intern (film) 241
International Labour Organization 97, 228, 246
Ireland 25
Israel 6

Jackson, Michael 267–8
Japan 36, 186
Jassy, Andy 129
Jennison, Jude 199
Jensen, Mary 178
jobs
    change in types 14–18
    classification 43
Jobs, Reed 194–5
Jobs, Steve 85, 172
Joel, Billy 62, 160
Judd, Ashley 162

Kadence 180
Kahneman, Daniel 46
Kalanick, Travis 215
Kellerman, Barbara 87
Kellogg, W. K. 96
Kenya 221
Kerouac, Jack 68
Keynes, John Maynard 97
Kickstarter 148
Kindertransport 272
King, Martin Luther 171
Kingsolver, Barbara 160
knowledge work
    home working 22
    predictive AI 51
    productivity 46
    replacement anxiety 56
    tools and technology 65

Krueger, Alan 46
Kuang, Rebecca F. 160
Kvam, Sondre 73

Lay, Kenneth 89
leadership
   bad types 87
   charismatic 90, 91
   generational bias to ways of working 122
   uncertainty 199, 264
'Lean on Me' (Red Box) 226
Learners 243–4
Leavers 243–4
legislation
   flexible working rights 25, 258
   health and safety 79
   'right to disconnect' xxiii
Letts, John 253–4
Levine, Matt 86
LinkedIn 14–15, 31, 39, 59, 143, 180, 216
Liquid Paper 69, 79
Lithuania 113
Littlejohn, Richard 31–2, 146
LLMs (large language models) *see* ChatGPT
London 108, 112, 124, 137, 269
London Book Fair 147
long Covid 6, 81, 194, 202, 214

MacDonald, Maril 9
McGough, Roger 11
McGowan, Denis 149
McGowan, Rose 162
Mad Men (TV series) 162
Magritte, René 20–1, 27
Mamet, David 147, 170
management
   flexible working attitudes 35–7
   generational shift 126
   hybrid working attitudes 24, 38, 42, 221, 229, 257–8
   return to office policies 23–4
manufacturing, assembly lines 53, 93, 216

Marans, Gabe 140
Maria Theresa, Empress 91–2
Mars (company) 221
mass consumerism 10, 267
mass production 53, 93, 216
May, Katherine 147–8
Mayhew, William 17
Mayo, Elton 26, 152, 153
Mazzon, Jen 180
MBAs 101–3, 167, 266
medical appointments, time off work 3
meritocracy 61
Meta Platforms Inc. 73, 165
metaverse 2, 50, 73–4, 123, 180–1, 260
#MeToo 161
Microsoft 22, 70
migration 108, 112
Millennials 126, 190, 224, 232, 235
Mills, Eleanor 245, 246
MindGym 76, 195
Miscovich, Peter 72, 115–28, 136, 161
misery index 46
MIT
   human gymnastics lab 28
   Media Lab 122
Modern Times (film) 1
Mollick, Ethan 213
The Momentous, Uneventful Day (Haigh) 114
Moneypenny 258
moon landings 174–7
Moore's Law 53
Morgan, Gareth 167
motherhood penalty 32–3
movies, narrative arc 17
Moyo, Dambisa 87, 91
Mr Bates vs The Post Office (TV series) 163
muesli 59–61
multiverse 2, 5
Multiverse 74
Murthy, Narayana 99
Murthy, Vivek 165
Museum of Industry, Baltimore 66–7

Musk, Elon 13, 24, 54, 75, 166, 183
My Fair Lady (film) 218
Myerson, Jeremy 186

Nadella, Satya 87
Naer 73–4
napping 46
narrative arc 17
National Hockey League 166
National Players' Federation 166
National Theatre, London 269–70
nature 147–8
networks 28, 61–2, 188
New York 123–4
The New York Times 70
Nicholson, Jack 68
Nike swoosh 133
'9 to 5' (Parton) 18, 190
Noon 246
The Nowhere Office (Hobsbawm) xvi, xvii, 178, 241
The Nowhere Office podcast xviii, 68–9, 101, 102
Nye, Joseph 146

Obama, Barack 1
Obama, Michelle 172
office buildings
    downsizing 149
    Great Refurb 136–8
    historical change of use 106
    mixed-use conversions 27, 259
    occupancy levels xxii, 2, 104, 108, 125, 143, 259
    see also real estate
The Office (TV series) xv, 201, 217
offices
    coffee 139–43
    social experience 27–8, 135, 137–8, 139, 186, 259
    start of careers 100, 208
    teamworking 28, 149
On the Road (Kerouac) 68
On Work (Thompson) 160–1
One Life (film) 272

OpenAI
    boardroom coup 85–8
    see also ChatGPT
opioid crisis 204
Orbach, Susie 201–2
Osborne, Michael 18
outsourcing 209, 212
Owen, Andi 37
Owen, Robert 93, 96–7
Oxford 113
Oxman, Neri 155

Paphides, Pete 60–1
Paris 112, 124
Parks and Recreation (TV series) 193
Parton, Dolly 18, 190
patent inflation 45
pay gap 32–3, 247
Paycheck, Johnny 18, 190, 265
Pentland, Sandy 28
plagiarism 155
planning, time horizons 261
poetry 11, 112, 255–6
Polywork 179
Poor Things (film) 263
Post Office 'Horizon' scandal 77, 163–4
POTATO working 129, 130
power shift to workers 25–6, 110–11, 125–6, 166
Pregnant Then Screwed campaign 247, 248
presenteeism
    backlash 23–4
    management attitudes xxii, 24–5, 34, 166
    pointless 138
    politics of 38–9, 45
    premium payments 40, 145–6
    proximity bias 169–70
printing, invention of 15, 53
privacy 54, 197
production lines 53, 93, 216
productivity
    changing assumptions 28
    collaboration 178

INDEX

emerging economies 99
Henry Ford and working week 93–4
hybrid working 42–4, 258
measurement 45–6
politics of 44–5, 166
property values, suburbia and beyond 26–7
prostitution 17–18
proximity bias 169–70
publishing industry 82–3, 147, 160
PWC 172, 199, 238
Pygmalion (Shaw) 218, 241

queenagers 76, 245–9
quiet quitting 20, 82, 244, 250

rail travel 127
Ray, John J, III 89, 91
real estate 26–7, 50, 72, 115–28, 132, 147
 see also office buildings
recruitment
 commencement speeches 170–4
 flexibility 23, 39
 Generation Z 236, 238
 post-Covid effect 20
 power shift to workers 26
 talent acquisition 74–5, 139, 216
 talent mobility 35–6
remote working 107–8, 116–17, 133, 135, 180
 see also hybrid working; WFH
replacement anxiety 52, 53–5, 152
resilience 202
reskilling 81–2, 102–3, 251, 269
retail sector transformation 121, 210–11
retail systems 66–7
retention
 call centers 210
 during Covid-19 pandemic 199
 Generation Z 236
 mass turnover 22, 171–2
 post-Covid effect 20
 power shift to workers 26, 110

retirement 81, 239, 240–1
return to office policies (RTO) 23–4, 126, 129, 217, 257–8
'right to disconnect' xxiii, 221
Ripley, Amanda 167
Rishi, Sanjay 161
robotics 8, 79–80
Rockefeller Center 151
Ross, Philip 186
Rumsfeld, Donald 14

Sadow, Rob 98
safety
 AI (artificial intelligence) 76–7, 79–80
 office buildings 136–7
 psychological 197
'salting' 82
San Francisco 124
Sandburg, Carl 112
Saudi Arabia 113
Savills Plc. 140
Scale (West) 113
Schein, Edgar 153
Schor, Juliet B. 99
Schwab, Klaus 9
Scoop (Waugh) 13
Seuss, Dr. 30, 35
Severance (TV series) xv, xvi
sexism 161–2, 215
Shakespeare, William 131
Shaw, George Bernard 218, 241
Shelley, Mary 53
Sherwood, Alice 51–2, 55
The Shining (film) 68
side hustles 58, 60–1
Silicon Valley 118
Silva-Tarouca, Emanuel da 92
Singapore 8, 124
Skills Future 8
'Skyscraper' (Sandburg) 112
Slack 178, 206
sleep 206, 207, 209
smartphones 231, 232, 267
Smith, Ben 228
smoking 221

293

Snow Crash (Stephenson) 180, 260
Snow White (film) 189
The Snowman (Briggs) 273
social experience 233
social media 164
The Social Problems of an Industrial Civilization (Mayo) 26
society, sense of belonging 152–3
Solomon, David 31, 130–1, 257–8
solopreneurs 58, 59–61, 88, 244
Sorrell, Martin 142
spaceships 255–6
Spotlight (film) 177
St George, Andrew xxiv, 68–9, 252–3
staff turnover 22
Standage, Tom 142
Standard Chartered 149
Stanton, Rick 183
Starbucks Corp. 26, 82, 83
Stephenson, Neal 180, 260
Stern, Stefan xviii
stop–start work 19–20
storytelling, narrative arc 17
Strata, Filippo de 15, 53
Straub, Richard 86
Streeten, Nicola xxiv
'The Strength of Weak Ties' (Granovetter) 62
stress
   AI in call centers 210
   burnout 189, 201–4, 205–8
   disease factor 55–6
   micro step behaviours 207
   technology 209
strikes 38, 54, 83
suburbia 26–7, 110–12
Succession (TV series) xxi, 85, 220
Sud, Anjali 229
Sugar, Alan 164
Suleyman, Mustafa 4, 51
'Super Screener' 74–5
surveillance systems 77, 197, 210–12
sustainability 14–15, 137
Sutherland, Rory 129–30
Sutskever, Ilya 86
Swash, Joanna 258

Takano, Mark 96
'Take This Job and Shove It' (Paycheck) 18, 190
talent acquisition 74–5, 139, 216
talent mobility 35, 217
Tarsus 146
Taylor, Frederick Winslow 46, 153, 216
teaching online 38–9
Teamraderie 39
Teams xv, 205
teamworking
   collaboration 178–82
   face to face 28
   globalization 35
   hybrid working 2
   moon landings 174–7
   office design 149
technology
   always-on xxi, 25, 168, 198, 222, 223–4
   change in job types 18, 68–70
   change in use 65–9
   collaboration 178–82
   complication and compatibility 70
   future predictions 255–6
   health and safety 79–80
   outdated 66–7, 70, 106
   reskilling 251
   robotics 8, 79–80
   solving problems with 209–10
   speed of change 48–9
   see also AI
teleconferencing 20, 27, 179, 205
Tesla 79–80, 166
Thai cave rescue 183, 184
Thanksgiving 173, 185–7
Then We Came to the End (Ferris) 138
Theranos 89–90
Things Change (film) 170
Thirteen Lives (film) 183
Thompson, Derek 160–1
Thrive Global 205, 206
Thwaite, Alice 76, 84
time and motion measurements 46
time, control of 94–5

time horizons, planning 261
time management 253
time zones 35, 99
Tippex 79, 80
'Toggling Tax' 180
Tomb, Greg 228
Toulson-Clarke, Simon 226
Tourish, Dennis 90
trade unions 25–6, 82–3
trains 127–8
transcription 76
Tsai, Diana 74–5
Tuckman, Bruce 178
turbulence 7–9, 46, 55, 81, 198–200, 261, 273
Twain, Mark 68
Twitter Inc. 165, 166
TW*T working 129–31
typing/typewriters 65–6, 68–9, 78–9
Tyson, Laura 7–8, 80

U-index 46
Uber 63, 108, 215
UK
    British Library cyberattack 77–8
    childcare costs 247
    flexible working rights 25
    Post Office 'Horizon' scandal 77, 163–4
    see also London
Ukraine 6
uncertainty 14, 198–200, 264
unconscious bias 155
United State of Work 46, 63, 261–73
universal basic income 100
universities
    commencement speeches 170–4
    Generation Z 234–5, 237–9
    pandemic pastoral care 7
Unworking (Myerson & Ross) 186
Upwage 74–5
urban apocalypse 132
urban design *see* city design
USA
    American Dream 265
    focus of this book xviii–xxii

    future predictions 265–6
    health insurance 99–100
    opioid crisis 204
    size of economy 63, 102, 266
    vacations 220
Utopia for Realists (Bregman) 97

vacations 219–22
values, driving behaviour 6–7
van Gennip, Karien 228
Van Gogh, Vincent 48
Vatcha, Naheed 90
Virgin Money 203–4
virtual reality 73–4, 181
voice recognition 76
von Polier, Frauke 259
Voyagers 147
VUCA theory 199

Wall Street (film) 83
Walsh, Marty 102, 228
war 6
The Waste Land (Eliot) 190
Watford, UK 26
Waugh, Evelyn 13
WeCrashed (TV series) 139
WEF *see* World Economic Forum
Weinstein, Harvey 162
wellbeing
    AI assistance 9, 210–12
    boundary management 219–22
    burnout 189, 201–4, 205–8
    corporate spend 196, 203
    misery index 46
    priority for workers 22
    see also health
West, Geoffrey 113
WeWork Inc. 27, 139, 242
W.F.A (Work from Anywhere) 148
WFH (work from home)
    attitudes to 31–2
    impact on city economies 109, 112
    knowledge work 22
    percentage of paid days xxii
    percentage of workers 41
    see also hybrid working

WhatsApp 188
'Where do we park our spaceships?' (Mr Gee) 255–6
white collar work
    change in attitude 19, 22
    impact of AI 15–16
    networks and meritocracy 61–2
White, E. B. 69, 105
Whitman, Walt xix
Wilde, Oscar 159, 161
Wilder, Billy 147, 193
Winnicott, Donald 51
Winton, Nicholas 272
Wipro 72
women
    change in family dynamics 240
    flexible working 33–4, 208, 247–8
    pay gap 32–3, 247
    portrayal by ChatGPT 107
    queenagers 245–9
    Seuss generation 30–1
    typing pools 68
    workplace bias 32–3
work
    common challenges 262
    completing tasks 65
    culture about xxi, xxiii, 1, 12, 18
    disengagement 62
    distributed workforce 273
    power shift to workers 166
    sense of purpose 3
    uncertain future 14
work culture
    always-on xxi, 25, 168, 198, 222, 223–4, 265
    brand message 156
    changing assumptions 28–9, 154, 191
    collaboration 178–82
    commencement speeches 170–4
    conflict 165–6, 167–8, 214
    future predictions 257–60, 269–71
    groupthink 167
    Hawthorne Effect 153–4, 264
    hierarchies 167, 233
    hybrid working 258
    keeping the human in the loop 262
    responsiveness 263–4
    sense of belonging 184, 186–7, 248
    Thanksgiving 185–7
    toxicity 163–4, 165–6, 193, 201–2
work from home *see* WFH
work–life balance
    boundary management 219–22
    change in attitude 20, 22, 37
    effect on city design 114
    'right to disconnect' campaign xxiii, 221
    side hustles 60–1
Work Trend Index (Microsoft) 22
workations 220–1
worker power shift 25–6, 110–11, 125–6, 166
'Workin' Day and Night' (Jackson) 267
'Working Assumptions' column, *Bloomberg* xvii–xviii
Working Identity (Ibarra) 59
working week, length of 10, 93–6, 216
The Workplace You Need Now (Rishi, Breslau & Miscovich) 161
WORKTECH Academy 138
World Economic Forum (WEF) 8–9, 14, 46, 146, 227–30
World Health Organization 197, 202, 203, 206
Wozniak, Steve 54
Wyman, Oliver 229

Yellowface (Kuang) 160

Zahidi, Saadia 8
Zoom xv, 135, 143, 179, 205, 228, 251

Printed in Great Britain
by Amazon